W9-CJQ-924

Revised and Updated To the Year 2005

The Minority Executives' Handbook

Revised and Updated To the Year 2005

The Minority Executives' Handbook

The Complete Guide To Career
Success In Today's Culturally
Diverse Workforce

Randolph W. Cameron

Amistad

New York, New York

First published in 1989 by Warner Books as an Amistad book.
First issued as an Amistad Press, Inc., trade paperback in 1996.

Amistad Press, Inc.
1271 Avenue of the Americas
New York, NY 10020

Distributed by:
St. Martin's Press c/o VHPS
175 Fifth Avenue
New York, NY 10010

Cover Design by Gilbert D. Fletcher
Designed by H. Roberts
Produced by Horowitz/Rae
1 2 3 4 5 6 7 8 9 10   96 97

Library of Congress Cataloging-in-Publication Data

Cameron, Randolph W. (Randolph Whitney)
    The minority executives' handbook : the complete guide to
career success in today's culturally diverse workforce /
Randolph W. Cameron. — Rev. and updated to the year 2005.
       p.   cm.
    Includes bibliographical references (p.   ) and index.
    ISBN 1-56743-021-X (pbk.) : $11.95
    1. Minority executives—United States—Handbooks,
manuals, etc.   I. Title.
HD38.25.U6C36   1996
658.4'09'08693—dc20
                                            96-12488
                                            CIP

This book is dedicated to my mother and father, Anneatta and Hugh J. Cameron, who made it possible for me to pursue a career in business when so many young black college graduates were discouraged from doing so and never tried.

In addition, my wife, Martha, and children, Michele and Randy; my aunt, Lolita Perry; my brothers, James and Donald Cameron; and my in-laws, Alice and William Boyce, are also remembered for their support and inspiration.

I also want to remember my father-in-law, Claude Billingsley; my uncle, Al Thompson; my dearest friends, Edith and James Morton, Iona and Calvin Pressley, Patricia Gibson, and Joseph and Barbara Bragg, for their love and inspiration.

Finally, I want to remember Ernest Talbert and John Price, my professors at Delaware State College, and my friend and mentor, D. Parke Gibson, whose wisdom showed me that "with faith, all things are possible."

Revised and Updated To the Year 2005

The Minority Executives' Handbook

ACKNOWLEDGMENTS

While I have spent much time trying to put some constructive ideas between the two covers of this book, I know that this book could not have been written without the help of my family and friends. Therefore, I would like to acknowledge their contributions:

Over the three years of writing this book, my wife, Martha Cameron, helped me to think through many of the ideas and became a constant source of inspiration. She gave me much wise counsel and editorial support.

Then there is my dear friend Edith Leitao, whom I affectionately call "Boss." I am indebted to her. Typing and retyping the manuscript was her way of showing me that my ideas were valid and my vision clear. For twelve years, Edith has helped me to document my observations in the corporate world.

I am also indebted to Carol Manago, who provided research support, Marie Brown, my agent, Malaika Adero, and Andrea Haight, with whom I have had many discussions, and who read, edited, and commented on a major part of the manuscript.

CONTENTS

Foreword   *xi*
Preface   *xv*
Introduction   *1*

I. / A Concept for Planning   9
Packaging Your Corporate Image   *12*
  The Right Attitude   *14*
  The Right Clothes   *16*
  The Right Speech   *18*
  The Right On-Time Habits   *21*
  The Right Prose   *21*
  The Right Presentation Skills   *22*
  The Right Politics   *25*
Personality and Skill Go Together   *27*
Tips on Marketing Your Skills   *29*

II. / Understanding Corporate Thinking   33
Corporate Players   *33*
Company Rules   *33*
Corporate Discretion   *35*

Executive Privileges and Power   36
Corporate Culture   39
What All Good Managers Know   52
A Checklist of Thoughts for Professional Survival
   and Corporate Success   55
Why and How People Get Promoted   59
Management Severance and Settlement Packages   69

III. / Corporate Pitfalls   77
Sexual Harassment   78
The Equal Employment Opportunity Commission (EEOC)   80
Image Assassination   82
The New Minority Employee   85
How to Protect Yourself From a Job Attack   92

IV. / Networking: Laying Your Corporate Foundation   107
The Power Broker   109
Learning to Network   109
Twelve Top Networking Characteristics   109
Creating Your Image   117
Working with Volunteer Organizations   119
Working with Trade Organizations   120
Joining Professional Associations   121
Writing Your Own Press Release   123
Mentors and Mentoring   125
The Need to Be Friendly   130
Job Hunting   132
   Preparing for a Job Search   132
   Building Self-confidence   133
   The Self-critique Process   136
   The Interview Process   137
   Dressing for an Interview   138
   Being on Time   139
   Speaking Successfully   139
   A Screening Process   140
   Salary and Benefits Negotiations   141
   Checklist for the Job-Research Process   144
   Preparation Time   145
   Target Market Research   145

Action Plan   *146*
Evaluation Process   *146*

V. / Managing Your Personal Life   149
Why Drinking Can Hurt Your Career   *149*
Dating on the Job   *151*
Using Sex to Get a Promotion   *153*
Married and Working Together   *155*
On "Doing Drugs"   *156*
The Weekly Paycheck Syndrome   *160*
Understanding and Coping with Corporate Stress   *164*
A Family Dilemma   *168*
How to Make a Five-Year Career Forecast That
   Works for You   *169*

VI. / Issues and Answers   177
Straightforward Talk   *177*
Thoughts for Career Wisdom and Success   *196*

VII. / Outlook for the 1990s–2005   201
Socioeconomic Issues and Expectations   *201*
Prospects for Employment   *203*
What About Tomorrow's Jobs?   *207*

**VIII. / Your Easy Reference Source for Mentoring,
   Networking, and Career Opportunities   223**
Directories   *224*
Where to Look for Information, Referrals, and
   Placement Services   *230*
Magazines   *232*
Major Daily Newspapers in the 50 Leading
   U.S. Markets   *232*
Black-oriented Newspapers   *234*
Hispanic Newspapers   *238*
Hispanic Magazines, Directories, and Periodicals   *239*
Native American Directories and Periodicals   *240*
Asian Directories, Periodicals, and Broadcasting   *240*
Minority Oriented Radio and Television Stations   *242*
Networking Opportunities   *247*

Selected Native American Organizations   247
Selected Asian Organizations   248
Selected Hispanic Organizations   249
State Political Caucuses   253
Selected Black Organizations   254
Black Colleges and Universities   261

Appendix I. Title VII: Prohibition of Employment Discrimination   265
Appendix II. Average Income by State   269
Recommended Reading   273
Index   275

FOREWORD

Randy Cameron has written a very timely and important book. It is a book for the future rather than the past; geared toward determining the history of minorities in America rather than recording it. The book is addressed to the minority executive, a career category whose ranks diminished during the Reagan years as the bright hopes of earlier *affirmative action* have been dimmed by the reality of *corporate reaction*. One can only wonder if an earlier writing of this book might not have affected that reality. But such speculation is fruitless, since the book derives from firsthand experience with those social attitudes and economic realities which have combined to produce the current corporate mood.

Simply put, black executives have disappeared from the corporate ranks in droves in the last few years. And, of course, Randy Cameron's book will be more of a painful reminder than a self-help guide in their hands. They need an *Unemployed and Disillusioned Minority Executives' Handbook*. Such a book might focus heavily on daily prayers and words of spiritual consolation and comfort. In the New York metropolitan area, for example, the pool of executive jobs has evaporated by 9 percent over the past couple of years, and well over half of the eliminated jobs were held by blacks. The recent lesson of black history in America is that blacks in executive positions are history!

The ranks of black executives have been decimated by a combination of disillusionment and retrenchment. During the late sixties and the seventies, when the phrases "affirmative action" and "equal employment opportunity" were in common vogue and not infrequent practice, black faces began to infiltrate the executive ranks in unprecedented (although by no means enormous) numbers. Although black executives were found disproportionately in public affairs, community relations, and human resource and social service categories, more than a few blacks found themselves with desks and paychecks in the private sector and in large corporations. It was a heady experience arising from a social and economic heyday in the land. Social service, employment training, and human resource development programs flourished under the banner of a Great Society, as did affirmative action efforts, and a substantial number of major corporations wore their social consciences on their pin-striped sleeves. Blacks had their foot in a door they had theretofore only long been kicking, and the promise of progress to the top seemed bright indeed.

But blacks in management soon found that it takes more than entering a door to be accepted inside. Blacks had "cracked the corporate community" but only a crack; they faced roadblocks and obstructions at every turn. When time for promotion came around, black managers found their office doors labeled with a familiar sign from a segregated past: For Blacks Only. White males held the working keys to promotion. Blacks hired to fill earmarked jobs simply stayed in them while nonblack others advanced. Not surprisingly, increasing numbers of disenchanted black managers and executives withdrew from the prospect of dead-end careers. Many took the entrepreneurial route, choosing to forge their own career paths as their own bosses.

Those blacks who stayed became victims of involuntary displacement as social responsibility gave way to economic reality. Corporations and other private sector enterprises which had been loose, accepting, and even flabby in their hiring practices during the economic heyday became lean and mean. Bottom-line figures of economic necessity displaced high-minded notions of equal opportunity. Profit took precedence over platitudes. Work force reductions made daily headlines: CBS News cut back 40 percent; TWA laid off 5,000 cabin attendants; GE cut back 25 percent, reducing its payroll by 100,000; AT&T eliminated more than 27,000 jobs. In the cutback process, the axiom "Last hired, first fired" was followed with vengeance. Jobs earmarked for blacks simply ceased to exist. The private sector, which had long operated as an effective "entitlement program" for whites, took on a less plentiful countenance, and in that process black faces disappeared.

At the same time, the political mood turned sour. The outpouring of government spending for human needs programs trickled to a near halt. The Great Society was transformed into a miserly community in which self-help and private charity were assigned to replace former government spending. The very programs and agencies which had been the primary sources of black managerial opportunity were mutilated by belt-tightening and many closed their doors.

In such a social, political, and economic climate, why a *Minority Executives' Handbook?* Its aim would appear to be akin to trying to sell ice to Eskimos. And the ozone layer has yet to be sufficiently depleted to make such a sales campaign worthwhile.

The Minority Executives' Handbook is geared to the realistic future. While there are others who will find it helpful and useful, the book will be valuable primarily to those young minority entrants into the employment market who have been neither sullied nor disenchanted by past experience. It speaks also to those bright, well-educated young minorities who have discarded corporate managerial settings as a career choice, largely because of the negative experiences of their elders. Many of them are disenchanted by default and choose to begin their careers along entrepreneurial lines.

Randy Cameron has written a guide which is an indispensable aid to even the best college and professional school education. It is an educational supplement which augments competence with an understanding of competitive reality. It draws upon the experiences of those who have gone before to enlighten the career path of those who will follow. As such, it is both a "how-to-book" and a survival manual.

Two quintessential realities emerge from the pages of *The Minority Executives' Handbook.* First is the recognition that racism is very much alive and operationally vital in the corporate culture, just as it is in the American culture at large. Any would-be minority executive who fails to take account of the pervasive, insidious, and sometimes blatant matter-of-factness of racism does so at his or her own peril. Corporate social responsibility always flows into practical policy through the filter of racism, even when merit is claimed as the singular policy-determining factor.

The second recognition is that of a distinct corporate culture, a cultural milieu with its own rules and regulations. But aspiring minority executives must know the rules to be able to follow them. Since corporate cultural expectations are generally assumed rather than taught, this book is an eye-opening necessity.

I commend this book to your reading, just as I commend Randy Cameron for having written it at precisely the right time. Hopefully, it will prove to be an important contribution to the history of black people and other minorities in the United States.

Calvin O. Pressley
Executive Director
Institute of Church Administration And Management

PREFACE

OUTLOOK FOR THE FUTURE

While the United States economy, in the 1990s, seems to be on the path to recovery, millions of people are out of work with no real prospects for future gainful employment. Recent college graduates are finding it increasingly difficult to get even the low-paying and entry-level jobs in their fields of choice, while thousands of their high school graduate counterparts are hard-pressed to find any meaningful work at all. Despite certain improvements in the economy, millions of Americans of all ages, levels of education, and work experience, are traumatized by a rapidly changing job market. Many low- and middle-income Americans feel a terrible sense of displacement and deprivation as the nation's leadership struggles to find solutions to the many job-related ills of the country. Without the means to establish a plan to put Americans back to work, a permanent class of unemployed and under-employed people is developing.

Since the first edition of *The Minority Executives' Handbook* was published in 1989, I've talked and worked with hundreds of men and women across the country. I asked them about their greatest needs and concerns on the job and in their careers. From hourly workers to established managers, two of the most-asked questions by men and women are: How do workers protect themselves against politically motivated job attacks? And, How can workers achieve upward mobility in an atmosphere of organizational downsizing and consolidation?

Downsizing has been an especially troubling phenomenon, particularly for older, more experienced workers, and it is continuing to occur in the corporate world at an alarming rate. Many organizations now find themselves in the throes of uncertainties and complexities: IBM laid off 125,000 workers worldwide; American Express laid off 1,700 people in its New York office; CBS made a 40 percent cutback in personnel, and GE pared 25 percent, reducing its payroll by 100,000 workers. TWA laid off 5,000 cabin attendants. Four thousand eight hundred workers were laid off at Aetna, and Sears cut its work force by 48,000 people. The list goes on and on.

Nine million Americans are jobless today and much of it stems from downsizing in both profit and non-profit organizations. Many of those who have been affected find that their lives have been changed forever. According to the Bureau of Labor Statistics, approximately 15 percent of all laid-off workers ever expect to return to their same jobs.

Dramatic changes have taken place in the American job market before—the farming industry makes a case in point. Sixty percent of employed Americans worked in farming in 1850. But, as new technologies were introduced, the available jobs in agriculture were reduced to 39 percent by 1900; 8.1 percent by 1960; and to 2.7 percent in 1990. This low percentage of workers is far more significant than it appears when you consider that this diminished work force is still productive enough to meet the food demands of this country, *and* export markets all around the world—with tons of surplus in the form of cheese and grain left over.

The Issue of Unemployment

There is much speculation about the cause of America's current unemployment problems. While our leadership has yet to identify all of the causes, the mindset of greed, which marked corporate America in the 1980s, is cited by many informed businesspeople as a contributing factor.

Profits have been declining for corporations in the largest industrial nations since the late 1960s. During periods of declining profits, businesses sometimes look for short-term gain to ease the pressure and to solve external and internal problems. Short-term gain can be derived from strategies and activities that look good on paper, but are sometimes unproven, unreliable, and actually harmful, in the long-term, to the growth and stability of companies. Junk bonds, mergers, and acquisitions were the 1980s versions of the short-term "quick fix" approach to business. But, there really appears to be no successful shortcut to sound, long-term growth and stability in America. The more sensible approaches focus on the development of new technologies, reliable market research, investment spending, and committed, motivated workers and management. The mistakes of the past should teach us lessons to create a better reality in the here and now, and in the future.

The Bureau of Labor Statistics forecasts that the United States economy will net about 1.7 million new jobs each year from now to the year 2005. This rate of new job development is considered slow. And, only a third of the jobs are opening up in big companies. The rest will have to come from small to mid-size companies, with an emphasis on service-related businesses. Reports say that many Fortune 500 company CEOs plan to keep their management ranks lean and aggressive. They don't look forward to any significant increase in their managerial ranks over the next two or three years.

The important point to remember is that new federal government attitudes toward equal employment opportunity, changing tax laws, changing markets, and changing technology prompt companies to reshape their businesses. Reshaping could mean that strategic plans, corporate "mission statements," personnel policy and procedures, corporate culture, staff size, and overhead budgets change.

New hiring among the big companies will tend to be temporary and selective. Temporary employees, freelance talent, and consultants will be used to meet many businesses' talent, and human resource, needs. Pay raises—once thought to be an automatic annual ritual—are now being replaced by employer "thank you notes." Bonuses will only be for those people who demonstrate outstanding work habits and accomplishments during the year.

You Make the Difference

While all of the commentary on downsizing, and reshaping, the American workplace may disturb you, and even cause you some concern and uneasiness about your future, the truth is you need not worry about these conditions because, in the final analysis, *you* make the difference between success and failure; particularly, if you remain focused and committed to your career goals and aspirations. Remember, no one ever said that the road to success in your field of endeavor would be easy.

Admittedly, the unemployment statistics reported by the federal government are real, but they do not give you the entire picture. They do not speak to every individual's career experience in the United States. Some people, for example, are doing well during this period of change, and will continue to do so over the years to come. They will change jobs when they are ready, get promoted when they are worthy, start new businesses of their own, and be successful, in spite of the government's unemployment statistics.

Unemployment statistics in the United States, for the most part, only reflect the experiences of the general United States workforce and not the individual worker such as yourself. Therefore, while you should be aware of and informed about the general conditions of the American workplace, you should not be disheartened about the future of the workplace in general, nor dispirited about your own opportunities for career success.

Millions of Americans will achieve career success this year and every year, thereafter, well into 2000. You can be one of those people if you really want to be. Let nothing or no one turn you around in your career pursuit, and let no one deny you the opportunity to achieve your goals. Believe in what you want from life and go after it with total dedication. Have the courage and personal discipline to develop a written career plan—one that clearly identifies your vision, mission, objectives, and strategy. Support your personal career plan with some sound contingencies: an operational budget, timetables, and an effective feedback system to evaluate your progress. Remember, career success will be determined by the quality of your action plans, and your desire to make them a reality.

Many people will fail at their first and second attempts to be successful in a corporation, not because they lack the academic skills or the technical know-how. They will fail because they lack the knowledge and experience to deal with the discipline of corporate culture.

INTRODUCTION

The Minority Executives' Handbook is a guidebook for aspiring minority people who want to be successful in business and industry and may not have the necessary support and guidance to achieve their goals. Further, it is a reference source to help people identify and overcome the hidden obstacles that impede their progress in the corporation.

With few exceptions, corporate life at the very top of our nation's major corporations is nonexistent for blacks and other nonwhite Americans. This void of nonwhite participation in the top executive positions of business and industry in America should not continue because there is no legitimate business reason for it to continue. Its existence denies corporate America the opportunity to benefit from the vast pool of talent that blacks and other nonwhite Americans bring to it. And it denies minority citizens the opportunity to reach their full potential in our society.

I have lectured on the subject of industrial race relations at corporations and colleges all around the country. I have talked with young people about their work-related experiences in the corporate world, and participated in more race relations seminars and workshops than I would care to remember. For over twenty-three years, I have had the opportunity to observe, both as consultant to major corporations and as a corporate executive, the experiences of blacks and other minorities working in corporate America.

The overwhelming majority of students, hourly employees, entry-level management people, and established executives have confirmed two key issues that impede the general progress and upward mobility of minorities in corporate America. They are racism and corporate culture.

This book has been written to help corporate-oriented people understand how racism operates in the private sector, how corporate culture impedes the upward mobility of minorities, and what minorities can do to help themselves.

This book is not just another book on the life and times of people who run business and industry in America today. It is also not a book that continues merely to state the problems that minority people face in corporate America without concern for needed answers.

Rather, this book is filled with practical "how-to" information and useful tools for people who really want to enjoy a successful corporate life. This is a handbook for every family in America who has an aspiring college student who might very well end up working with some corporation in this country. More important, this is a guidebook for people who are actively pursuing a successful career in the corporate world right now and have need to develop a "game plan" that works for them. Not a plan to enable them simply to survive, but a plan to thrive in a highly complex, ever-changing, competitive corporate culture, one where it is often thought that "winning is everything" and "bigger is better."

Books written about the experiences of blacks in corporate America today have stated and restated the problems with which blacks have been confronted in adjusting to an unfamiliar organizational environment. This book, in addition to discussing these problems, identifies ways that concerned people can make an appropriate response to the challenging situations found on the job. This book suggests ways to negotiate many of the problems found in the corporate culture to a successful conclusion.

Many people will fail at their first and second attempts to be successful in a corporation, not because they lack the academic skills or the technical know-how. They will fail because they lack the knowledge and experience to deal with the discipline of corporate culture. There are rules, regulations, outside influences that corporate people are guided by when seeking job security, upward mobility, financial success, and power. These rules, regulations, and influences are not easily accessible, because the information and insight are not openly discussed anywhere in the corporation, or published, for that matter.

The Minority Executives' Handbook identifies corporate culture in very practical terms. This book enables the reader to change his or her corporate life by changing his or her thinking. There is a checklist for survival and corporate success, a concept for personal planning, and tips on marketing one's skills. There are also case histories to work with that give readers an opportunity to think through situations that could actually happen to them.

Many people in corporate life talk about the need to network, but few really become good at it. *The Minority Executives' Handbook* not only defines the concept of networking, it provides a step-by-step guide for developing effective corporate networking skills.

Most business schools do not deal with the subject of corporate culture, because they do not see the significance of the issue at this time. And, with some few exceptions, there is little personal family experience in this area for minorities to take advantage of. As a result, many blacks simply will not survive the initial exposure to the corporate world.

Minority corporate people, today, must do more than merely go through their own personal experiences; they must learn to grow through their experiences, turn around and help the next group of minority personnel entering the corporation.

The more experienced corporate people have a responsibility to see that the younger inexperienced people have a fair chance of surviving the corporate culture shock that seems to make so many unnecessary casualties out of entry-level minority personnel. It is not an impossible challenge to overcome, but it does mean that experienced people in corporations must be willing to establish mentoring relationships with minorities that help to reduce the margin for error, as they adjust to their environment.

Knowing what to expect from competition, how to respond to management, and how to relate to the corporate style of doing things can make all the difference in the world if you are a new employee in the company. The best technical skills in the business will not amount to very much if the new employee cannot cope with the internal politics of the organization, or fails to observe corporate customs, tradition, and life-styles.

All too often, it is not the lack of technical skill that defeats the aspiring minority person, but his inability to relate to the culture of the organization and react accordingly.

Corporations are constantly changing, and minority employees, particularly the new entry-level management people, need to be sensitive to the changing environment, or face the danger of becoming expendable... the last in, first out method of reorganization. In fact, it has been said that the minority employment picture in the United States is a good economic indicator, because minorities have traditionally been the last group hired during an economic upturn, and the first group laid off during an economic downturn. Every time the business environment changes, corporations rethink their position in the marketplace, and readjust the size of the organization to protect profits.

The important point to remember is that changing federal government attitudes toward equal employment opportunity, changing tax laws, changing markets, and changing technology all tend to make companies reshape their businesses. This could mean that strategic plans change, corporate "mission statements" change, personnel policy and procedures change, management's attitude toward EEO changes, corporate culture changes, and overhead and staff reductions are mandated.

Knowing how to survive and thrive in a time of organizational changes requires job proficiency, coping skills, a strong personality, and knowledge of the corporate culture. Without these tools, few minorities can survive on their business acumen alone.

Unfortunately, colleges and universities in the United States have not yet recognized the need to provide students with the coping skills for corporate culture shock. Although they could very easily provide the support with supplemental career counseling, seminars, and workshops, this does not appear to be a priority at this time.

If minority graduates from our nation's colleges and universities are to succeed in the corporate world, beyond a token few, institutions of higher education must keep pace with the changing complexity of business and industry. They must concentrate on preparing graduates for employment in industry who are not only academically sound but psychologically ready. Without the interpersonal skills for coping with the environmental imperfections of corporate life in America, minorities will not progress, in any appreciable numbers, in management for years to come.

Colleges and universities should be in the business of analyzing the success and failure rate of its graduates as they move through the business world. They need to get honest feedback data on what students experience once they enter the corporate world and why some are successful and others are not. They need to know, for example, what combination of factors tends to produce a successful career in the corporate world for minorities and what factors suggest failure. Colleges and universities also need to make an ongoing evaluation of the mood of corporate America and the mood of the federal bureaucracy as they relate to qualitative and quantitative employment practices of minorities, and they need to publish their findings. Institutions of higher education have a role to play in preparing young people for a successful transition into the business world, and, currently, this is not being done to the degree that it could be done. They also have a role to play in helping corporate America, as a recipient of the graduates they produce, take a hard look at the imperfections of its corporate culture.

Most of America's leadership, today, will agree that we have moved from an industrial society to an information society. They will also agree that the globalization of information is the one clear sign confirming the information age we now live in.

Satellites, telecommunications, cable television, and computers are transforming our personal lives, business lives, and educational experience at an incredibly rapid rate, whether we like it or not. Marshall McLuhan said, some years ago, that television would bring about a "global village," and I suppose that with the help of these other communications technologies, McLuhan's description of the world today was quite accurate.

However, with all of the new technology available and all of the information moving around the earth at lightning speed, some Americans will still lack the insight to survive and prosper in this information society. For as much as we now know about building information systems and technology, very little is known about the interpersonal skills required to survive and prosper among the people who run these organizations, or among the people who use the technology for profit-making activities.

There is an information gap in corporate America that suggests that without some very specific knowledge about the right interpersonal skills, minorities will have a difficult time trying to participate fully in the corporate mainstream management of this new information society.

Without corporate career counseling and mentoring relationships, few minorities will be able to negotiate the subjective criteria long established by the old traditional executives. The criteria for the most part have served more to screen minorities out of management jobs than into management jobs.

Most minority people entering the corporate world will experience some degree of corporate culture shock within the first two to three years of their career. Chances are that their desire for recognition, increased salary, and promotion will bring about a head-on collision with the built-in competition that today's corporate culture helps to create.

Simply stated, American corporations are a part of an imperfect society in which its minority citizens, for the most part, must still struggle for equality of opportunity on many levels. While it is true that corporations have greatly improved the conditions of the American society (minorities included), they have really not stood apart from the American society in a leadership position with greater moral or economic commitment to EEO.

Overall, the economic gains that minorities made in corporate America during the sixties and seventies have been as a result of the pressure that blacks and concerned whites have placed on society to act responsibly. Corporations, for the most part, have reacted to the temper and mood of the federal government and the will of the people by developing something they call corporate social responsibility.

Corporations tend to be reactionary to social environmental conditions, and you will generally find that corporate social responsibility activity over the years has been only as strong as the federal government and social activist groups in society pressured corporations to make it. While it is true that corporate social responsibility has become a consistent budget item for a number of major corporations, the level of participation now varies according to the degree of social and governmental environmental pressure in society.

In addition, the major corporations in America carry almost the total cost of corporate social responsibility programs because of their high visibility. With some few exceptions, medium-size and small corporations in America do very little to share the cost of implementing corporate social responsibility programs, because they have relatively low visibility and no real government and community pressure to do so. But think of what America could achieve if more corporations were involved.

The attitudinal conditions that prevail in the larger American society, at any given period of time, tend to be reflected to a degree in the corporate environment and, consequently, the corporate culture as well... it may be liberal or it may be conservative. Again, corporations are reactionary by nature and they react not only to market changes and technological changes but to changes in the temper and mood of society as well.

For example, people generally do not leave their political opinions, value systems, religious beliefs, cultural bias, and preconceived ideas about other people at home. They generally bring these things with them to the workplace, and depending upon their level of authority in the organization, and the temper and mood of the majority population in the country, they influence the shape and form of the corporate environment and ultimately the corporate culture of the organization.

These personal attitudes are quite often consciously or unconsciously carried over into the formal decision-making process of companies and, if left unchecked, will even find their way into things like personnel policy and procedure. This means, for example, that instead of organizational decisions being made from purely objective thinking, they are made more from the subjective feelings of the decision makers. It may be relative to the qualitative and quantitative employment practices of minorities and women, or it may involve the entire range of corporate social responsibility programs and activities: consumerism, safety, environmentalism, etc.

The point we want to remember here is that issues related to how fast or how high a minority or a woman can move up in nontraditional jobs in an organization may have more to do with what corporate people (decision makers) are currently reacting to in the larger American social environment than we are willing to admit.

Executives who learn to perfect the art of networking often go on in business to become "power brokers," and power brokers in business are the people who make things happen.

It has been said that the best time to look for a job is when you already have one. This executive handbook helps the reader to take a close look at the challenge of corporate job hunting, and offers a positive "how-to" approach to an often difficult experience. For example, it addresses the idea of how to build your self-confidence, develop a personalized job-search strategy, and deal with the job interview process.

During the 1960s and 1970s, many corporations retained management consultants to design and run management sensitivity training programs that went a long way toward helping some middle and upper levels of white executives understand and cope with the problems of integrating staff and meeting corporate equal employment opportunity goals as required by federal law. But how many of the minority employees entering those same corporations were actually prepared for the new experience that awaited them within the corporate culture? How many of them, for example, were aware of the rules and regulations that govern corporate life? How many of them were prepared to deal with its power to elevate human existence and change life-styles, or to create disorientation and anger and self-doubt?

Frankly, very few blacks and other minorities are adequately prepared even today for the corporate culture shock, despite the business management training that they might have received in school.

I

A Concept for Planning

Every person who wants to succeed in the corporate world should have his or her own plan for success. The plan, basically, should be developed along the lines of a strategic marketing plan with the author positioned as the prime product and the "bottom line."

Each plan should begin with some solid research that includes internal and external environmental scanning. You need to know, for example, the company's official view of its own purposes—often available in a formal "mission statement." And you need to know how the company proposes to accomplish its mission. You cannot expect to grow and develop in a highly competitive work environment if you don't really know or understand where the company is trying to go and how it plans to get there.

Sophisticated companies have a strategic plan of some sort and you need to know what that plan is. The company's plan, among other things, will indicate its direction for the future. It will show the short-range and the medium-range tasks that management is expected to perform; competitive activity; changes in corporate image that are being sought; financial sources available; and the corporate plan for personnel deployment and development.

In formulating your plan for success, be sure that you take into account the company's plan for the future and how it will implement that plan. The two plans should be compatible, from the viewpoint of personnel deployment and development. Therefore, you will also need to be sure that your skills and personality are consistent with what management will need to reach its goals and objectives.

Be guided by the fact that corporations are made up of skilled individuals performing specific tasks that relate to some overall plan. Corporations that are serious about their plans must have skilled operational-type people to carry out their plans, or those plans will not work. Consequently, you must have the skills the company needs, according to plan, or the company will not need you.

Your planning process may reveal that you need to go back to school, or take some classes in a subject that will enhance your value and importance to the company. The point here is that when the opportunity comes up to fill a certain job or perform a certain task, you need to be ready to step forward and assure the company that you are the person they are looking for.

An interesting thing about the planning process is that it forces you to be aggressive at the scanning stage. It is not enough to have very general information about the company and the direction it is moving in. You need to be as specific as you can be. This means that you are going to have to develop a networking system that extends into the personnel department, the finance and marketing departments, the corporate planning department, and any other area of the business that gives answers to your questions. In other words, your networking activity is an important part of your research efforts, and you need to have information that you can depend on.

While the subject of networking is discussed at length in a subsequent chapter of this book, it is important at this point to note that networking and networks are an essential ingredient in your career planning process.

Networking might best be defined as that interpersonal activity that results in positive professional and/or social relations, relations that are both supportive in nature and reciprocal. Regular contact is generally required in order to keep networking relationships alive and well. Successful American managerial and professional people of every variety depend quite heavily on networking and networks as potential power tools for advancement. They clearly understand that to grow and prosper in an American institution or organization they must have good networking skills and network resources. The power to win friends and influence people cannot be discounted in any way.

When beginning your planning process, always put it in writing so that you can review it from time to time and even change it when you need to. As indicated, planning is such a basic tool in successful corporations that most companies will routinely assemble a five-year written plan; this includes their alternative approaches to the business and contingency plans that can be implemented at the lowest operating level if need be.

You can also have a five-year written plan for your career, if you want to, and it doesn't take a lot of hard work to do it, either. The first step is to develop a strong positive mental attitude. If you don't like the direction your career is going in, believe that you can change it by altering any negative thoughts about yourself and your skills. By changing your consciousness from negative to positive, you immediately start to develop a strong mental positive attitude that puts you in charge of your career path.

Think in terms of a planning process that starts with a set of specific objectives. For example, it may be that your objective is to become the manager of sales promotion, in your existing company, within three years, and a director of sales promotion within five years. This specific objective should take you to the next step, which is to begin some networking activity, followed by an external and internal environmental scan.

Externally, you need to look at your objective from an industry point of view. For example, what is the future of the sales promotion executive's job within the industry? Is there a growing demand for these executives, or is there a limited future? If your scanning efforts show that there will be a low priority for sales promotion executives in the future of the industry, you may want to reconsider.

On the internal side of the scanning process, you will certainly want to evaluate your chances for the job and the future of that position in the company. There is no point in pursuing a dead-end job. Also don't forget to consider the potential power the position will carry within the company and the compensation. Some jobs pay more than others in a company because they are considered more important to the company's overall success. You will want to consider that.

If your research indicates that you need to improve your dress code, or upgrade your presentation skills, quickly factor these things into your planning. Whatever your basic fact-finding efforts produce, assign each issue a degree of importance, on a scale of one to ten, and include them in the plan in a priority order.

Remember that a real test of your ability to develop a meaningful plan for success will come when you can show honesty in your assessment of yourself, good information-gathering skills, good analyzing and interpretation skills, and a clear understanding of your environment.

Also remember that management understands and respects executives who have a realistic plan of direction and actively pursue the jobs they want in an aggressive but professional way. Your networking skills will show management what you are pursuing, and you will have to master this skill if you want to make real progress in your corporate career. As a footnote to good planning skills, always clearly identify your goals, objectives and strategy, and back that up with contingency plans, a timetable, a budget, a feedback system, and good supportive research.

PACKAGING YOUR CORPORATE IMAGE:
The Seven Corporate Noble Truths

An entry-level management employee who is not aware of the seven "Corporate Noble Truths"—the Right Attitude, the Right Clothes, the Right Speech, the Right On-Time Habits, the Right Prose, the Right Presentation Skills, and the Right Politics—is likely to be in serious trouble, sooner or later.

PLANNING MODEL

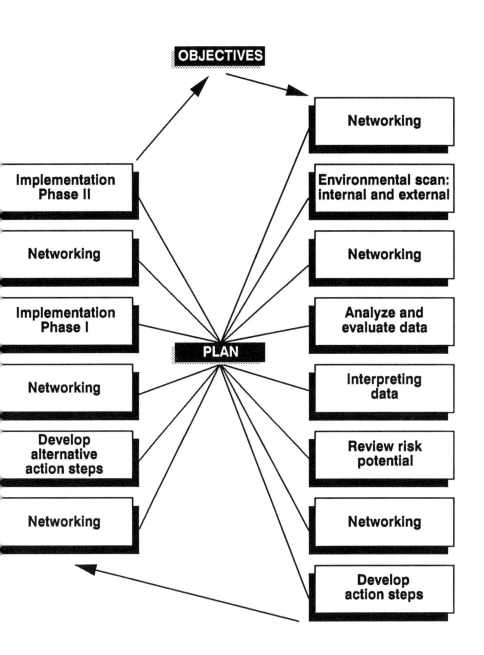

The Right Attitude

The so-called right attitude is not always clearly definable, which is why so many people get "shot down" on not having the proper attitude and they almost never really quite understand just what management means when the subject comes up. Corporate attitude, for the most part, is a subjective area that management uses to evaluate its employees' behavior patterns. It is that one thing that almost always escapes the new and the inexperienced employee, because it has a great deal to do with what the boss thinks about your ability to be a "team player," to be in the right place at the right time and say the right thing at the right time, to show great enthusiasm, no matter what the task at hand, no matter how ridiculous it may seem, or how long it may take to get the job done.

Judgments about people's attitudes are always subjective and are most often left to the interpretation of an employee's immediate supervisor. This means that your year-end evaluation may be based totally on your boss's or supervisor's definition of "right attitude," and it would pay you to know what that definition is. When your boss wants to criticize you in this area, he or she will generally say that you are not a "team player" or that you don't seem to fit in. Be very sensitive to this area and regularly get a reading on how you are doing as a member of the "team."

Also be mindful that no one is suggesting that you should play the role of an "Uncle Tom" or get into the "brown-nose game," but don't wait until your annual appraisal to try to find out what your supervisor really thinks about you. By that time, it might well be too late. Moreover, if you really don't know what your supervisor's definition is of a "good team player," you had better ask someone in the department who has earned the reputation of doing well in this area. Chances are that he or she knows the supervisor very well and knows how he or she thinks.

If the mere thought of having to change your attitude to suit your boss makes you feel like you are relinquishing some important part of your personality, or selling your soul for a job, then get some good objective counsel on the outside. You have to make sure that you *see it right—before you attempt to set it right.*

Always remember that as a paid employee of the company

you work for, you have agreed to support the organization by helping it to achieve its stated goals, objectives, and reason for being. This generally means that you have agreed not only to do your job to the best of your ability but that you will be cooperative, helpful, and pleasant to your fellow employees. In exchange for your salary and company benefits, you, as an employee, have a responsibility to try to be a positive and not a negative force in the department. This could involve getting to work early and staying late, in order to complete a project on time. It could also mean working on weekends, along with your associates, as a team effort to get a job done. The whole point is that having the "right attitude" in the corporate world generally means that you are willing to do all that you can do to help the company achieve its goals and objectives in a true spirit of cooperation.

Having the right attitude does not mean that you should be treated unfairly by your boss or your fellow employees and never say anything about it. It also does not mean that you should allow your co-workers to dump their work assignments on you, when they are responsible for their own work. There is no comfort in silent suffering. However, being a team player in the corporate world should mean sharing work assignments and sharing a positive team spirit. It should also mean taking responsibility for your part of the assignment and doing the best you can to make the project successful. When more than one person is assigned to a project, all of the members of the project are responsible. In a group project, the whole team is depending upon each team member to be accountable for his or her part, or the project could be a failure. Often, the difference between being successful and failing in a group project is personal accountability. As a professional, you will want to take pride in your work and be willing to be accountable.

Most people starting on their first jobs are not familiar with organizational behavior in the corporate world. The pressure to conform in this environment can have a tremendous negative effect on young people, who have recently obtained some level of higher education and perhaps subconsciously feel that they are beyond this type of behavior. For minority groups, the pressure can be even more difficult to adjust to, if it is interpreted as being directed at them in some special or unequal way. Therefore, you may have to take yourself through some real mental gymnastics to overcome feelings that changing your "attitude" means that you are going to have to become something less than a person that you can live with.

Realizing that some minority employees tend to have problems in this area, let us take a moment and look at at least one possible reason. Most entry-level managers come to the organizational structure in a spirit of confidence and individualism (having recently completed some level of higher education). Sometimes they are not emotionally prepared to immediately turn around and subject themselves to the stress of being "low man" on the organizational ladder. Because minorities have been told that education is the way to break through racially oriented social and psychological restrictions, pressures toward conformity within corporations can present some special adjustment challenges for spirited minority college graduates.

While the spirit of individualism may be a valued quality, once you get some power in the corporation, it is most often discouraged at the lower levels of management. Certainly, blacks and Hispanics have generally reached the doors of corporate America by utilizing their individual spirit, the same spirit that says to the world, "If you give me a chance, I'll show you what I can do!" Ironically, that same strong spirit, if not channeled properly in the corporate environment, can turn out to be a force working against an otherwise bright, talented young person.

The Right Clothes

Standards on dress in the United States are so diverse that you would find it difficult, at best, to impose a single dress code on the whole country. However, while it may be true that Americans, as a group, feel very comfortable about their varied dress styles, some sectors of American society have rigid ideas about what people should wear on the job, and apparently no one is really ready to challenge them. At least, no one working in the offices of a corporation. Corporations all over the United States tend to be conservative when it comes to the way they expect their management employees to dress, and anyone who is interested in a long and successful career in a corporation had better be sensitive to what the standards of dress are on the job.

Now, you might well ask what is meant by the "right clothes" in the corporate environment. The answer is simple. You should try to look as much like the members of senior management as you possibly can. Within reason, of course. While it is not expected that entry-level management people will have the financial means to buy expensive clothing, it is expected that they will make an effort to wear the same basic business-oriented styles that management wears. Right down to colors, color combinations, and even fabric. For whatever reasons, some corporate management people will be reluctant to let you know that you are wearing the wrong kind of clothes. They will simply observe your dress style over a period of time, and use your lack of awareness of your personal appearance as a strike against you. It is like having bad breath—no one will tell you about it. So you need to be your own boss when it comes to your wardrobe. Don't hesitate to subscribe to fashion magazines that tell you what successful business people are wearing. If you want to be successful in business, try to look the part and act the part of a successful business person. Your professional image is very important and you need to invest some money in a wardrobe that is fitting for an up-and-coming successful executive. Your investment will pay off for you in the long run.

In addition, if fashion magazines are not much help to you, you may want to get some professional advice on what to buy and how to manage your wardrobe. There are many books on the market that tell business people how to dress for a successful career. Buy one and see if you can learn something to help your career.

There are other grooming habits and skills that women should be aware of. For instance, knowing the difference between daytime makeup and evening makeup and knowing how to apply makeup so that it does not call attention to itself but tends to enhance the natural beauty.

Black and Hispanic corporate career-minded men should also be aware that most white corporate males in senior-level management do not wear facial hair. They feel that facial hair does not give them the "clean-cut" look that they desire, and the so-called clean-cut look is still preferred in today's corporate world, with some very few exceptions. The clean-cut look is also a cultural image development that has been encouraged in the corporate world by group image pressure among white males.

So, because over 90 percent of black and Hispanic males wear some degree of facial hair, this may or may not be a factor to consider when you are being evaluated for appearance as a member of the management team. Nevertheless, it is safe to say that a modest amount of facial hair is acceptable in corporate America today. But minority males should probably consider restricting their facial hair to the traditional mustache and nothing more, at least until they get to a level of real management power.

Yes, I know that this all sounds rather limiting and tends to infringe on expression of your own personality and tastes, but that's the way it is and it's hard to get around it. The reality is that you will need to take into account the corporate dress code when you join a company; and that code should be within reason for you, because conforming to it will have to be a part of your overall corporate plan.

The Right Speech

Everyone can improve his speech and many can become good speakers if they are willing to invest some time and effort. If you want to improve your speaking skills, you have to work at it. Step by step you must build on a foundation of good grammar, vocabulary, and style.

Here are some tips and techniques on effective speaking that can point you in the right direction.

• Think before you talk. Think about what you want to say and how you can best frame your commentary before you say anything. You don't have to know word for word what you are going to say, but it helps if you have a general idea. So don't try to memorize the points you want to make, just let your ideas and words flow naturally. Make your point or points, but be brief and concise.

• Show self-confidence when you talk. Don't be intimidated by your audience. Remember, if you feel that you have something to contribute to a discussion or if you want to inform people about some information that you have, speak and speak with self-confidence. When speaking, also remember to use eye contact to get the attention of your audience.

• Don't be afraid to use hand gestures to help express an idea or a feeling. A good speaker often makes gestures with his or her hands or arms to stress something he or she is saying. The use of gestures, however, should be natural and not exaggerated.

• Don't be afraid to disagree in a group meeting or a public forum. People are not impressed by those who have something constructive to contribute to a meeting or forum but fail to express their own mind or opinions.

• When it is necessary for you to disagree with other people in a meeting, use a natural tone and manner, and don't exaggerate.

• Always try to stay in control of your emotions even when someone is saying something outrageous. Self-control is a good sign of professionalism.

• If you find yourself in a debate on a particular issue, handle objections to your remarks smoothly. Also, try to anticipate obvious objections to a point that you plan to make in a debate. And counter the objection without losing your composure. Generally, the best counter for negative comments is sound positive rebuttal.

• It is generally good to show enthusiasm for your commentary. As a thinking individual, you have earned the right to contribute to a discussion if you are invited to the meeting. Your opinion may not be insightful or profound, but you are entitled to actively participate. *The important idea here is that you should try to add something constructive to the discussion; don't waste the group's time with unnecessary talk.*

• Regardless of the size of the meeting, there are four communication objectives that you need to consider before you decide to actively participate and speak out. Select and incorporate as many of the following objectives in your remarks as you believe necessary to get your point or points across to your audience: (1) persuade or get action from your audience; (2) inform your audience; (3) impress and convince your audience; and (4) entertain your audience.

Looking the part of a well-groomed executive is an important step for getting management's attention. But what is even more important than looking good is what comes out of the executive's mouth. It is not only *what* the executive says that counts, but also when he says it and how he says it that makes his or her image complete.

Effective oral communication skills and know-how should be developed early in a manager's career if the manager wants to move up in the organization. Remember, your success on the job could easily rest on your ability to communicate orally. Check your career survival plan at this point and make sure that it includes a provision for learning effective oral communication.

If necessary, identify people in your organization who handle oral communication well and try to borrow some of their strong points while developing your own personal style. Build a good vocabulary and learn to use words correctly. Don't try to overdo things by using a "big" word that draws people's attention, when you could just as easily have used a simple word that means the same thing. People are sensitive to other people who try to impress with "big" words.

If you are not confident about the way you speak, work hard on improving it. Go to a night school, if you have to, and get some professional instruction. What we are talking about here is an investment in the future, so whatever it costs to get the job done, do it!

Once you get a reputation in the company as a person with a speech deficiency or poor oral communication skills, it tends to stick with you. For example, if your first boss decides (for whatever the reason) to label you and he says that you do not speak very well, chances are that he will pass this negative judgment about you on to your next boss. At this point, you will be lucky if you even have a chance to defend yourself and try to change this negative image. So, if you are not articulate, you should think about changing that condition, because it could make the difference between success and failure on a particular job.

The Right On-Time Habits

Being on time in the corporate world is equivalent to saving the company money. In fact, to be trite, time *is* money to any serious business person, and when someone makes a habit of being late, that person is, in effect, stealing money from his or her employer.

You will be hard-pressed to find any company in the United States that is willing to tolerate lateness, of any kind, on an ongoing basis. Habitual lateness is just not one of the things that will earn you a promotion in the corporate world, or anything else, except a notice to leave—so why get into that habit?

On the other hand, coming to work early and always getting to meetings on time is a very admirable quality in corporate life. Don't get me wrong: I am not saying that getting to work early will in and by itself get you a promotion, but I do believe that it will certainly earn you a good reputation among management people, and together with your other good performance areas, it could lead to your being considered an outstanding candidate for better job opportunities.

Finally, don't be one of those people who try to justify their lateness by saying that they stay and work after closing hours. I can assure you that management really does not want to hear that kind of talk. Believe me, if your company's work schedule calls for a 9-to-5 working day, then you had better be there on time, if not before the scheduled time.

The Right Prose

We live in a society that places a great deal of emphasis on the written word (the pen *is* mightier than the sword), and corporate America is no different from the rest of our society on this subject. In fact, your ability to write well is so important to your success in the corporate world that one badly written piece of communication on an important subject to a member of senior management could cost you your job. Good communication skills in a company are worth money to management. Generally, people who write well in a company are singled out for important assignments for senior management, and over a period of time, management begins to depend on these people for their talents. Obviously, this kind of exposure to top management will never hurt your stock in the company.

The point to make here is that some people in positions of power in corporate America don't expect minorities to have good writing skills. If you don't know all of the company's approved idiomatic expressions, learn them and use them to show management that you can write and write well, using language that they understand. Remember that if you want to move up the corporate ladder, there is no way to get around poor writing skills.

There are many business-writing courses, seminars, and workshops that you can attend if you really want to improve your skills. In fact, many companies will even pay for studies if you ask them. Learning to write good business letters and other corporate communications is not a difficult thing to master. You can really start quite simply by getting copies of well-written communication material and work at home. Practice until you are really good, develop your own style of writing that is within the standard format, and you will earn respect and a good name for yourself.

The Right Presentation Skills

Over the years, many executives have made or lost their reputations on the basis of a single presentation. In fact, at some companies, a single presentation can be the catalyst for promotional opportunities for an entry-level executive, if the right senior management people see it and like it.

What makes the presentation such a highly touted forum remains something of a mystery. However, the corporate presentation does reflect the shape and form of real show business, and because America created Hollywood, we know that Americans love to be entertained. While the presentation concept has its basic intent to inform, the information given must be presented in such a way that it pleases the senses of management. The presentation must also fit the form and style that management is accustomed to seeing, or it will not be received well.

Importantly, management's demand for information actually extends well beyond mere facts, figures, and creative ideas. What we see in this case is a rather strong display of institutional conformity. It is not only what you say that counts but how well you say it, according to company tradition.

A candidate for our nation's highest office, today, must have the presentation skills of a professional actor, or he will most certainly lose points in the great American television debating forum. Whether right or wrong, our society, with the encouragement of the television news media, demands that our presidential candidates all look, speak, and present the issues with the confidence and charm of professional broadcasters or actors. This is institutional conformity in politics. In some respects it is similar to institutional conformity within corporations.

Management really wants to see good presentations. Presentations have become one of management's primary tools for measuring personnel potential. Now, to make a good presentation, you must know something about the style of the company and how management likes things presented. It is almost like developing a Broadway production around knowledge of what the public wants to see.

Obviously, the level of perfection required and the demand for excellence do vary from company to company, but the central idea here is that information imparted to management must be done "right." Cost is not a major consideration for many companies when it comes to putting on a good show for management. The importance of the information, of course, should have a relationship to the cost of the presentation, but it really does not always have to justify it altogether.

How the presenter dresses is an important factor. Management likes to see their people in very traditional dress when making a presentation. You must never wear anything that offends management's eye, or you will most certainly get silent demerits for personal appearance. Dressing properly for the presentation is so important that it has been reported that some management people have been turned off on the presenter because they could not stand the way the presenter looked.

The next crucial factor is your skill as a presenter. This relates to what you say, how well you say it, and how long it takes you to say it. Pay particular attention to things like diction, projection, accent, vocabulary, and pace. Listeners are distracted from the content if they cannot easily understand what is being said.

Remember, the real secret to being a good corporate presenter starts with having reliable and relevant data on your target audience. For example, who are the people you are going to present to and what do you know about them? In addition, how familiar is the intended audience with your subject and how much do they really want to know? Do they want a brief overview of the subject matter or do they want to know everything there is to know?

Next, you need to be able to anticipate the questions that will follow the presentation. The question-and-answer session of any presentation is like the icing on a cake. Why bake a good cake and then turn around and put a lousy icing on it?

Along these same lines, there is really no substitute for knowing your subject matter well and rehearsing it over and over and over again. In fact, if it is at all possible, try to have a few dress rehearsals in front of people who are sincere and knowledgeable about both your subject and the makeup of the intended audience. They could give you some valuable feedback before you do the final show. They could help you check your voice projection, pace, flow, content, closing, and so on. All of these things are extremely important in a presentation to a group of corporate executives, particularly if they are a group of top executives.

If you plan to have visual backup support, make sure that everything is in perfect working order ahead of time, and that you have a way to correct any mechanical failures. Mechanical failures have been the death of many potentially good presentations, because management generally holds the presenter responsible for any and all mishaps connected with the entire show, from the beginning to the end.

Finally, if you have the opportunity to look over the conference room where you will be making your presentation, check the lighting and sound systems and decide exactly where you should stand to make the presentation, for maximum effect. Also look at the seating arrangement and make sure that you have your audience seated where you want them, and not just anywhere they end up sitting because no one ever directed them to sit elsewhere. As the presenter, you are almost always given the opportunity to "set the stage."

The Right Politics

The "right politics" in any company is a relative thing, and what makes your politics the right politics in any company is that your political efforts produce favorable results when you have a need to call on political allies.

In the final analysis, the right politics is being in a position to identify yourself with, or ally yourself with, a politically powerful person or group of people within the company who can provide short-term or long-term job security and job opportunities.

Long before you decide to ally yourself with a particular group of politically influential executives, you should understand what makes them tick:

1. These executives are held together by association and mutual support of one another.

2. If they disagree with one another, they almost never do so in public view.

3. Their coming together on issues is the basis of their strength, and this makes the group a real force to deal with.

4. Should a member of the group come under attack, the group will support him or her.

5. Leadership in the group is predicated on rank and power in the group.

6. Ambition is a prevalent characteristic within the group.

7. The group maintains itself by selective informal recruitment.

8. The promise of job security and job opportunity is the major attraction to the group.

Can you expect to be approached formally to join a politically influential group within the corporation? The answer is *no*! Do not expect ever to receive a formal invitation to join such a group, because there *is* no formal invitation or indoctrination of any kind. Technically, the group does not exist at all, and no one will ever admit to its existence in public.

How do you join a politically active and influential group of executives within a company? In most instances, it is by identification, group association, and most important, group acceptance. Generally speaking, someone who is an existing member of the group first extends his or her hand in friendship, which really serves as a kind of prescreening exercise. Eventually, if that person likes you and thinks that you will "fit in" in the group, he will act as a sponsoring person by introducing you to the right people. New recruits are important to groups like these, because they need support from bright and talented people within the ranks.

In addition, bright and talented young executives make good, bright, talented top management. These people can be moved up quickly within the organization, without the need to justify or defend their movement over other people who are not part of the political group, and who have been around a long time. Remember, management always reserves the right to say who moves up in the organization, so the idea that everyone in the company has an equal chance to be a part of senior management is not entirely true. Some people are "handpicked," while others will never be invited, for one reason or another.

Now, if all of these group dynamics are still not clear to you, think of them as being like the workings of a professional fraternity, and you will be very close to an understanding of how and why corporate politics works in large American corporations.

Playing company politics can be a very risky business, and you should understand the pros and cons before you decide to be a player. If you can't stand to lose the game, don't get into the game. From a political point of view, the bigger the opportunity, the greater risk of getting hurt by the opposition group or a competitive person involved. Nevertheless, people who want success relatively quickly almost inevitably become players.

On the other hand, *if you elect not to be a political player,* someone who is a player may very well come along and use you as his or her political stepping-stone. Call it an "unfriendly takeover" if you will. So the question of whether you should get involved in company politics may be an academic one, if competition is playing the game and you need to protect yourself from people who are more actively ambitious than you are.

PERSONALITY AND SKILL GO TOGETHER

How well you do in corporate life in America, or how long you are able to survive, has a lot to do with your skills and personality. You must maintain a good balance between these two assets at all times, or you will not be successful. Remember that your skills cannot exist without a good personality to promote them and your good personality does not mean very much without skill or talent to earn respect for you. They must coexist and one must never lose sight of the other.

Your success in corporate life will also have a lot to do with your ability to market your skills and your personality effectively. There is really no substitute for developing a favorable personality and some type of expertise that makes you an asset to a company instead of a liability.

Corporations, for the most part, are in the business of buying and selling goods and services of one kind or another, and they do need experienced people who are able to work together to help them achieve their corporate goals and objectives in a cost-effective way. Demonstrate that you have what business needs, and your value to business and industry will be greater than you can imagine, greater in compensation and greater in prestige.

Developing a good personality, suited for corporate life, may not be easy. While you will come in contact with many helpful, sincere, and supportive people, chances are you will also come in contact with an equal number of destructive, insincere people, who are eager to impede your progress. Obviously, you will have to learn how to go around the corporate "gatekeepers to progress," or you will fail from the personality point of view.

In any event, it is not an impossible challenge. It means, however, that you will have to study your opponent's weaknesses and strengths like a prizefighter in a boxing ring. You must learn when to punch and duck, dodge and stay away from low corporate blows.

This is all part of your preparation for becoming a "seasoned corporate professional," because you must learn these tactics without losing your composure 99 percent of the time. When you lose your composure, you lose your ability to think clearly, and when you cannot think clearly, chances are that your opponent will take advantage of you.

If you push a spider off an object, that spider has the capability of spinning a silk thread instantaneously and reattaching itself to another object before it meets disaster. In other words, there are very strong instincts for survival in a spider and you can learn a lot about instincts for survival by observing other forms of life and their habitat.

You should not hesitate to observe the seasoned corporate professional who has mastered the interpersonal skills to be successful in the organization. He or she, more than anyone else, can help you in a real "tight spot." In fact, you are encouraged not to wait until you are in a tight spot to seek out a mentoring relationship with someone who is in a position to guide you in the art of developing the necessary coping skills to be successful. Anticipate the fact that in a highly competitive environment, where the stakes are high, you will at some point need some good advice about how to handle a situation or person that threatens your position in the company.

Management has a lot of respect for talented people who have basic survival instincts: the ability to get the job done, despite the obstacles of personality that might stand in the way. Companies will pay a lot of money for people who can work effectively under challenging conditions, and if you are a minority person who can do this, you will not go unnoticed in a corporation that respects and needs talented people.

Marketing your personality in a corporation can become a matter of giving management the opportunity to observe you under trying conditions for a period of time and earning a favorable reputation, or having other people, inside and outside of the company, comment favorably about your positivity and personality. Remember, everyone likes a positive personality. If you can demonstrate a positive outlook working under trying circumstances, chances are that you will influence people in a very favorable way.

Now, being a minority person and working in a corporate environment can create some added challenges that a nonminority person would not have to contend with. For example, it could be that you are resented for having a position of authority, and you are expected by management to give nonminority people direction that they are unwilling to accept.

If your race ever becomes a factor in your ability to discharge your duties, you need to document it and seek counsel and advice from management. This is also a time to get advice from your mentoring relationship with a seasoned professional manager as well, one who knows the company and the people who make the decisions that really count.

Biased or unfair treatment based on race is not something you should treat lightly. It can grow well out of proportion if left unchecked early. In a highly competitive working environment, discrimination based on race can appear at any time, and it then becomes a question of how you are going to handle it. Your personality will have a lot to do with your reaction to discrimination of any kind. If you are given to immediate, strong emotional response, chances are that you will be defeated in your attempt to handle the situation. If, on the other hand, you remain calm and seek expert advice and counsel, chances are that you will end up in good shape, regardless of how long or how difficult the process of growing through the experience may be.

In the final analysis, where discrimination exists to the extent that you cannot perform your assigned job, you will find that there are generally three issues that you will ultimately have to address:

1. Will management support you because of your skill (value to the business) and strong positive mental attitude?

2. Will management change your assignment or department and try to resolve the problem?

3. Do you want to work at a company that has so little interest in your career that they will neither support you in your assigned job nor remove you from the problem area?

TIPS ON MARKETING YOUR SKILLS

Business and industry have the money to pay for the talent they need. Therefore, it will pay you to package and sell your skills much the same way a company markets its products. You must research the business, identify their needs, place your product in the most attractive package possible, and sell them on what you have to offer.

Marketing your skills is not a difficult thing to do, but it does require some creative thinking and effort. Here are some suggestions on how to get started:

• Identify all of the key professional organizations and associations in your field and take out a membership in the organization that can best help you professionally; for example, the American Management Association, the American Marketing Association, the National Association of Market Developers.

• Once you have joined an important professional group, become active in that group and earn the respect and admiration of your associates.

• If given the opportunity, write articles for your professional journals and trade publications to demonstrate your knowledge and insights in your field. If it requires time and effort to research a subject to write a good article, invest the time and effort; it will pay off for you in the future.

• If given an opportunity to make presentations before other professionals in your field, accept the offers and establish yourself as a good public speaker.

• Don't be afraid to take on special assignments that give you exposure to your industry associates. These groups often have direct pipelines to the senior management of corporations, and management is always looking for young talent that is capable of earning the respect and the admiration of people in the industry.

• If you are scheduled to be recognized by some trade association or respected professional group, let your management know about it. Invite them to the dinner or luncheon, or whatever, and let them be a witness to your achievements. Don't hide your recognition opportunity, because this is a very important part of your marketing process.

• Finally, to be successful at marketing your skills and talents, you must create a good corporate image by promoting yourself as a positive, capable, and self-confident person. Don't be reluctant to tell people that you enjoy your work and the company that you work for. Business people admire other business people who enjoy their work and who appear committed to their business.

II

Understanding Corporate Thinking

CORPORATE PLAYERS

Who are the people who can help or hurt your career? And how important is it that you know who the important corporate players are? Without knowing who the important players are in the company and how much influence they have, one always runs the risk of making enemies of the wrong people, and this sort of thing can come back to haunt you later on in your career. Always remember that some of the most important people in the company may not necessarily be the senior-ranking people, but rather people who hold key positions in the company and who are in a position to do you harm, if they really want to, for example, the personnel manager or director.

COMPANY RULES

Policies and procedures in any company are an important consideration. Therefore, your plan for a successful career in a company must also take into account all of the relevant rules and regulations, particularly the policies that could affect you and your well-being. This is like learning the law of the land. Every entry-level management employee should make it a point to research the company's personnel practices and meet some of the people who run that department. Also remember that you have a personnel file that you should be intimate with as long as you are working for that organization. There should never be any surprises in your official corporate record. In fact, why not review it every six months?

Be aware that business cannot function well in the presence of chaos. Therefore, policies and procedures are created to help management run the business in an orderly environment. If there is any serious threat to that orderly environment, the offenders will be dealt with swiftly.

Needless to say, with few exceptions, management-level employees who participate in, or strongly support, employee causes of one kind or another generally do not last long in a company. There are some exceptions, of course, but normally, company policy and procedures are supposed to cover the employee channels of redress. If, on the other hand, an issue arises that is not covered by the existing company regulations, it is quite possible that you can convince management to rewrite or revise the rules. This type of activity, however, must be well thought out and well orchestrated within company channels.

Also be aware that in most corporations, there are two sets of rules and regulations. One set is based on the written stated policy and the other is based on unwritten policy. Unwritten policy is generally a matter of long-established company tradition, custom, and management style. Know that this concomitant policy does exist, and consider its importance when developing your survival plan.

Corporate-level research information can be looked at from a departmental point of view as well. Strong corporations, today, establish departments that have a positive effect on the overall organization and, more important, make an effective fit into the strategic plan. This includes the company's goals, objectives, tasks, style, policies, procedures, resources, personnel communication practices, and so forth.

CORPORATE DISCRETION

Understanding how the corporate "grapevines" work in the company you work for may be more important than you would expect. In fact, these channels of information exist on many levels in every large company and tend to interchange at various points like railroad switching stations, giving data to human talking trains scurrying from floor to floor and department to department.

If you are lucky enough to know the people who actually operate these information switching stations, and if they like you, you are considered a person with valuable contacts. And, in fact, the information made available to you by these informal channels may on occasion prove extremely useful.

Generally speaking, however, people who actively participate in the unofficial internal information gathering and dissemination systems are not the corporate master politicians. Politicians may, in fact, use them, but these individuals are people who, for the most part, just spread rumors. These people have the capacity to be both very dangerous and very helpful at the same time. It all depends on whom they happen to be talking about on any given day, and what they are telling their many co-informants that will circulate throughout a company facility—and maybe even throughout the company's worldwide facilities, if it happens to be a multinational corporation and the victim is an important personality in the organization.

The real point to learn here is that the important internal information conduits seldom, if ever, care whom they are giving the information to; they just love the status of being a major source of information and feel, somehow, that it is their duty to get the job done, regardless of who may be hurt. Whether or not they personally know the individual they are talking about, or whether the rumor is based on fact, is really unimportant. The most important thing that they have to do is pass the information on to their contacts. It is not their job to verify the data.

Corporate pipelines or grapevines exist on virtually every level in the corporate world. Often these channels of information transcend age, sex, race, and job title. A rumor may travel via secretaries, supervisors, and managers to vice-presidents and above. Every level participates in some way. Few corporate departments worth their salt are excluded. Therefore, discretion is a matter of self-defense in the corporate world—not merely a question of choice or style, but a basic necessity.

EXECUTIVE PRIVILEGES AND POWER

Did you ever stop to think why the competition for jobs in the corporate world is so intense? What is so special about the corporate world that people not only want to work in corporations but also want to be very successful in them?

Do all who pursue a career in the corporate world, for example, share the same motivations and therefore aspire to the same goals? For several years now, students in great numbers have been abandoning the more conventional studies in our colleges and universities to actively pursue business-related studies that could ultimately lead to a career in the corporate world. Why, then, the sudden shift toward business and industry? And why this desire for corporate jobs?

If you have never really concerned yourself with such questions, then take a moment or two and seriously think about them. Ask yourself questions such as: What direction is the country now leaning in and where do I fit in all of this? The conclusions that you draw could be very helpful to you in better understanding what is taking place (vocationally) all around you, and, more important, how you can benefit from this newfound insight. For example, there is no doubt that the private sector (corporate life in particular) is currently the hottest game in town. Compare the corporate salaries and benefits with those in other fields of endeavor, if you are not quite convinced of this.

The fact of the matter is that most people in our society prefer prosperity to poverty, and corporations today represent the key to America's continued prosperity. Few people will argue this point.

While it is true that equality of opportunity has not yet been fully obtained in corporate America, corporations still offer one of the greatest single opportunities to dramatically improve your income and status in this society.

Some years ago, a Harvard University professor by the name of Dr. David C. McClelland, together with his associates, investigated some of the primary factors related to *individual motivation in corporate America*. The results of their studies led them to develop a "three-motive theory of psychological motivation." The three motives were *"Need for Achievement," "Need for Power,"* and *"Need for Affiliation."*

The Need for Achievement, as explained by Dr. McClelland, is reflected in the desire to excel or to do a good job. The Need for Affiliation is shown when there is a desire to establish, maintain, or prolong a positive emotional relationship with others. And, finally, the Need for Power exists when a person has a particular goal in mind that involves the exercising of authority over other people.

The whole point in mentioning Dr. McClelland's work is that corporations today really do understand what motivates people to work hard, and they are more than willing to provide the incentives that create the atmosphere for corporate people to meet their needs. When you stop to think that some executives in these organizations have the responsibility for managing millions and billions of dollars, it is, after all, in the corporation's best interest to keep the "captains of industry" happy, by creating an environment in which the managers can meet their own needs. Whether we are talking about achievement, power, or affiliation, all of the support systems are made available to managers in corporations. In this instance, corporate America really does do its homework.

Corporations in America know, for example, through various "needs assessment studies," what most American people "really want" and what it will take to keep them reasonably happy. It all, then, becomes a matter of creating the environment in which the owners can make money and, concurrently, reward the people who do the best job of running their business. Now, what exactly do corporations reward the people with who do the best job of running their business?

For the most part, owners reward corporate people with executive privileges and with power over other people in the organization. Power to hire and the power to fire, the power to promote one employee over another, and the right to send someone anywhere in the world, providing the employee is willing to go. The degree of power depends on the rank and responsibility of the executive in the organization. The bigger the company, the greater the privileges and the power, as a rule.

Executive privileges can be so vast that they almost stagger the imagination. Try to think of personally having or having access to the following:

• Stock options, bonuses, and a big salary—six or seven figures
• Corporate jets, limousines, a company-owned apartment, rent-free
• Expenses for entertainment, a company car, and a gasoline credit card
• Housing in the best suburban communities of the country
• Vacation expenses for family members
• The use of practically all corporate facilities and professional personnel for personal needs
• Travel privileges, for both professional enhancement and personal need, as well as travel time out of the office
• General dining privileges of all varieties
• Paid tickets or company-reserved seating for plays, movies, championship events of every kind imaginable: basketball, baseball, football, tennis, and the like

The list of executive privileges for some corporate people is almost endless. It all depends upon how important the executive is to the business and how big the business. That is, how big its sales and profits are. Now, how does that list strike you just for starters?

What does all of this discussion about executive privileges and power have to do with "how to survive in the corporate world"?

Many people experience some degree of trauma in the early stages of making an adjustment to corporate life. They find that they are dealing with uncharted territory, and this unmarked ground does not always afford them the luxury of knowing how and when to respond favorably to the infrastructure of the corporation. As a result, some new managers find themselves overreacting to the hierarchy on certain occasions, and some find themselves not reacting at all, even when they should. Some even find themselves reacting to the right people in the company, but for all the wrong reasons. That is why you really have to try to understand the motives of upper-level executives as early in your career as possible.

Knowing when to react and how to react and with whom to react is very important for a young executive after joining a company. But reading corporate signs and signals can be a tricky exercise, even for experienced executives. That is why, should they not know how to respond to some situation, they will first check things out by way of their network system.

The idea that you might be able to hide indefinitely and thereby avoid any confrontations with the hierarchy is unrealistic. Invariably, you will have to take responsibility for some assignment, and it is at this point that you could become open for attack, should some senior-level executive feel the need to exercise his or her executive power. The whole point here is that because the senior executive has executive privileges and power, he can determine when it is to his advantage or pleasure to use it.

Having power over other people, by virtue of your rank in a company, can be a very ego-gratifying experience. It is important to try to understand this motivating force within the corporation, because it is one of the main reasons people place so much importance on executive privileges and power. If you keep this in mind, it may be easier for you to grasp the important fact that an attack on an employee who is a member of the minority group is not necessarily racially oriented. In fact, it may not be personal at all. Rather, it may be a simple matter of someone having the privilege or power and wanting to use it.

CORPORATE CULTURE

Much has been written recently about the "corporate culture." Some corporations are touted as being excellent companies because they have strong corporate cultures, while others have gone through painful, and often expensive, struggles to identify or even create a corporate culture. Every corporation has its own style, a way of doing business that encompasses everything from how executives manage, how assignments and promotions are made, to how meetings are conducted, products marketed, and consumers treated. That style becomes corporate culture when it also includes common values, beliefs, and behavior that motivate employees to work toward a shared objective. Corporate culture determines what is acceptable and expected behavior for all employees.

Since most companies do not train new employees in their corporate culture, it is up to the employees to learn it for themselves. Having a mentor in the company can facilitate this learning process for a new employee. Minority employees are often at a disadvantage in this learning process, because they are less likely than their white counterparts to have a mentor in the company or strong networking resources. Therefore, it is vital for minority employees to observe successful older employees and learn as much as they can about how people function in the company or the acceptable behavior of the corporate culture. A lack of this knowledge is no excuse for mistakes in judgment and inappropriate behavior which could result in serious setbacks in an employee's career, if not the loss of his job.

Corporate culture is used to encourage employee productivity and is exercised in a myriad of ways in the everyday functioning of a company. It is not unusual for employees to be expected to place the company and its needs before their own. While the individual's right to succeed and aspire to the highest ranks of the company is as American as apple pie, the life and success of the company must be the common goal of all its employees.

What does this mean in terms of the minority manager? Is he any different in the corporate culture from the white manager? The minority manager is different in the sense that some acts or behavior of the corporate culture directed at him can be interpreted as being racially motivated, whether they are or not. The black manager has the challenge of not only learning the corporate culture but also having to determine sometimes if it is being used to disguise acts of racism or discrimination against him.

Is It Racism or Corporate Culture?

I. For the moment, imagine that you are a member of a sales management team attending a two-day company sales conference at a fashionable suburban conference center and country club. This annual motivational and recognition event brings together the top sales achievers of the company and a very select group of senior management people.

During the cocktail hour on the first day, you and several of your associates are standing in a group talking and enjoying a sociable drink. The group is composed of several members of the company's senior management and a few members of middle-level management. In this circle of six to eight people, you are the only black person; the others are all white. In fact, out of a group of ninety to one hundred people attending the conference, there are only four minority employees present, one Asian, one Hispanic, and two black executives, including yourself.

Suddenly, the president of the company enters the reception room and walks directly over to your group. Somewhat taken aback by his appearance, one of the senior vice-presidents steps forward to greet him and then asks him what he would like to drink. When the president replies, the vice-president turns to you and volunteers you to go and get the president's drink. When you return with the drink, the vice-president takes it from your hand and gives it to the president. Is this an act of racism, or is it an act of one person using his rank and privilege to achieve an end?

It could have been an act of racism, but it could also have been simply an act of the corporate culture, in this case, using one's rank and privilege. Let us assume for now that it was by chance that the person the vice-president volunteered was the only black person in the group. Let us also assume that it was not entirely unreasonable for the black manager to feel that he was singled out to perform what he considered a degrading service. After all, black people have historically been servants in this country, and the vice-president didn't ask one of the several white executives in the group to get the president a drink. Did he on some level of consciousness view the black manager as a servant and not the peer of the other executives in the group?

On the other hand, it is not uncommon in any corporation for a senior management person to ask a junior management person to perform a trivial task. Senior managers consider such requests routine matters, and complying with them is an important part of being a "good team player." It is entirely conceivable that any of the white junior managers present would have jumped at the chance to be singled out to get the president a drink, that he would have viewed it as an opportunity, no matter how fleeting, to gain the president's attention.

Having power over other people because of one's rank or status in a company can be a real ego-gratifying experience. It is critical that minority managers understand this ego-gratifying concept and be able to distinguish when someone is using his rank and station to exercise power and when someone is behaving in a racially motivated way. If minority executives can routinely make this distinction, it will be easier for them to grasp the fact that certain behavior directed at them may not be racist or even personal. It may be merely an opportunity for some high-ranking executive in the organization to use his or her rank and privilege of power.

When it is questionable whether behavior is racially motivated or part of the corporate style, black employees should make the distinction by using patterns of behavior, rather than a single act, for confirmation. They can begin this process by considering the following questions:

• Could the act or behavior directed at the black employee be directed at a white employee in the same manner?
• Was this behavior an isolated act or part of a pattern of behavior?
• Have other people been observed behaving in the same way with white employees?

Although black employees have to learn the behavior of the corporate culture and recognize that everything unpleasant directed at them is not racially motivated, they must not be too willing to consign any suspicions of racism to the corporate culture. Certainly, some employees, senior management included, are guilty of racist acts. Blacks and other minorities should not be afraid to use their instincts. Instinct can be a good barometer for measuring subtle acts of racism, but instinct alone is not enough. As with most members of minorities, the black manager had had enough experience with racism to be aware of the subtle signs by the time he reached the corporate world, and everything in his experience, background, and history told him that this was a racial incident. However, signs or indications of racism in the corporate world are not always enough to suggest or warrant action or reaction. Unsubstantiated charges of racism are simply charges and nothing more. The black manager must be able to prove what he believes to be true. And, in this case as in any similar case, proof of racism calls for written and/or corroborative evidence from credible people who are willing to go on record and confirm your charges.

II. You have just received a promotion to the position of director of market research and are pleased with the progress you have made in the company over the last ten years. While life in the corporation has not been easy, you have managed to avoid many of the problem areas while developing a slow but progressive career path.

In a department of twenty-five staff people, five are minority people, including you. You are well respected in the department, and you enjoy the reputation of being a good manager.

One day your boss invites you to join her on a business trip to California to research a new computer system that could help to generate substantially more business for the company. The trip will require that the two of you travel together and spend several days evaluating the new concept. This is the first business trip the two of you have made together since your new promotion to the director level. Things have not always been perfect between the two of you, but the relationship has not been a negative one, either. For the most part, the two of you have worked well together, and there are no problems between you at this time.

Flying at forty thousand feet, the two of you have just completed lunch and some casual conversation about world affairs when your boss turns toward you with a pleasant facial expression and says, "Amy, you know you are so well accepted in our department now that I don't even think of you as being black. You seem to fit in so well."

Is the vice-president's statement a sign of racism or is it something else? How would you respond to the boss's remark under the circumstances, or would you respond at all?

In this example, there is evidence of unconscious racism which can be a very dangerous form of racism in a corporate environment. Often, some professed liberals in the corporate world are really "closet racists," who may go undetected for years. Racist tendencies, conscious or unconscious, supported by a powerful position in a corporation can have a far-reaching effect on minority personnel.

In this case, it can be reasonably assumed that this form of racism was unconscious, because the context in which the remark was made was pleasant and friendly. In fact, the director's boss was really trying to compliment the director, and in her insensitive attempt, ended up making a racist remark. Incidentally, this is not uncommon in the corporate world with regard to minority and nonminority relationships and communications between management people at many levels.

However, in order to resolve this issue the director needs to quickly decide if her response or lack of response will (1) significantly influence a favorable change in the boss's unconscious attitude, (2) heighten the boss's race relations awareness level, (3) confuse the boss and perhaps create a strained relationship, (4) gain assurance for herself that her dignity has not been destroyed or her principles compromised.

Based upon the fact that the director has had a good working relationship with her boss and that there is no history of racial remarks in their relationship, she has two distinct choices: (1) ignore the remark and see if any racial remarks come up again before she attempts to clear things up; (2) use the opportunity to do some race relations consciousness-raising. If she chooses the latter, the director could explain to her boss that while she understood that the boss was paying her a compliment, which she appreciated, the statement was the kind that some blacks might find offensive. She could then explain the sensitivity that some blacks might have in such a situation. She could then reassure her boss that she realized no negative connotation was implied or intended.

An open and friendly discussion of race relations sensitivities between management people can often be quite helpful, because it establishes an awareness and an opportunity for people to be candid if they want to without being threatened.

III. You are a Hispanic executive assistant working for the vice-president of manufacturing operations. You are the first and only Hispanic person to hold this staff position in the fifty-year history of the company. With fourteen years of executive staff experience in the company, you felt quite comfortable in accepting this job, because you had earned the promotion and you were the next staff executive person in line for the job. Although you did not know very much about your new reporting officer before accepting the position, you were highly regarded by most management-level people in the company because of your skills and years of good standing in the company.

After two months on the new job, you discover that there are certain routine fact-gathering and decision-making activities in your job description that your boss has not asked you to perform. Being the concerned professional that you are, you decide to investigate this matter by asking a few questions of the other executive assistants who perform basically the same duties for other officers. You ask if they are aware of any duties in their job descriptions that their bosses do not permit them to perform, such as reviewing salary increases for the branch management personnel and staff performance appraisals based on policy guidelines. They all say that they handle these duties as routine, confidential matters.

Three months later when it is time for all vice-presidents in the company to review salary increase recommendations and performance appraisals screened and processed by their executive assistants, you realize that your boss has not involved you in these activities. As a result, you become disturbed and decide to call your boss's former executive assistant who retired but said that he would help you if you needed his support. You ask him about the salary and appraisal issues, and he confirms that he always handled those matters for the vice-president without any problems at all. He further says that he does not know why you have not been asked to perform these duties, because they are definitely part of your job. All of the executive assistants handle this information and make decisions about it. He can't understand why you were not given these responsibilities, since you are certainly skilled and highly qualified.

Surprised and disappointed at the same time, you are convinced that the only way to clear up this issue is to discuss it with your boss and see what he has to say about it. However, before you have a chance to speak with him about the matter, you learn from a friend that your boss has been secretly sending all of the branch salary and evaluation data up to the group vice-president's office for processing. This, of course, is highly irregular and suggests that you are not to be trusted in matters of decision making and confidentiality. In addition, you are reminded that your own performance appraisal could be subject to question on matters related to salary guidelines, policy, and handling confidential information. This is traditionally a most important part of the executive assistant's job, and your lack of experience in this area could negatively affect your future success at the company.

After much thought and deliberation, you decide to discuss administrative procedures with your boss. Your approach is tactful but direct. You tell him that you are eager to see that his department runs efficiently and that all work submitted to the group vice-president is up to company standards. You also want to be sure that he has no concerns about your capability. He assures you that he has no such concerns. You then remind him that he must submit the salary recommendations and performance appraisal material to the group vice-president and assure him that you are ready to do the administrative workup on this whenever he is ready. This forces your boss to admit that he has taken care of this task already. You ask him if there was any reason he did not call on you to handle the assignment, and he cannot give you any good reasons for his behavior except to say that he wanted to do it that way, that it was his decision not to involve you this time. After all, you were new on the job.

A week later you learn from a white executive, who is part of your network, that your boss does not have a history of being liberal on issues around women and minorities and that you would do well to get out of his department ·as soon and as quietly as possible.

Is your boss exercising his executive privilege within the corporate culture, or is his behavior racially motivated?

The executive assistant has valid and collaborative support for his belief that the vice-president's behavior is outside the corporate culture of the company and that it is racially motivated. Every other employee with his job title and description, including his predecessor, performed these confidential, decision-making duties routinely. Further, he was told by someone he trusted and who was in a position to know that his boss was not favorably disposed toward women and minorities.

The vice-president's excuse that the executive assistant was new on the job was not sufficient, since he was skilled and experienced enough to get the job in the first place. Certainly his newness on the job could not justify the vice-president's behavior in having these duties performed by other people without the assistant's knowledge. His explanation that he did it because he wanted it that way did not leave the door open for further communication about his actions and their effect on the assistant.

Working directly for someone who is biased and behaves in a prejudicial manner is a sure way to have an unsuccessful, stressful career experience. It would be unproductive, if not destructive to the executive assistant's career, to continue to confront his boss on these issues and others that are sure to emerge. If the executive assistant wants to remain in the company and continue to progress, he must develop a plan of action to transfer to another department. All too often people who work under unsatisfactory conditions or with unreasonable bosses stay too long in their jobs. They tend to have repeated confrontations with their bosses before they decide to try to transfer to another department or leave the company. The executive assistant is at an advantage at this point, because his boss does not know that the assistant is aware of his views or his behavior. Further, there has not developed between them at this point a confrontational, adversarial relationship. Once the executive assistant develops his plan of action and starts his internal, or external, job search, the chances are good that the vice-president will not try to impede his moves. A good strategy for dealing effectively with a boss that proves to be an adversary is not to let him know what you are thinking or planning until it is too late for him to react negatively and try to hinder your progress.

While this approach is easily suggested, it is not as easily implemented. It requires tact and diplomacy for explaining the desire to change positions without criticizing the boss. It requires promoting one's skills and experience, career aspirations, and desire to contribute to the company in the most positive way possible. A written plan must be drawn up that identifies networking opportunities, job opportunities, and a timetable for positive action.

From Another Perspective

For the last several pages in this chapter, the subject of corporate culture has been discussed from a practical point of view using the case-study method to reinforce certain concepts and concurrently bring certain issues to light. Now let's look at this same subject matter from a slightly different vantage point and see if a more comprehensive picture can be presented.

As your career expands, you will need the ability to scrutinize corporate culture very quickly and make judgment calls that could have an effect on your professional growth and development for years to come. To fully understand the corporate world, you must first recognize that no two organizations operate the same way. Every organization (profit or nonprofit) has its own concept of reality that sets it apart from the rest of the world. This individual tone, flavor, or personality of the organization is created not by historical accident, but by the quality of the people who manage the organization... from the Board of Directors right down the line of executive decision makers.

You might think that your exposure to and knowledge of the corporate culture at one organization would guarantee your success at any corporation. Unfortunately, this is not the case. Each and every work experience you encounter requires that you research the organization well. This means that one of the first things you will want to do after joining a new organization is to make sure that you understand the political realities of the company. Then you can take the necessary steps to adjust your management style and coping skills to fit the new organization.

A Specialist Talks About
Corporate Culture

Human resource specialist William M. Boyce, adjunct professor at Cornell University School of Industrial and Labor Relations, and presently Human Resources Director of Yonkers General Hospital, believes that corporate culture is a primary ingredient in the total makeup of a healthy, vibrant company. However, says Boyce, corporate culture is not necessarily a force for good. On one hand, it can serve as a force to encourage productivity, unity of purpose, and a strong bottom line. On the other hand, it can serve as a force to promote poor employee morale, lackluster employee performance, and a weak bottom line. "It all depends on the chief executive officer's beliefs, strengths, and management style." The company's written procedures and policies are the obvious things to examine. But the chief executive officer's values, perceptions, and sensitivity to employees are another matter altogether. These are unwritten factors that make a significant impact on the company culture, and they are not found in personnel manuals. For example, if the CEO is lacking in positive values, good perception skills, and sensitivity to people, chances are his organization's culture will weaken over a period of time.

The need for corporations to monitor their cultural climate is so important, says Boyce, that he recommends that American companies, and foreign-owned companies in particular, retain the services of a top-level consultant to routinely examine the climate of the company and report the findings directly to the CEO.

The consultant should carefully monitor all of the organization's values, customs, procedures, and policies in place to determine the precise effect they are having on the organization. Once the CEO is in a position to measure the effect that his internal policies, procedures, and ideology are having on his organization, he can take corrective action on a timely basis if necessary. If, however, the CEO doesn't get reliable feedback on this subject, and he is not aware of existing problem areas, the organization could be in for some serious trouble. Bill Boyce says the reason he recommends that a CEO retain an outside consultant to monitor his company's cultural climate is to provide objectivity and expertise in the evaluation and recommendation process. "Few executives who are responsible for running the day-to-day operations of an organization can routinely step back and provide the CEO with an objective analysis and evaluation of the organization's culture, particularly when they are a part of the body politic of the company."

Boyce defines corporate culture as a major part of the "personality" of an organization which is established by the CEO and reinforced by his senior staff members. The chief executive officer's concept of the "right management style" and ideology can make all the difference in the world, says Boyce.

A Corporate Culture Checklist

Understanding corporate culture can provide both job opportunity and job security for people who really want to be successful in the profit and nonprofit world. Here are some valuable points to consider as you move along your career path:

Job Search Activity

• When looking for a job in the private, public, and nonprofit sectors, take the time to research the history of the organization's values, customs, habits, and folkways. This includes the organization's affirmative action and equal employment opportunity record as well.

• Before you make the final decision to join an organization, see if they will allow you an opportunity to spend some time with an established and respected member of the company. Make this request of the company before you agree to the final employment terms. Ideally, the employee you talk with should be able to discuss the "personality" of the firm from a historical perspective as well as the direction the company appears to be moving in. Colleges and universities that seek to recruit talented students regularly encourage established students to talk with prospective candidates, so why shouldn't employers encourage the same approach if they are sincerely interested in you?

• If it appears that a prospective employer does not encourage contact with his employees prior to employment, try networking on your own without the help of the company. It may mean that you will end up taking a little longer to check out the company relative to the cultural issue, but the insight that you get could be the piece that you need to complete the total picture of a company that could play an important part in your career. Don't forget, this is your career path and you should do all that you can to ensure your success.

Research and Networking Techniques
for Corporate Culture Information

• Seek out information from personnel agencies, trade associations, the Better Business Bureau, local and national Chambers of Commerce, investment analysis, stockbrokers, search firms, and community leaders (business, civic, social, and religious), including elected officials.

• Talk with vendors that service the organization with creative work, equipment and supplies, etc. (e.g., advertising, public relations, accounting, and legal services businesses).

• Check the biography of the CEO if possible. That can tell you much about the person and his or her beliefs/philosophy. Also check his/her organization memberships and volunteer activity. You can get a sense of what socioeconomic leanings one has by knowing the organizations to which he or she belongs.

• *The Wall Street Journal* and the *New York Times* provide excellent information through public libraries' microfilm of newspapers.

After You Are Hired and
During the Orientation Period

• Be sure that you can identify with and relate to the management procedures and policies that drive the organization on a day-to-day basis.

• Be sure that you can relate to and identify with the practices and procedures that guide your specific department. Each department will no doubt have departmental (written and unwritten) procedures that are peculiar to that department.

• Be sure that you identify the people in the organization that make or influence policies and procedures during the orientation stage of your employment. Don't wait until you have made a mistake before you decide to find out whom you have to deal with and how it should be done. Also try to get a good reading on the personality and management style of these individuals (conservative vs. liberal, methodical vs. reactionary, etc.).

• Don't forget to network with older, more established employees. You can learn a lot by simply being pleasant and friendly during the orientation period—but don't overdo it.

WHAT ALL GOOD MANAGERS KNOW

1. *All good managers know* that without the full cooperation and support of their staffs, they would not be able to achieve the goals and objectives of the department or the company.

2. *All good managers know* that a cooperative approach to managing people tends to produce greater harmony, unity of purpose, effective teamwork, and productivity than an authoritarian approach.

3. *All good managers know* that in the management of people it is more important to be perceived as a fair person than a well-liked person. A management style that embodies fairness includes a concern for equality of opportunity and therefore places each member of the department or team on an equal footing at the outset. This then affords the opportunity for recognition to go to staff members according to their performance on the job.

4. *All good managers know* that every staff member in the department or company must have the opportunity to fail. Good management skills evolve by trial and error. (Few inexperienced management people ever come to a position in a state of perfection.) Therefore, a good manager knows that the experience of failure is as important in the learning process as the experience of success.

5. *All good managers know* that it is not really possible to motivate anyone. In reality, people motivate themselves when a conducive atmosphere is provided. Therefore, the manager's challenge is to create the proper atmosphere so that people can actually motivate themselves.

6. *All good managers know* that financial compensation is only one of the answers to creating a conducive atmosphere for self-motivation. Another very important part of the equation is personal recognition. In fact, some people even crave recognition beyond all financial rewards. The final part to the puzzle is job satisfaction. There is no substitute for job satisfaction.

7. *All good managers know* that in order to be a manager of a project or organization and to do it well, and reach objectives, there must be a concisely developed approach to it. If there is no system—no "method to your madness" that is tailored to the task—it will be difficult to manage well or reach objectives. (It is true that you may stumble onto some of your objectives by chance, without a concisely developed approach, but it is unlikely that you will ever know how you reached your goal. So if you are ever required to duplicate your efforts, it will be extremely difficult, if not impossible, for you to do so.)

8. *All good managers know* that every organization is constantly in the process of changing. Therefore, flexibility is a desirable management characteristic and inflexibility is a millstone around a manager's neck.

9. *All good managers know* that it is important to be perceived as a "team player." Team players for the most part are people who are almost always in the right place at the right time, say the right things at the right time, are dependable, and show great enthusiasm no matter what the task at hand may be. They do their fair share of the work and they don't complain.

10. *All good managers know* that a good corporate "game plan" is always needed for survival. This should include, among other things, getting important task work assignments from management, earning a reputation for being dependable, develop-ing a favorable internal and external corporate image, and maintaining a good relationship with senior management.

11. *All good managers know* that while it cannot be said that everyone in the corporation who gets promoted earns that promo-tion, based upon hard work, there must be some limits as to what a person will do to get ahead. No company should be able to get you to do something unethical or buy your self-respect. That is too high a price to pay for any promotion.

12. *All good managers know* that people who drink exces-sively during the workday have a tendency to send out confusing and conflicting messages to their fellow associates, relative to their own career goals and objectives. They also, generally, end up saying the wrong things to the wrong people at the wrong time.

13. *All good managers know* that the use of drugs in the workplace serves no legitimate purpose and may get you a quick exit from the company.

14. *All good managers know* that it pays to have some sound business investments outside of your own company. Few smart business people put all of their eggs in one basket. When your income is on sound footing, you are apt to be free to do a better job for your company.

15. *All good managers know* that a positive business image is an important "commodity" to have, both internally and externally. They also know that you have to work at acquiring a favorable image on an ongoing basis, and that takes time, effort, and know-how.

16. *All good managers know* that there is no substitute for being a *good manager*. To be a good manager, you have to earn it! That means ongoing study in the areas of state-of-the-art technol-ogy, management, and interpersonal skills. It also means lots and lots of long hours of hard work and it means finding a need in the company's strategic plan and filling it.

Go with the flow and grow with the company.

A CHECKLIST OF THOUGHTS FOR
PROFESSIONAL SURVIVAL AND CORPORATE SUCCESS

Many of the thoughts contained in this list are so important that you will need to review them over and over, just to make sure that you clearly understand the principles behind the thinking:

1. Be yourself. Remember that to a large extent you create your own identity by the choices you make.

2. Be committed to your work and demonstrate your commitment.

3. Try to grow by learning something new every day.

4. Learn to enjoy your work. Don't just work to make a living.

5. Know that you are more than a job, and seek to become all that you can be. If you fail at a single task or even a job, believe that you can go on to other achievements, if you are willing to try.

6. Respect time and guide yourself by it, but don't become driven by it. When the time available to you is divided properly and viewed realistically, you can make a reasonable attempt to separate the possible from the impossible.

7. Set realistic goals and be guided by realistic plans to reach them. Goals that are unrealistically set are perhaps not goals at all, but wishful thinking and egotism.

8. Learn to prioritize. The key to handling stressful work is prioritizing on a day-to-day and week-to-week basis.

9. When working under stressful management and management assignments, learn to be flexible...go with the flow of things.

10. Plan and replan all challenging jobs and assignments. Good planning skills have no substitute, and to plan properly one must fully understand the challenge.

11. Learn to delegate when given an opportunity. It gives you the chance to see what else needs to be done. Don't be an egotist; share the work and the credit.

12. Be quick to recognize those who support and help you and give them full credit.

13. The way to developing insight into a problem is to ask many good questions and listen more than you talk. Talking a lot is not a sign of intelligence and it often shows just how little you really know.

14. When listening, learn to listen on two levels: what was said and what was not mentioned at all. Often, what was not said is the more important thing.

15. There is no shame in knowing your limitations. If you know you need more detailed instructions, say so—sooner rather than later. A brave-spirited person, not knowing his limitations, may reach for the next rung on the ladder and take his chances on success, but only a fool, knowing his limitations, would reach out knowing that neither the rung nor the ladder is to be had.

16. True success is measured by one's inner standards, but to appear successful in business, one must look successful, speak of successful deeds, and generally act successful. Successful people in business have an image that reflects confidence and authority. It is an attitude, a posture, if you will, that generally can be seen in the manner of dress, speech, bearing, and manner of presentation.

17. Learn to communicate on many levels and communicate well, verbally and nonverbally, in written and body language.

18. Don't be afraid to take on responsibility even though it may involve risk. Responsibility is a great sign of maturity, and few benefits are to be had without taking some responsibility and risk.

19. If you can accept the worst that can happen to you in any given situation, then it may be worth the risk. But if you cannot take the heat, then get out of the kitchen as quickly as possible. Remember there are friendly fires. A friendly fire is one where you get burned, but you live on after the lesson is learned. An unfriendly fire is one that kills your career with the organization, forever.

20. Study the art of risk taking. Learn to evaluate good risks and bad ones; it can make the difference between an early successful career, a late successful career, or no success at all.

21. Remember that in business, time is money. Meet deadlines, be punctual, and have respect for other people's time.

22. A business person's reputation is generally earned by his

reliability and responsibility. It can take years to establish a good reputation, which can be lost by a single misjudgment or act of bad faith.

23. Study the art of setting realistic expectations. False expectations, set for yourself or set by others, can spell instant failure.

24. We all have the right to fail. The most reliable kind of learning comes from trial and error. We accept that process in scientific research, so why not in business? To lose the right to fail suggests that you have but one opportunity to succeed and then you are dead!

25. A business person wears many hats, professional, social, civic, religious, and political. Keep your business hat on when you are working or dealing in business matters. Wearing more than one hat in a business environment can send out conflicting messages that clog up effective channels of communication.

26. Stress kills, so why not learn to manage stress before it kills you? And, equally important, why create stress to kill others? You can change your life and reduce stress by simply changing your perception of what is important and what is not important.

27. In the corporate world, there are players and nonplayers of corporate games. If you decide to become a player, be sure to study the game well and, above all, learn the rules.

28. Corporate gamesmanship is a political craft that has to be perfected over the years. Therefore, never underestimate your opponent, particularly if he has age and experience on his side. And be very careful about whom you trust. Many old-timers, for example, have uncollected indebtedness that they can collect on if they ever need to, and it could be the CEO that is indebted to them.

29. The Godfather Game is a necessary evil in corporate life. Having the wrong Godfather is like stepping into a boxing ring with both hands tied behind your back. Nevertheless, when trouble comes, it sure pays to have somebody who can keep the pressure off you.

30. Getting the right Godfather is a combination of luck, knowing who really controls the corporate action, and being in the right place at the right time.

31. Corporate regimes are great if you are a member of the ruling party. However, should the regime ever change in favor of another party, be ready to run for cover—because things can really get bad.

32. More people fail in corporate life because of their personality than for any other reason. Learn the art of winning friends and influencing people. It can really pay off. Most corporate senior people are not mental giants, but they are generally adequate and they are generally liked by someone who runs the show.

33. Some corporate people are exceptional. Learn to recognize a legitimate rising star; it could be helpful in later years.

34. A corporation is not a democratic institution, so don't be a fool and pretend that it is.

35. For the most part, all corporate people serve at the pleasure of the "King" (chief executive officer) and if you fail to serve the King, or if the King no longer has need of your services, then you will have a very short life in the corporate kingdom.

36. What price will you pay for glory? If you are willing to pay any price, then it may only be a matter of time before you will be bought for a handful of dollars. If you are willing to put yourself up for sale, the corporation may try to buy you. Once you have been acquired, you forfeit your right to say no to the corporation, even though it may end your existence, as you know it. Understand the "purchasing agent" when he comes to call and know what you are agreeing to do. Every relationship has a contract... ask yourself if you clearly understand the terms of the contract before you agree to pay the price. "What does a man profit if he gains the world and loses his soul?"

37. In a time of corporate economic crisis (prolonged poor sales), or a downturn in the overall economy, some jobs are expendable. Try not to have one of those jobs! If you do have one, make sure you are covered by your Godfather, or you could be looking for another job, when and if staff cuts are made.

38. The name of the game in corporate life is to make as much money as you can, for as long as you can, and then invest it well. Even the CEO will one day outlive his usefulness to the corporation, and God help you if you don't have some money put away for a rainy day.

39. The best time to look for a job is when you have one. Therefore, always keep your lines of communication open to the marketplace . . . it allows you to negotiate from strength.

WHY AND HOW PEOPLE GET PROMOTED

Getting promoted within your existing company or organization is difficult for most people. People hope that by simply accomplishing "jobs well done," their superiors will take notice, or they wait for some "right moment" to land an account, or pull off a coup. They aspire to and desire advancement but seldom do what is really necessary to make their aspirations materialize.

If you don't happen to be the boss's son or daughter, which sometimes assures your advancement in the organization, getting serious about earning a promotion means being "promotion-minded." The effort could require you to make changes in how you use your time and energy and could, consequently, affect your personal, and professional, life. It could mean a less active social life and/or less time and energy to spend with your family. It often requires a total commitment and could end up being a full-time preoccupation.

Promotion-minded people are very focused: They know what they want and systematically work to achieve their objectives. They learn to visualize their opportunities in great detail, plan strategies that enable them to move forward, gain support to strengthen their efforts, and sustain their resolve until success is achieved. Promotion-minded people tend to be goal-oriented people. They support their goals with strategies, tactics, and reasonable timetables that all come together for effective results.

It stands to reason that the current climate of corporate downsizing means that fewer positions are likely to be open for people to be promoted into. Competition could be keen, and people who are serious about advancement need to keep that in mind. Take the competition on in a mature and methodical way. Networking, mentoring, and political influence are only some of the many methods you can use to overcome your competition. So, don't forget to factor these into your planning process.

Cultivating Opportunity

Contrary to the cliché, opportunity does not knock. It is cultivated, long before you are able to open the door and let it in. There are many ways to develop opportunity, but among the most effective is to draw on your relationships with colleagues and co-workers who are more experienced than you. You might be pleasantly surprised to find that people who have successfully advanced their own careers are willing and, sometimes, delighted to share valuable tips, techniques, and information. Good relationships with your more experienced colleagues can help you to identify, track, and qualify for new positions and future growth areas in your organization. Your colleagues can help you to be ahead of the competition, and target a position before the job opening is openly discussed or publicly announced.

Here are some specific steps that you can take to cultivate opportunities for yourself:

Step 1. Attitude

Your company may be willing to teach you the new skills and techniques that are required to do an effective job for them, but they cannot give you a positive attitude toward your work. Make being positive a habit, because no one likes to be around people who are pessimistic and complaining. Generally speaking, negative individuals are not the first to advance in an organization. Managers are human. They want to be at ease with the members of their team, and tend to think of people they are comfortable with when positions open up.

Enthusiasm breeds enthusiasm, and usually builds energy that produces positive results. Few organizations thrive or survive over time with too many negative people employed. By the same token, much of an organization's success comes from its ability to recruit and maintain a core of positive and enthusiastic people.

Step 2. Volunteer

Be willing to do more than your job actually calls for. Going above and beyond what is required is not something everyone in the organization can easily do. Some people have a difficult enough time keeping up with their regular work assignments. However, if you are looking for ways to enhance your image in the company, extending yourself is an excellent strategy. That is, if your voluntary efforts are welcomed by your boss. Ask first. Ideally, you should make your activities visible to senior management. But, do so in a natural way, without flaunting or constantly bragging about yourself. That will make your intentions suspect and defeat your purpose.

Volunteering to help support your department, in general, and your boss, in particular, will be noticed when it is time for your performance review. Always remember that every department, or unit within a department, has a set of goals to reach. Employees who regularly volunteer to help the boss, and the unit, reach those objectives will usually receive some form of commendation for their efforts.

While there are no guarantees that every boss or supervisor will recognize you for your voluntary effort, it is one of the best ways to earn favorable points in a performance review. It is also a good way to get the attention of management when they are looking for talent to advance within the organization.

Step 3. Skill Development

You may need to invest time and money in training, or retraining, to make yourself more marketable. With this in mind, survey the potential areas of advancement in your company that seem right for you. Then, analyze your existing skills. By assessing your company's present and future personnel needs, you can decide what further training and education you could use. Remember that organizations need state-of-the-art input from their employees in order to remain competitive in the domestic and world markets.

Professional training and retraining is a multi-billion-dollar business in the United States for good reasons. It is essentially driven by technical advancements, new marketing concepts, and new computer systems of every variety.

Take every opportunity you have to attend the various management training schools, workshops, and seminars. Check with your Human Resources Department, because they can tell you what training opportunities exist, and which ones are free. Evaluate the training program to be sure that it is appropriate for your level of knowledge and experience. People sometimes sign up for workshops or seminars that don't offer them what they really need. Once you've done your research and find that the program will address your needs, go for it. You cannot afford to miss out on any opportunity that will provide you with a good competitive advantage over other candidates.

Be creative in the ways you develop skills and experience. Attend, for example, industry trade conferences and conventions. They can provide good opportunities to network and to attend other important workshops and seminars.

There are many ways to justify your travel expenses and participation in a business-related conference, over and above your own personal learning experience. Use your imagination, and do the necessary research to be prepared to address any issue your boss may bring up regarding your desire to attend a particular conference. In many cases, your company will pay for your conference travel and out-of-pocket expenses if you can show how the company can benefit from your participation.

Some people bring back data and materials from the conference they attended to share with their supervisor and department members. Other people write summary reports when they return, and present their findings to their entire department at a subsequent staff meeting.

Another skill-development exercise, that is relatively easy to accomplish, is industry-related reading. Make a habit of reading books, reports, and articles on the facts, figures, and trends that are relevant to your business. Your associates and supervisors will begin to look to you as a good reference source and as a knowledgeable person. The reading takes time, but it's worth it. You will, in effect, become a consultant for your unit or department, and your visibility, value, and stature in the company will be improved.

Subscribe to key company- and industry-related publications. The United States government publishes lots of free information through the National Printing Office in Washington, D.C. Add your name to mailing lists to receive various government publications.

Step 4. Marketing Your Skills and Abilities

Learn to market your professional skills and abilities in your organization for maximum results. See yourself as a quality product worthy of advertisement and promotion. As most marketing professionals will tell you, you must know your product well and believe in it yourself if you are going to persuade others of the same. Unfortunately, people, sometimes, seek promotions knowing that they do not have all the qualities required for the advanced job, and are not really ready for the additional responsibility. Try not to be one of these people. Make sure that you are ready, willing, and able to handle a job advancement whenever you decide to reach out for a promotion.

Marketing professionals will also tell you that the packaging of a product is also a key to success. So, make sure you sound and look the part. Evaluate your style of dress, your ability to present business matters in a professional manner, your verbal and nonverbal communication skills, your attitude and enthusiasm, your knowledge of the business, and your demonstrated abilities. There is no substitute for having a good track record when it comes to demonstrated abilities. Having done good work and gotten credit for it is one of the most effective things you can do when you are career-minded and looking for a promotion. Doing good work is important, but doing good work and getting credit for it is one of the best marketing strategies that you can have. Unfortunately, not everyone knows how to do a good job of getting credit for work well done. It almost takes a special instinct for being in the right place at the right time, or for saying the right things to the right people. Those who do it well actually work at it all the time. For example, they know what meetings to attend—when certain senior management people will be present—and take the opportunity to informally talk about their accomplishments.

A more difficult challenge is to get your boss or some high official in the organization to say good things about your work in public meetings and/or in meetings that are well attended by other senior officers. You seldom have control of this, but the "third party endorsement" concept is really the most effective advertisement and promotion you can get. It is a credible way for people to receive information about you. On those occasions when a colleague or manager thanks or praises you verbally, ask him or her to write a note to the individual or individuals who are key to the promotion you're seeking. You might also ask your boss if he or she would mind putting a complimentary note into your personnel file. In this way, you will have a record when your performance review comes up later on.

Get involved with the trade associations in your field. Call and find out if your skills are needed for any important association effort. If they ask you to work with them on a volunteer basis, be sure to get your boss to approve of your participation. Do your best on the project you're assigned to, and seek ways to get visibility and recognition. For example, trade associations, often, are more than happy to send letters of commendation to company leadership, and to any other key individuals in the company.

Sometimes, visibility is achieved through publicity in an industry trade publication. A published photograph of you, with important people or executives from other companies, is a good public relations technique that can get the attention of your own senior management. So, keep your eye out for photo opportunities, particularly when important people are present, or the subject that is associated with the picture is important to your company. Most trade associations have public relations people who are paid to publicize industry members. Get to know association P.R. people. They will tell you about important events and what committees to volunteer for, for good credit and photo opportunities.

The Need To Reinvent the Company

Companies have a real need to reinvent themselves every so many years. It is a renewal process designed to invigorate and prolong the life of the organization. Every organization has a natural life cycle: a beginning, a middle, and an end. No organization can live forever—at least not in its original structural and conceptual form. Those that achieve longevity do so because they are flexible enough to meet changing market demands. Small companies may grow to become big companies, and big companies may break themselves up and become mid-size or small companies in order to survive and thrive. Regardless of the direction that a company chooses to take, it must rely on the will, creative talent, and strength of its human resources to make things happen—money alone cannot fulfill the changing needs of an organization.

Remember, companies fire, hire, train, or promote personnel, not necessarily because they like them or dislike them, but because it is in their best interests to do so. It is important for career-minded people to be very clear about what companies need and want, as well as what companies will do to reward employees who meet their needs.

People who really want to advance their careers will do what needs to be done to find the solution to problems at work. This is true whether the person is working in the accounting department or the manufacturing end of the business. Every business has its share of problems at almost every level of its operations, and every business has a need to employ people who can step in and solve them. See yourself as an innovator and become an innovator at the right time. Clearly it is not an easy thing to do and it will not happen merely because you wish for it. The truth is, you have to know and understand what is causing the problems. You also have to research the issues, be imaginative in drawing conclusions and making recommendations, and you have to take chances. If you draw the wrong conclusions and make mistakes, you have to be big enough to admit it. If you can do this for your company, chances are management will take notice and advance your career—you can count on it.

Find a Need and Fill It!

A man by the name of Art Fry became a celebrated company innovator simply because he identified a company's need and filled it.

As the story goes, every Sunday Mr. Art Fry actively participated in his church choir, but with a great deal of discomfort. It seems that every time Fry attempted to hold his hymnal up to sing, he would lose his place in the hymn book, because his bookmark kept falling down within the book or out of it completely. Fry felt very uncomfortable about this situation, because he always took his work with the choir very seriously.

After getting a degree in chemical engineering from the University of Minnesota, Mr. Fry got a job in product development at the 3M Corporation in Rochester, Minnesota. And, while the 3M Company did not request that he develop a product that would make money for it, fill a need in the marketplace, or solve Fry's own personal problem, that is what actually happened.

Fry began to experiment with different types of adhesive material to solve his bookmark problem. He wanted something that would keep his bookmark in place and not damage the hymnal in any way. He developed a special adhesive that worked so well he decided to expand on its use, and provide space to write a little note. Fry's vision included a memo pad with pages that could stick without causing damage to original documents or create adhesive permanency.

At first, no one in Fry's company seemed interested in his invention. However, after he began to distribute his little memo pads, free of charge, to people around his company, they started to use them.

One day, a senior member of the 3M Company saw the little note pads, used one, liked it, and called Fry. The rest of the story is history for Fry, the 3M Company, and the world. Today, 3M makes millions of dollars from Fry's invention. He now enjoys a well-paying senior management position.

Remember, people who manage to make significant contributions to the well-being of their organizations end up investing a lot of personal time and effort in the process. They often find it necessary to go well beyond the boundaries of the organization's traditional way of doing things. You take a risk, but that's a positive thing. Without some risk there is little opportunity to bring about something new and better. Believe in yourself, believe that you can make a difference, and you will!

ADVANCEMENT OUTSIDE OF YOUR ORGANIZATION

The alternative to promotion and advancement from within your company is to seek a better position outside of your current place of employment. If your current employer appears to feel no sense of immediacy in advancing your career, why not do it yourself? You might find yourself expecting your boss to provide you with certain career opportunities and then show signs of discontent if they are not forthcoming in a reasonable amount of time. So why not consider a new place of employment—sooner rather than later? Remember, you control your career; no one else does.

You may find it uncomfortable to think about leaving your employer, but leaving should, at least, be an option. If you think this way, you operate from a position of power and you will feel a personal sense of ownership relative to your own future. No other person, place, or thing should ever appear to possess the power to decide the circumstances of your personal or professional life.

This kind of self-determination promotes and encourages a wonderful sense of mental, physical, and emotional freedom. Embrace it, believe it, and maintain it, at any cost. Self-determination is a critical part of a sound formula for personal and professional growth and development. Without it, there is little likelihood that you will ever be able to develop your own career, not to even mention your ability to self-actualize.

Few people are skillful enough to hide, for an indefinite period of time, their true feelings about their job, particularly if they are unhappy. So, know that what you feel inside will come out. Unhappiness can come out in subtle, and dramatic, ways. Either way, people who work with or around you can usually tell. Your boss can often tell if he or she is a perceptive person. Each of us forms patterns of behavior in our work environment: When we are stressed-out or unhappy about work situations, we often communicate it through changes in our behavior, *e.g.*, lackluster performance, poor interpersonal relations, and sloppy work habits. There are many ways people pick up on our discontent and desire to leave our jobs.

Look around you and count the number of people who routinely come to work late, frequently show signs of poor performance, and, often, have problems in their interpersonal relationships. It is likely that these same people are unhappy with their positions and would rather work somewhere else. People who are unhappy with their jobs generally leave their spirit and mind at home.

For the most part, these people can be characterized as those who want to leave their jobs but feel trapped. They don't enjoy a sense of self-determination and, for whatever reason, do not believe that they are free to self-actualize under the circumstances. They tend to lack the quality of personal empowerment that would enable them to size up a situation, make a decision, act on it, and have no regrets.

Your ability to achieve a sense of personal empowerment in your career is determined by your ability to take charge of your feelings and ideas, making them work for you, not against you. It means having a strong sense of who you are in relation to the world around you. Self-awareness has everything to do with your sense of self-worth and self-esteem—so be careful not to see yourself in narrow terms. Have a vision, because visions give rise to aspirations and, ultimately, to success.

What to Look for in Choosing a Company or a Job

• Growth Opportunity: New areas in your company or industry where you develop your skills and grow in ways that will enhance your career.

• Job Satisfaction: The position that you consider seriously should be challenging, offer real personal, and professional, growth. Look for work that you can enjoy doing. The more you enjoy your work, the better you'll perform.

• Culture: It would pay for you to get some insight into the organization's or the department's culture. It includes the organization's values and beliefs, and informs the behavior of all of its personnel. Every organization has its own style of doing business that encompasses everything from how executives manage and how assignments and promotions are made, to how meetings are conducted and how clients and customers are treated.

• Compensation: The compensation package should be one that allows you to meet your personal and professional obligations, and, concurrently, gives you a sense of financial reward for the time and effort involved.

• Location: The location of your workplace should be as accessible and convenient as possible.

• Lifecycle: Consider the stage of the company's development: Is the company growing, standing still, or dying? You want to be with an organization that isn't on its way to demise.

A Job Search Checklist

• Research: Know something about the history of the organization, its mission, culture, and status in its industry. Check out, as best you can, the organization's management and get a sense of its leadership skills.

• Strategize: Have a planned approach to your job search.

1. A good professional resume.

2. Good reasons why the organization should hire you. Know what you can do to better the organization.

3. Dress for success and make your potential employer feel that your appearance will enhance the professional image of the organization.

4. Check your interviewing skills and make sure that you are really comfortable in any situation.

5. Know what you are worth in the marketplace. Do some research and know what to ask for when it comes to compensation.

6. Be an aggressive networker.

7. Work with as many executive search firms as you can, but make sure they are good firms with a track record.

8. Seek career counseling if you need it. It can save you time and effort. Good career counselors help you research, follow up, evaluate, interview, and negotiate the best deal for you.

Be very clear about what's motivating you to consider a job/career change. Write the motives down and discuss them with a trusted associate or a career counselor. It can help you be certain about what you want and why you want it.

MANAGEMENT SEVERANCE AND SETTLEMENT PACKAGES

Most companies in America have a style and tradition that have evolved out of the personalities of their founding fathers. The style and tradition generally reflect the attitudes and principles set down by the founders and each succeeding president of the company thereafter.

The principles serve as a guide for future-generation management and the way they will run the company. The style, the tradition, management attitudes and principles, speak to the questions of how the company will grow and develop in the marketplace, how it chooses to be perceived in the marketplace, and how it treats its employees. The employees, being the people who make the company become whatever it is, play a major role in all of this.

It is within this context and background that the issue of severance and settlement packages is raised. What the company does or doesn't do for its employees and those who are about to leave, be they retirees, layoffs, or dismissals, is somehow rooted in the company's overall style and tradition.

Moreover, these actions are related to how management wants the employees, the stockholders, and the general community to feel about its methods of operation. For example, negative actions toward employees, on the part of management, can cause the company's Board of Directors and stockholders to lose confidence in the judgment of management. Poor managerial judgment over a period of time impacts negatively on the bottom line of the company. Therefore, it is in management's best interest to try to keep everyone happy, so that the company can continue to make money in a reasonably issue- or crisis-free environment.

Subject a company to too many side issues and crises and its management becomes distracted and loses sight of its primary objective, which is generally to increase sales and profits. So it follows that when people leave a company, particularly those who have had years of good service, they should leave with a reasonably good feeling. No company wants its existing employees, its Board of Directors, its stockholders, and most important, its consumers to feel that the company is in the habit of treating loyal and committed employees badly. This would, in effect, turn the clock back fifty to seventy-five years, when the management of companies ran "sweatshops."

What does all of this have to do with severance and settlement packages? Merely this: Severance packages or settlement packages, as packages go in corporate America, are by definition the price the company pays to disassociate itself from you, on a full-time permanent basis, no matter what the reason may be. Should you leave as an employee in good standing, that severance figure, in dollars and benefits, could be very generous. However, should the circumstances surrounding your departure from the company be less than ideal, the settlement figure could be anywhere from minimal to absolutely nothing at all.

The whole point here is that your going-out figure depends substantially on the following:

1. Length of service
2. Title or position in the company
3. Recognized contributions to the company
4. Current image in the company
5. Knowledge and exposure to confidential information
6. Standard personnel policies and practices
7. Rights as stated under local, state, and federal government regulations.

Under Severance Conditions

Those employees that are about to leave the company under relatively good conditions tend to make management feel that it owes them something for the years of loyalty, overall contribution to the growth and prosperity of the company, and good corporate citizenship. Good corporate citizenship, coincidentally, is figured into a company's "goodwill." Therefore, if you as an employee have in fact contributed to the social responsibility of a business organization, you have contributed to the net worth of the company.

Again, if you are fortunate enough to be leaving the company under generally good terms, management should be inclined to show some concern for the well-being of you and your family. No company wants to earn the reputation of turning its people out into the street without any concern for the person's well-being. This is true particularly among the employees who remain and invariably identify with the departing person.

Under Settlement Conditions

On the other hand, should you have to leave the company under less than favorable conditions, the company may still be willing to make you a settlement package. Remember, however, the company is not obligated to do this if no employment discrimination can be proven. The difference in this case is that the company may recognize that a former disgruntled employee can give away company secrets, expose company "sins," and generally make life difficult for an entity that needs an atmosphere of relative tranquillity to conduct business as usual.

A company has many publics that it must guard against for very obvious reasons, and I will name just a few groups that could be interested in what a single knowledgeable disgruntled employee might have to say: competitors; major stockholders; the Wall Street community (security analyst); federal, state, and local equal opportunity commissions; women's rights and environmentalist groups; consumers; existing labor-oriented employees; and last but certainly not least, the working press . . . à la *60 Minutes* on television.

The fact that the company no longer feels that it has a need for your services, or that your departure is on a mutual-agreement basis, does not mean that the company will not take care of you in some way. Again, the company is not obligated but you never know what the climate will be like at the time you are leaving.

Under Retirement Conditions

Every employee in the company serves at the pleasure of the King (chairman), and when the King and/or his trusted advisors no longer feel that you are of value to the company, they will more than likely let you go. Nobody gets a free ride in corporate America. That is, unless you are considered someone that they owe a favor to for previous service rendered and are near retirement. Then they will generally seat you on the sidelines, in some small office with an occasional assignment or two, until your retirement date comes up or some period near that date.

Management in most instances will make some kind of severance package for its executives when it is time for them to leave the company. The big questions are how much and for how long.

Recognizing that each person's package is, in truth, tailored to the person's situation, needs, rank, years of service, and reputation in the company, let's identify a few things that might trigger some creative thinking for a person faced with having to negotiate a going-out package.

Always remember that whenever you are negotiating, you should follow the unwritten rule that says, "If you don't ask, you don't get."

Going-Out Packages: Things to Consider

For Employees with One to Two Years Service

- Back pay for unused vacation time
- Use of the copy equipment, word processor, personal computer, and telephone before the final day of separation
- Flex time to look for a new job while on the company payroll from a week to two weeks
- Access to special insurance and health benefits at your own expense
- A letter stating that you were employed at the company for the one- to two-year period, with no negative commentary

For Employees with Two to Five Years Service

- Back pay for unused vacation time
- Use of the copy equipment, word processor, personal computer, and telephone before the final day of separation
- Flex time to look for a new job while on the company payroll from two weeks to four weeks
- Access to special insurance and health benefits at your own expense
- A letter stating that you were employed at the company for the two- to five-year period, with no negative commentary
- Buying out the employee's employment contract if the agreement is not completed
- The use of secretarial help to look for a new job before the day of termination

For Employees with Six to Twelve Years Service

- Back pay for unused vacation time
- Use of the copy equipment, word processor, personal computer, and telephone before the final day of separation
- Flex time to look for a new job while on the company payroll from thirty to ninety days
- The use of secretarial help to look for a new job before the day of termination
- The use of a small office and telephone while looking for a new job for a period of time
- Access to special insurance and health benefits at your own expense
- A letter stating that you were employed at the company for the six- to ten-year period, with no negative commentary
- Buying out the employee's employment contract if the agreement is not completed
- All vesting rights and retirement rights
- Expense-free outplacement services from an outside agency

For Employees with Thirteen to Twenty Years Service

- Back pay for unused vacation time
- Travel expenses (ground and air) back to the city where you were hired, if needed
- Use of the office copy equipment, word processor, personal computer, before the final day of separation
- The use of a small office and telephone while looking for a new job for a period of time
- The use of secretarial help to look for a new job before the final day of separation
- Access to special insurance and health benefits at your own expense
- A letter stating that you were employed at the company for the thirteen- to twenty-year period, with no negative commentary
- Combinations of flex time on the company payroll, relocation expenses, and expense-free outplacement services from an outside agency

• Special consulting contract for some service the company needs that they feel you can handle as a consultant

• A special "bridge," which represents an opportunity to stay on the company payroll, even though you do not physically come to the office. This bridge may be for a period of three months to one year to tide you over until retirement date.

• All vesting rights and retirement rights

For Employees with Twenty or More Years Service

• Back pay for unused vacation time

• Travel expenses (ground and air) back to the city where you were hired, if needed

• Use of the office copy equipment, word processor, personal computer, before the final day of separation

• The use of a small office and telephone while looking for a new job for a period of time

• The use of secretarial help to look for a new job before the final day of separation

• Access to special insurance and health benefits at your own expense

• A letter stating that you were employed at the company for the twenty-year or longer period, with no negative commentary

• Combinations of flex time on the company payroll, relocation expenses, and expense-free outplacement services from an outside agency

• Special consulting contract for some service the company needs that they feel you can handle as a consultant

• Special "bridge," which represents an opportunity to stay on the company payroll, even though you do not physically come to the office. This bridge may be for a period of a year or two—until official retirement date.

• Buying out the employee's employment contract if the agreement is not completed

• Use of company-expensed credit cards for a very limited period of time (telephone, gasoline, meals, etc.)

• Investment counseling services at the company's expense

• All vesting rights and retirement rights

In summary, remember to think creatively. Cash is not the only means of compensation. Use leverage to negotiate. Leverage is the vantage point because of your personal relationship with the company, the position or positions you have held during your career with the company, and the relationships you may have had with key top management in the company (vice-president, executive vice-president, president, and chairman of the board).

III

Corporate Pitfalls

A corporate pitfall is a dangerous hidden condition that could threaten your reputation or job security. It is a pit contrived for entrapping an unsuspecting victim. Pitfalls in the corporate world can be so complex that they sometimes appear to have the overtones of a first-class spy novel. On the other hand, some corporate pits are so slight that you don't even realize that you have fallen into one until you feel the impact from the fall. The corporate intrigue and subterfuge that surround some of the circumstances can be amazing.

A pitfall in the corporate world can result in a minor condition that does only temporary damage to your reputation, and your reputation can be repaired over a period of time. It can also result in a condition that is so serious, it ends your career with your employer. For this reason, let us examine some of the many different pitfalls that you can take and then see if you cannot better understand how they come about, and what, if anything, you can do should you ever be confronted with them.

The scenarios in this chapter are all hypothetical and you may never experience a single one of the pitfalls described in them, but it will not hurt you to be aware that these things do happen to people and that you could very easily become a victim on any day.

SEXUAL HARASSMENT

You are a single, female, new entry-level management employee and after you have been on the job only six months, your vice-president invites you to his office for a general discussion of your progress in his department—problems, concerns, and so on. During the course of the conversation, he implies that a person with your looks and intelligence could progress rapidly in his department if you followed his advice and counsel. Subsequent to this meeting, you begin to receive personal invitations from the V.P. for after-work-hours cocktails to discuss your progress and aspirations in the company. You sense that all of this attention is leading up to a compromising situation involving a personal relationship between yourself and the boss. To avoid an even more unpleasant confrontation later, you decide to reject his advances now.

Suddenly, your immediate supervisor, who is a male manager, and who is trying very hard to get ahead in the company, starts expressing some dissatisfaction in your work. At first, it appears to be a very simple thing that dissatisfies him, but as time goes on, the problems, alleged mistakes, and poor direction seem to increase. You observe that the manager is afraid of the V.P. and will do anything to keep him happy. You also think that in some way the rejected V.P. is influencing the manager's opinion about your competence, but you can't prove it.

Finally, you get your first annual performance appraisal and your performance is rated unsatisfactory. Your manager tells you that unless your performance improves greatly in the next three months, he will have to reconsider your future with the company.

It is difficult to decide what to do about this situation. You really need the job to manage your personal affairs, but you will not let anyone take advantage of you. The problem is that you can't prove that the V.P. is using his influence to get you out of the company.

What Do You Think?

• Do you think you have a serious problem, and if so, what do you think that problem is?
• Do you think you helped to create the problem by your decision to reject your V.P.?
• How are you going to handle this situation?
  a. What is the first thing you are going to do?
  b. What is the second thing you're going to do?
  c. What is the one thing you are *not* going to do?

Obviously, there are any number of courses you could take in such a situation, from doing nothing at all and hoping that the whole situation will soon go away, to inviting your boyfriend to come down to the company and beat up the V.P. (five minutes after your resignation).

Realistically, you have to decide what practical alternatives you have and which ones you should take to save yourself as much personal pain and discomfort as possible. For argument's sake, let us assume that you have decided that you want to continue your career with the company and that you are going to try to develop a plan to counteract the V.P. who is trying to use his influence on your supervisor to get you fired.

Sexual Harassment Counteraction

One possible first step might be for you to share the problem with someone in the company, like the vice-president of personnel, and seek his or her advice as to how you should handle such a situation. If the situation cannot be resolved to your advantage, it may be necessary for you to get the vice-president's help to transfer out of the present department without letting your vice-president or managing supervisor know your plans until it is too late for them to stop you.

By sharing the problem with the vice-president of personnel, you create an opportunity to gain support from a high-ranking executive who should be sympathetic to your problem of sexual harassment and who also does not want the company to get the bad publicity that would result from a lawsuit by the Human Rights Commission.

Next, you try to document every incident that suggested sexual harassment in any way. Armed with this documentation, you write letters to your own personnel file and indicate names, dates, and places where you believe sexual harassment took place. You keep the letters at home until you feel there is a need to produce them. You do not send them to the personnel department at this point. You may also very discreetly find out if your vice-president has ever harassed any other females in the department and, if so, document that alleged information in your file at home. This is an example of the kind of support that you would need for a good Human Rights Commission sex discrimination case.

With regard to the supervisor, you can try to turn the performance appraisal around quickly by making him take responsibility for your success or failure in the department. This can be done by requesting weekly review meetings and daily meetings, if necessary, to determine what is going well and what is not going well, and more important, what he is prepared to do to help you become successful. Now, should the manager be unwilling to cooperate in this exercise, then you must document your efforts by writing memorandums to your personnel file and concurrently seeking the support of the vice-president of personnel.

Don't pay attention to anyone who tells you to seek the help of a low-level person in the personnel department; it is really critical that you go to the top on matters like these. Finally, should the vice-president of personnel be reluctant to help in any way, your last resort might be to seek outside help from a private lawyer or city or state agency experienced in these matters.

The Equal Employment Opportunity Commission (EEOC)

Guidelines establishing what constitutes sexual harassment were completed by the Equal Employment Opportunity Commission in late 1980. These guidelines were written in response to the increasing number of reported incidences of sexual harassment of female employees, and retaliation from supervisors or employers when employees rejected their advances.

Women involved in legal action of one type or another, prior to 1980, actually established the court precedent for federal sexual harassment guidelines. The whole issue of what constitutes sexual harassment or sex discrimination in corporate settings is a very difficult one for business and industry and for government regulatory agencies, because an alleged case of harassment or discrimination often boils down to one person's word against another's. However, where a person is able to establish reasonable proof, for example co-worker corroboration and documentation, satisfaction in the form of justice can be obtained for the victim.

The time element for resolving such cases will vary, depending on the type of case being considered and how much the company stands to lose. In most instances, it is a matter of money and company prestige (among stockholders, customers, and other employees) that the organization is trying to protect.

Some cases, for example those involving an isolated incident of sexual harassment, may be settled quite easily out of court by an agency investigator, hearing officer, and the corporate personnel department, supported by in-house legal staff. On the other hand, legal suits involving several people or company practices of sex discrimination (not giving equal pay for equal work, etc.) can go on for years, depending on the courts and the number of cases the agency has to deal with. The ability of the company in question to pay the cost of staff counsel and outside legal counsel needed to fight the charges is another consideration that can affect how fast a settlement is reached.

Finally, remember that the legal definition of sexual harassment is not a narrow one. The EEOC states that "uninvited or unwelcomed sexual advances of all types, requests for sexual favors of any kind, including verbal or physical conduct of a sexual nature, constitutes sexual harassment, when submission to such conduct is made either explicitly or implicitly a term or condition of an individual's employment, when submission to or rejection of such conduct by an individual is used as the basis for employment decisions affecting such individual, or such conduct has the purpose or effect of unreasonably interfering with an individual's work performance or creating an intimidating, hostile, or offensive working environment."

The guidelines further state that in deciding whether alleged conduct constitutes sexual harassment, the commission will review the record in its entirety, and then the totality of the circumstances, such as the nature of the sexual advances and the context in which the alleged incidents occurred. The determination of the legality of a particular action will be made from the facts on a case-by-case basis.

IMAGE ASSASSINATION

You are a black manager of a marketing department at a major consumer products company and you have six years experience. During the course of your annual performance appraisal, your supervisor tells you in an offhand way that he was at a cocktail party a few weeks before and that a certain senior plant manager happened to tell him that when you visited his facility a few years ago, you made a very poor presentation. Futhermore, your supervisor says that the only reason he is telling you this is that some people (for example, the senior plant manager) feel that *your presentation skills might be somewhat lacking.* However, your supervisor quickly follows his negative information with a statement that says, in effect, that he personally thinks your presentation skills are fine, but he just wanted to let you know how John Doe, senior plant manager in Colorado, really feels about you.

You quickly respond to your supervisor by telling him that you never made a presentation to John Doe, so you don't see how he could say anything about the quality of your presentation skills, much less that they are lacking in some way. During the next few minutes of conversation, you and your boss establish the fact that while you did not make a presentation to John Doe, you did have a brief meeting with him a few years ago. Moreover, you emphatically state that the meeting was so brief you are hard-pressed to figure out why he would say something like that to your boss, particularly at a cocktail party, and what is even more suspicious is that he would say it two years after it was alleged to have happened and not immediately after the incident took place, if in fact it did.

In any event, your boss suggests that he really did not mean to upset you about this, because he knows that you can make a good presentation, and that the only reason he brought the subject up was that he wanted you to be careful when you visit plant facilities in the future. He then suggests that you forget about the matter, and the two of you complete your appraisal session for the year. Incidentally, your boss gives you a good rating on your annual performance review, and while you are not happy about the John Doe issue, you decide to let the matter rest.

Exactly one year later, you find yourself sitting in the same office, having your annual performance review with the same person. This time your boss starts out by saying some really nice things about your performance for the year, and you can see that you are going to get another good rating on your performance appraisal. However, just at the time that your boss is about to bring the meeting to a close, he stops, pauses, and then proceeds to bring up the John Doe incident, as if it were now a reality and you need to pay attention to your presentation skills in general.

What Do You Think?

• Do you think the black marketing manager has an image problem, and if so, what is it?

• Do you believe that John Doe, plant manager, really made that statement about the black manager, and why?

• Why do you think the marketing manager's director told him what John Doe said about him at the cocktail party? Was the director trying to be sincere and helpful, or did he have another motive?

• Why do you think the marketing manager's director continues to bring up this alleged incident during the manager's performance review? Is this coincidental, or is it in some way related to how the director really feels about the manager, only he will not come out and say it to his face?

• How would you handle the situation?
  a. The first time it came up
  b. The following year—the second time
  c. On any future discussion of the incident by the
     supervisor

Image Assassination Counteraction

In this case, the black manager does have a problem on his
hands, but the extent of the problem is not known because of the
manager's rather limited information. In other words, it appears
that the whole case could really be something his boss has created
and that John Doe really did not say anything about the manager
at all; or it could be that John Doe did say something to the
manager's boss about his impression of the manager, and now the
boss feels that he has a weapon he can use to keep the manager in
line, should he ever have any ideas of competing for his job or
trying for a promotion for another job that the boss does not want
him to have. Unfortunately, this is a psychological game that is
sometimes played in the corporation to try to make subordinates
fear the boss.

In any event, the manager at least has an opportunity to
try to neutralize the psychological game the boss may be
playing, by simply requesting an opportunity to confront John
Doe in the director's presence and try to clear up any mistake.
But at this point in the game, the manager's boss will more
than likely not want to follow his suggestion, because if John
Doe really did not make the statement in the first place, the
manager's boss would obviously be exposed as a liar. Further-
more, if the plant manager did make the statement, he certainly does not want the marketing manager to know that he has
been circulating negative things about him and certainly not
two years after the incident was alleged to have happened.
This kind of behavior could open the door to all kinds of
accusations, ranging from poor management judgment to out-
right discrimination.

The important point here is that the manager has need of a

tactic he can use to protect himself from his boss. By unemotionally asking to have this alleged incident discussed in an open forum, he has a good chance of putting a stop to the harassment and preventing the continued threat of image assassination.

THE NEW MINORITY EMPLOYEE

You have just been hired as a management trainee in a midwestern company. The company is in the consumer products business and you are the first Hispanic—in fact, the first minority person—to be hired by the company in a management trainee position. While you have worked for the company very successfully for over three years in a sales position, you have not had extended exposure to the company's home office and all that goes on there from day to day.

Your job as a salesperson was strictly field-related, and you operated from your home, using the mail and telephone for communication with company headquarters. With the exception of a one-week sales training course that was given at the home office, you have not been there in years. By word of mouth, you learn that the company has invited you to come and work in the home office for a number of reasons, one being that within the seventy-five-year history of the company there has never been a minority person in a management position at the home office. Minorities have held clerical, field sales, and labor-oriented positions with the company for the last twenty-five years, but not a single management-level job.

In addition, you have surmised that the company is now a little concerned about its image in the eyes of state and city EEO agencies, and about how its consumers (some of whom are minorities) and stockholders may feel about a company that is operating outside of the federal law, under Title VII of the Civil Rights Act of 1964 (see Appendix I).

While you had three and a half years of successful experience as a salesperson, you realize that, as a Hispanic person, you may not be accepted by everyone in the new environment and that you may even encounter some problems of prejudice and discrimination. On the first day in the office you start to feel the psychological pressure of being the "first" minority management trainee in the history of the company.

You have learned that it does not pay to overreact to anything, so you ignore the rather cool reception on your first day. In fact, you even find yourself smiling at the thought that you would probably have gone into shock and felt really embarrassed if the company had rolled out the red carpet and made a big deal out of your first day on the job. After seventy-five years, you could hardly imagine that the company would want to draw a lot of attention to the fact that it was just getting around to hiring its first minority management employee.

Time moves on, and you find that your orientation period at the home office for the first two weeks is going reasonably well. That is, until the Friday of the second week. You are invited by one of your associates for a drink at the local watering hole before going home for the weekend. As you enter the bar, you find that virtually every male lower-level management person in the home office is there with a drink in his hand. The noise level, the joking, and the loud music are overpowering. As you try to fit into the flow of things, you realize that much of the laughter and shouting is a result of gossip about the sexual activities of various male and female employees after work hours, and telling racial and ethnic jokes.

At this point, you start to feel uncomfortable. Not that you are shocked by stories about the secretaries, who continue to ignore you every day and will not even answer your telephone if you are away from your desk, but the ethnic jokes are just not your style, particularly when they are at someone else's expense. Somehow you manage to get through the two hours of drinking and joking around without drawing much attention to yourself. But the fact of the matter is that just anticipating the first time the group will start in with Hispanic jokes, the same way they told the Polish and Jewish jokes, is enough to get you uptight. So after a few weeks of the same social scene, you decide to avoid the weekly gathering.

The idea of drinking in a local bar for two hours after work on a Friday evening is not your idea of fun. When you add to that the not-too-subtle dating games that are being played by various male and female employees around the office, everybody knowing who is dating whom, you are convinced that this "Peyton Place" environment is not for you. So you decide to make a 180-degree turn in your relationships in the office.

You are friendly at work, but you never go to the local bar. Generally, you go on coffee breaks with fellow department members, but sometimes you have lunch with people in other departments, and on many occasions, you sit in the cafeteria and have lunch with other minority employees who are not on the managerial level.

Your main purpose is simply to create some diversity for yourself. However, you also want to let the other minority employees know that while you are a member of the management group, you are friendly, approachable, and not someone who tries to deny that he is a member of a minority group.

After this conscious effort on your part to expand your working environment, by talking with and eating with people from other departments and other working levels, you begin to notice some signs of resentment from the people within your own department. First, there are small things like not getting the word that a staff meeting date has been changed, or that someone left a telephone message for you while you were at lunch. Secretaries sometime seem to mimic their bosses' attitudes; anyone the boss does not like receives abrupt treatment from the secretary. When this happens, you realize that you are at a disadvantage, because you don't have a secretary yet to do battle for you. As a new member of the management group, you are obligated to draw your secretarial help from the pool, and it is very hard to develop relationships with any one person, because the typists in the pool change from day to day.

Finally, you are given your first big assignment as a management trainee and you suddenly realize that you have no one in your immediate group that you trust enough to ask for help when you need it. Your supervisor seems to be busy or out of the office, and you are afraid to let him know that you don't always understand him after he has explained something to you; you don't want him to think that you can't learn quickly. As time goes on, the assignment becomes even more difficult to complete, because the people who have experience in the department are not friendly with you and seem unwilling to extend themselves to you.

It becomes quite clear that your decision to function socially outside of the department's immediate group has prompted your associates to isolate you from them, and without the support systems of the group, you begin to experience some difficulty in getting your assignments done properly, at least the ones that require information based on the experience of your associates.

Over the next six months, you encounter several negative situations, situations that could have been positive if you had had some friendly support from your co-workers. However, you decided early on that you would not beg your co-workers to support you, even if it meant losing your job. You have a lot of pride and you refuse to be put in the position of having to go around begging your co-workers to help you save your job. Basically, you are firm in your belief that you do not want to be part of the office social and political games, but you did not realize at first that you would have to pay a big price for operating socially outside of the group.

Operating outside of the group has some great advantages, like not having to put up with the office gossip and drinking sessions. But on the other hand, operating outside of the group has also meant that you are virtually cut off from office politics and viewed as a nonconformist. Over the next six months you notice that you have been in a series of ongoing arguments with your supervisor, and it is apparent that the two of you cannot get along with each other. Everything you do seems to draw critical remarks from him, no matter how well you do it.

At the end of the year, you go in to meet with your supervisor for your annual appraisal. It is not surprising at all that you mutually agree that this management experience has really not been a good one for you and the company, and that in the interest of your career, you would do well to look for another job, outside of the company. Particularly, your boss says that he cannot give you a good recommendation if you try to transfer to another department, but if you decide to leave the company quietly, he will not give an unfavorable reference. So you resign on the spot.

What Do You Think?

• Did the new minority employee take the right approach when he decided to keep his distance (socially) from his co-workers?
• Even though he resented the gossip and interoffice socializing, should the new employee have compromised his feelings and actively participated in whatever was going on within the department, so that he could have maintained good, friendly relationships with his colleagues?
• Should the new employee have compromised his feelings so that he could get the support needed from his associates to keep his job?
• Was it possible for the employee to have enjoyed both his convictions and the friendly support of his co-workers, and if so, how?
• How would you have handled this situation if you were the new minority management employee?

The New Minority Employee Counteraction

You may recall reading, early in the book, that although most people looking to join the corporate world feel that the biggest immediate challenge they face is getting a good job, in reality the greatest challenge is keeping the job after you get it.

Reviewing the new minority employee's situation, we see that a difficult and challenging set of problems can develop very quickly. In fact, from the very first day that you join a department, you may have to make decisions about group and peer relationships, because every department and every company has a certain way or style of relating to one another. You can call it the corporate culture of the organization in which there can be several subgroups operating within the overall culture of the company. Nevertheless, the new employee who is perceptive and knows how to do more listening than talking will quickly find out what the group dynamics are in his or her department. The trick in handling the new corporate experience is in getting a good, fast people-assessment. You can easily do that by simply looking, listening, and asking good questions.

The second thing you need to do is immediately display a pleasant personality, one that encourages people in the department to want to be nice to you. Being on good terms with as many people as possible will be important in impending political games, existing political games, and old political games that may recur. Your observations will tell you which people in the department could be a real problem for you by close association, and which people will help you out when you encounter difficult work assignments.

Our new minority employee, in this example, never anticipated or understood the importance of influencing people and winning friends; therefore, he never got a chance to make a good impression on any of the people in his department. The subject of how to win friends and influence people should be taught in every college and business school in the country, because it is the basis of what it takes to survive and thrive in most professions and corporations. To prove my point, try making a lot of enemies on a new job and see how long you last.

I will go so far as to repeat what almost everyone knows, and that is that it is not always what you know that helps make you a success in a people-oriented environment, but whom you know and how well they like you, and how much power and influence they have in that environment, be it corporate or otherwise. This is not to suggest that skill and talent don't mean very much, but when skilled competition is great and talent is available, you can bet that your personality means a lot.

Finally, the problems described in our example of a new minority employee trying to negotiate the office socializing rituals and department politics are not uncommon ones for new people. Many people find themselves getting totally involved in this type of activity, to the extent that they can't handle it and end up making serious mistakes. Your early maneuvers and the tactics you employ are extremely important, because your success in the department to a large extent depends on how quickly you are able to establish a positive image, a good first impression.

You may be a nice person, but for whatever the reason, people in your new environment do not see you that way, and, therefore, you are perceived wrongly. This is a case of what is known as stepping off on the wrong foot, or starting off on the wrong foot. The established group is marching to one cadence and the new person to another.

Like it or not, perceptions are important. Once people in the department perceive you to be a "nice" person, most of them will go out of their way to help you in your orientation stage. Remember that, competitively, you are not a threat to anyone at this point. Therefore, you are in a position to disarm potential enemies—in other words, to make it hard for most, if not all, of the people in your group *not* to like you from the very first day.

Obviously, there may be some people in the department who are not going to like you immediately and will not extend a helping hand. That situation is all right as long as they don't try to hurt you or impede your progress in any way. You must be positive in your approach to the new group and basically ignore the negative forces, if there are any. If you are able to get one or more key people in the department to be receptive to your positive attitude, the whole orientation period should go relatively well. Again, what we are really discussing here is establishing a working relationship on the job: not trying to get people to *love* you, but being positive in approach to them and getting your foot in the door. Your effort, in this regard, should go beyond key management types and include the more established secretaries as well. For example, the boss's secretary might be an excellent person to try to establish a friendly relationship with.

Why are these particular individuals suggested? Basically because the established employee is the one who is well informed in the corporate setting, and you do need some supportive relationship early on in your experience. Don't let the situation get out of hand like the example of the new employee, particularly if you can prevent it. He became isolated from his group in the orientation stage. Try to keep the channels of communication open as much as possible, so you will know what is going on in the department.

The orientation process is very important to the new employee. Therefore, you are going to need some help in understanding the work assignment and methods employed to get the job done. Remember, positive relationships with more-established employees in a group can not only help keep you informed but help protect you as well.

The bottom line on this issue is that a new minority management trainee should try to exercise tact and good interpersonal skills when joining an established corporate management group. It may not be easy but you will find you can do well by working at it. Be positive and be determined. It is the depth of your determination that will help you meet your career goals. Let no one turn you around!

HOW TO PROTECT YOURSELF FROM A JOB ATTACK

Chances are, the longer you work for a corporation or a non-profit organization, the greater your risk of having your job security threatened by someone who does not like you, or who cannot really appreciate the skills and talents that you bring to your job.

While it is true that longevity has its influence in the world of work, longevity does not exempt you from being the target of someone's attempt to get you fired. The person who is actually responsible for the campaign against you does not have to know you personally, but they must believe that they will profit from your loss.

From a chief executive officer of a major corporation, to the lowest-level person in an organization, a job attack can happen to anyone, at anytime.

If you read and listen to the business media, you know it is not uncommon to have a member of your firm's board of directors attack the CEO of the business. Nor is it uncommon for people to draw conclusions, and make decisions where you are concerned, based on a political agenda that opposes you in some way. It happens that people use others as personal stepping-stones to success.

As long as there is a single employee around who has more ambition than talent or ethics, or a person willing to run the risk of being exposed as politically dangerous and devious, no one is ever completely protected from a well-planned, and executed, job attack. Sometimes people who work with you are secretly envious of your authority and status in your organization. While you might say, in such a situation, so what if they do envy me, what can they really do to me? The truth is, they *can* do damage if they take the time and energy, and are skillful enough to launch a well-planned attack. People who work with you may actually consider themselves to be a better professional than you are, but, sometimes, have no legitimate way of demonstrating their feelings to management. People's attitudes about race, sex, and age can be at the root of their behavior: Feelings of superiority, envy, and blind ambition can cause them to believe that they are justified in striking out at you.

The Highly Ambitious

There are a number of people working in corporations and non-profit organizations, today, that consider themselves to be highly ambitious, competitive, and political. Unfortunately, their career strategies often include tactics that are designed to propel themselves forward by eliminating the competition, by any means necessary.

The most common mistake that targets of attack make is to react. The first rule, in combating any job crisis, is to make sure that you see the situation right before you attempt to set it right. You must act in a planned and calculated way. It may save your job. The last thing you want to do, when under attack, is panic.

Factors and Risks Involved in a Job Attack

In a job attack there are, generally, two levels of risk involved. One level identifies the risks for the victim and the other identifies the risks for the perpetrator. In any event, both levels of risk can be considerable.

The Victims' Risks:

- Denial of promotional opportunities
- Image assassination/loss of credibility
- Demotion
- Dismissal

The Perpetrators' Risks:

• Exposure for a wrongful political act directed at a fellow employee
• Backfire, due to the exposure
• Counterattack from the intended victim

Strategies for Survival—
Environmental Scanning and Fact Gathering

Before you decide to take action against a suspected job attack, you should have as much information as you can get. By having good, reliable information, you are in a position to take intelligent measures. This is when your networking skills can pay off. Effective networking has traditionally been a good way to gather needed information, but, you may want to network with, on a confidential basis, only those people you feel certain you can trust. Remember, never give out more information than is necessary to get the information that you require. Generally, the fewer people who know about your problem, the better off you are.

Once you are convinced that you have obtained all of the information you need, analyze the data to make sure that all of the bits and pieces fit together. Aim for as complete a picture as you can. Hopefully, you will have more than one source with which to compare or confirm data. Remember that each giver of information will have a particular point-of-view. Their perceptions may be different from yours, also.

An outside opinion may be of great value when you are ready to draw conclusions. People outside of your organization may not know the individuals involved, but may be quite familiar with the circumstances surrounding the situation. Their detachment and objectivity may be an asset in helping you to arrive at sound conclusions.

Evaluate and Recommend

Now you're ready to evaluate your information. On a scale of 1 to 10, identify and rate your data. Pay careful attention to:

- The importance of the information
- The accuracy of the information
- The reliability of the source of the information
- The quality of the information
- The quantity of information
- Examples of any similar cases
- The content of objective opinions
- Your own instincts

In order to make a good evaluation, you really need to look at your case from the perpetrator's point-of-view and be sure that you have established a *motive*. Rumors are not the best data for establishing motive, but, admittedly, rumors can help if you have no other information to work with. The problem of working with a rumor is that you have to confirm the information before you can act on it with any degree of confidence. After all, "hearsay" information can be very dangerous.

At the recommendation stage of your plan to preempt the attack, you will want to be sure to identify as many options as you can and rate your options for potential effectiveness on a scale of 1 to 10.

These are possible options for you:

1. Do nothing about your situation and hope that the whole thing will somehow go away.

2. Try to renegotiate the situation personally by blocking and defending your position, or reversing the situation with a strong counter measure.

3. Get an influential person in the organization to run interference for you. In other words, get them to either speak for you or use their position of power to change the outcome of the situation.

4. Leave the department or company.

No matter which option you decide to take, always ask yourself this question before you take action: "What is the worst thing that can happen to me if I take this route? Can I accept the outcome of that situation no matter what happens?" If you feel that you cannot accept the outcome resulting from your choice, then rethink it. Your plan should have a sound contingency activity built into it. Contingency plans are supplemental actions that provide you with an opportunity to make alternative moves based on factors you may not have anticipated. No matter what option you choose, remember that the choice is yours, not someone else's. Go with your plan of action and stand by it.

MANAGING UNDER FIRE:
Defensive and Offensive Strategy to Consider

The loss of a job is not the only thing at risk in a job attack: your personal and professional image could be, as well.

When defending yourself against a job attack, nothing should happen in or around your territory that you are not aware of. You should be familiar with all staff assignments and the status of the assignments. People in your department or on your personal staff should not be doing things that you have no knowledge of, nor should they be doing things that are your responsibility in one way or another.

When managing from a defensive position, listening becomes more important than ever before: What a person does not say could be more important than what he actually says. Your manager may never really say that you are in trouble. But, you will usually notice a difference in mood, behavior, and conversation. You may, for example, not receive an invitation to a corporate event that you normally would go to. You could be excluded from certain meetings. You might also find yourself excluded from the traditional management roster to receive memoranda. Being "left out of the loop" like this is a clear negative message to a staff person in trouble.

The best barometer for measuring the atmospheric conditions among senior management and colleagues in your organization are your senses. Trust your instincts and take a periodic interpersonal-relations reading to see if any significant changes in attitude and behavior among your supervisors and colleagues have occurred. Many managers are not good at concealing their true feelings about their associates and subordinates, if and when those associates and/or subordinates come under fire.

Most, in fact, suffer from a form of *group pressure* or *peer pressure* that forces them to keep their distance from an associate in trouble. People often run for cover when one of the members in the group is under attack. Generally, only the strong and trusted friends of the victim can be counted upon to be supportive when trouble comes to call. Often, you really don't know who your real friends are in the organization until you find yourself under a personal attack.

Unfortunately, what a job attack does, in effect, is to create an organization-wide disturbance that affects every employee: the rhythm and workflow within the organizational environment is disturbed. Neither management, nor those who report to them, welcomes this type of unrest among its employees because it is typically counterproductive. The smooth operational flow of the business depends on good company morale. Employees end up spending a lot of time speculating on the outcome of job attacks, and sometimes they even get involved in the attack themselves believing that some injustice has been done, or that their involvement will prevent an attack against them. When a situation like this happens, management intervention is usually required to keep matters in control.

Managing from a Defensive Posture

When delegating work assignments to subordinates, try to use reliable people who can get the job done right. Don't take chances if you are not sure about your people. And, don't be afraid to test their loyalty. When you are managing under fire, you need to know whom you can trust and count on for support. If your subordinates have a history of being disloyal, don't expect to get their loyalty when you are operating under pressure. Here are a few suggestions for successful managing in a troubled environment:

• Spend additional time designing systems that allow for checks and balances. Reduce the margin for error by checking and rechecking important assignments.

• Spend needed time with the operational people or people in the field. In other words, work closely with the people who make things happen and impact on your "bottom line."

• Find ways to help motivate your people without stressful tactics, and don't forget to reward the people who support you in time of trouble.

• Be sure to have the paperwork in order—reports, budgets, forecasts, etc., should be done well and on time. Document, document, and document a little more to be sure that you have covered yourself completely. Read everything that comes across your desk. This can be a tremendous help to you in organizing your defense.

• Don't be afraid to spend extra time and effort communicating with colleagues vertically and horizontally. Add more staff meetings to your scheduled activities, if needed. Make more telephone calls to communicate and/or follow up on items that are in various stages of development. But, don't make unnecessary work for yourself and staff. The whole idea is that you need to "tighten up" your operation so that no one can say that you run your affairs poorly.

• When you are not defending your operation, spend time networking for needed information. Finally, always keep the person who is attacking you in sight. Know what he/she is doing at all times!

• Make sure you have studied your attacker's strategy and tactics well and then counter each move with one of your own. In some situations you may elect to confront your attacker face-to-face. In other situations, you may elect to work behind the scenes. The important thing here is that you want to be sure you *appropriately* address all of the issues.

• Timing is critical when you choose to combat your attacker. Be careful. You may decide to hit your attacker with something when you are traveling or on vacation. In this way, it would be hard for him to accuse you of something when you were not actually around the company during the time that it happened. Beware of appearing deceitful.

• Consider some public relations techniques to include in your defensive strategies. It may be necessary to try and repair your image after the fight with your attacker is over. So, think about some image enhancement measures that you could employ.

Managing from an Offensive Posture

The style of the offensive-minded manager—in profit-making and non-profit organizations, tends to be aggressive, vigorously energetic, and assertive.

Offensive-minded people also tend to be less concerned with protecting their flanks and more interested in taking risks. Their focus is more on quantity than the defensive-minded manager who plays it safe by cutting back on volume and concentrating on the quality of what they are producing. They are quick to initiate, suggest, recommend, create, and produce. They are constantly looking for new and better ways of doing things, and they don't mind letting others know all about their good works.

Offensive managers are more vulnerable to attack. They also tend to suffer more from burnout due to prolonged high-energy output in a high-profile fashion. Their strategy works, but not for everybody all the time.

Here are some suggested offensive tactics that can undergird your plan to counter a job attacker:

- Seek to improve your existing "turn-around time" on management projects and assignments.
- Try to attend more management meetings than ever before and actively participate in a positive way—be more visible.
- When discussing sensitive business issues with management, have a positive outlook on things no matter what the challenge. This is not the time to push the negative side of things.
- Seek to increase your opportunity to improve production levels by motivating staff.
- Keep good project records and be prepared to present them to management at a minute's notice. Also, keep on top of all management reports according to their due dates.
- Stay in line with your budget commitments.
- When and where possible, recommend system improve-

ments to show that you are looking for more cost-effective measures—don't be afraid to recommend if you know what you are doing.

• Don't be afraid to take appropriate cost-cutting steps if management shows some interest.

• Seek to have a number of creative ideas ready that you can present to management at the appropriate time.

• Networking with key management people to include frequent luncheon dates and after-work meetings can help also. While the opportunity is present to talk under less stressful conditions, remember that the company business comes first. Make good use of this opportunity.

• Seek to get in the office early every day, and when possible, use the extra time to prepare for the day's activities and talk informally with your boss if he or she makes a practice of getting to work early.

• To generate on-going image enhancement, consider the use of requesting and circulating selected management letters of commendation for work well done.

Protecting Your Welfare

It is one thing to be the member of a whole department that is "under fire," but it is something altogether different when you have been singled out for attack and you have to deal with the situation without the aid and support of your entire department.

Being able to stay focused on a daily basis is not an easy thing to do when you are personally challenged to a professional fight. Most people working under these conditions constantly find themselves having to manage their feelings of resentment and anger before they can get around to managing their daily tasks. What might normally be considered a routine assignment, for example, now becomes a real challenge simply because you are angry and those feelings of resentment keep coming up and getting in the way of your ability to concentrate on what you are doing. Also, having to watch, constantly, what you say to people, and having always to let your office know where you are at all times, is a distracting and distasteful experience.

What you are now discovering is that you can generally function rather well working under short periods of stress, but now you have even taken this negative job experience home with you. For whatever reason, you suddenly find it very difficult to stop thinking about this problem and it is somehow affecting your relations with your family and also affecting your sleep. You seem to be angry all the time, when you are at work and when you come home—you just can't seem to turn the "anger thing" off!

The real problem here is that you know that prolonged feelings of anger and resentment can have an extremely negative impact on your physical, mental, and emotional health. In fact, there are many documented cases of depressed people whose depression resulted from work-related harassment and stress, due to threatened job security. Therefore, the need to keep cool, to keep things under control, and to function well becomes a real concern. Not only because you need to perform well at work, but also because you need to protect your health and your relationships at home.

Do the Right Things

To ensure that you are physically, mentally, and emotionally fit to manage your affairs during a prolonged period of stressful working conditions, consider the following steps for protecting your welfare:

• Don't be afraid to discuss work-related problems with your family and trusted friends. Particularly if the problems are affecting you emotionally. Often, simply talking about your anger and resentment to someone close to you can help relieve some of the constant pressure. The process is called discharging your feelings, and it really works. If, on the other hand, you find that discharging your feelings with friends or family is not working for you, don't be afraid to get some professional help just to get you over this experience.

• Daily physical exercise is another good way to keep the pressure levels down when stress, due to work-related conditions, starts to build up. In fact, the more the stress builds, the more you need to exercise. If you have physical limitations, see your doctor for advice, but don't let things get out of hand. And, don't drink alcohol, smoke, or use drugs to manage or find a solution for this problem—these things do not work.

• Also, make sure that you get plenty of rest and relaxation. Spend the money and take the time to go to plays, movies, and places that offer personal enjoyment. Take weekend trips to see things, and visit people that make you feel good. After all, the investment in your personal welfare is worth the cost.

• Buy good books that you truly enjoy reading. Also, try to spend time with people who are positive and make you laugh. Do fun things together and get your mind off your work-related problems. Laughter is one of the best things to combat stressful experiences, anger, and resentment.

• Don't forget to eat a good balanced diet everyday. Eat more fruit and vegetables than normal, and drink lots of water. Six to eight glasses of water everyday will clean your body and make you feel better.

• Try not to talk to people who are negative all the time or who tend to depress you. Avoid this type of person until you feel emotionally strong enough to manage their negativity and to manage your own problems.

• Daily meditation can help you stay focused on your personal welfare and your will to win the work-related battle you now face. Meditation from a positive point-of-view can help you see the true reality of hostile encounters or engagements. The reality in such a situation is based on truth. And, the truth is that you can change your situation by changing the way you look at it, and the way you manage your feelings about it.

When the time is right, you may also want to consider conducting some special "search and dispel" missions aimed at neutralizing your attacker. Search and dispel missions need not be negative covert operations. Rather, they are an opportunity to dispel rumors, improve relations with key management people, and block the negative activity of your attacker. Therefore, don't be afraid to pinpoint problem areas and develop effective solutions— see things right so that you can set them right!

In the Final Analysis

In the final analysis, it really doesn't matter very much if you win the battle in a job attack, but lose your health in the process of fighting the battle. Winning is important, but it really is not everything. In fact, no job is worth the loss of personal health. So always remember, if you have your health—you really do have everything. It's much easier to replace a job and income than it is to restore the loss of good health. What is critical to the successful outcome of any corporate job attack is the ability of the attacked victim to walk away from the job attack in good mental, physical, and spiritual health.

To do that, you need to constantly monitor your stress levels to be sure that you are not vulnerable to some type of negative health condition. And, remember to take the appropriate steps to protect yourself physically, mentally, and emotionally. The whole idea is to keep yourself fit all of the time and able to meet the daily challenges of the job assault. For most people, this generally means developing a regimen of daily exercise, eating a daily balanced diet, getting the correct amount of rest needed to feel good and be alert, and developing a spiritual exercise to reinforce the spiritual self.

A Case History of a Corporate Job Attack

Virtually every person in an organization has some vulnerability to job attack. It is just a matter of someone studying the person's weakest points, applying the right pressure, and nine times out of ten, the biggest corporate executives will fall. Here is a case history that can give you some more insight on how a seasoned manager might attempt to defend himself or herself in a job attack.

Susan Jones, an internal publications manager, with over ten years experience in the company, walks into her office at 8:45 on a Thursday and begins her daily routine of administrative activity. She has had an outstanding history of performance reviews, is liked and respected throughout the company, and, therefore, feels relatively secure in her position. At 9 A.M. her immediate supervisor walks into her office and asks her to drop whatever she is working on, and quickly assemble the following data, which is needed for the vice-president of the department by no later than 2 P.M. that same day: a complete analysis of her department's budget, *i.e.*, expenditures to date and the balance; the current performance appraisals for all ten management-level people in her group; the files on all of the programs and projects in place; and a summary of the goals and objectives of that department for the entire year. She has been told by her boss that she does not know what is going on, but she will tell her as soon as she receives some information from senior management.

At 2 P.M. our manager is asked to report to a vice-president's office. He tells her that some of her department is going to be transferred soon. Half of her group is going to be reassigned to a newly-developed department and the balance is going to remain in the existing department within the corporate headquarters, as presently assigned.

She is also told that because of her performance record, she will be allowed to decide whether or not she would prefer to go with half of her group to set up what will be called a communications department, or remain with the existing department and the balance of her staff. Ms. Jones now feels the need to find out the rationale for the change. She needs to know the structure of the new department: it's hierarchy; budgets; the scope of its activities; and the anticipated size of the staff. It's obvious that some extensive reorganization is in progress, but she has been given virtually no information to make a decision about her own future, not to mention the future of the people in her group. She knows that whenever reorganization occurs, some people benefit from the change and others don't. She knows that she needs to know who is doing the horse trading, so she can make some maneuvers to protect her interests. Horse trading, in this instance, refers to those involved in the process of reshuffling personnel so as to meet the needs of top management, at a particular time and place. The reshuffling may be a part of a plan to make budget adjustments, create new corporate strategy, compensate for weak senior management activity, and so on.

The fact of the matter is that whenever decisions like these are made, it is generally top management's effort to achieve a corporate objective that has nothing to do with individual employees. The corporate leadership likes to feel that its *modus operandi* is predicated on a team concept, and executives such as Susan Jones should be willing to sacrifice their personal ambitions or developmental needs to help support the objectives of top management at the moment.

Understanding corporate thinking on these matters, our manager feels that she might well make the wrong decision regarding her own future and the reorganization. Fortunately, she finds out from a friend, who happens to be an insider, that what is really taking place is a management manpower "takeover," engineered by a senior vice-president.

The takeover, in effect, would give a particular first-line vice-president in the new department an opportunity to grab additional territory, additional staff members, and a larger budget—in the interest of strengthening the senior vice-president's position in the company. Power in a corporation is often related to the size of the territory the executive controls, the number of staff people in the department, and the size of the department's budget.

Now, while all of this may be good for the business, it obviously does not take into account the careers of the lower-level management people involved, *i.e.*, clerical workers, secretaries, and so on. Using her corporate contacts, our manager finds out that if she decides to go over to the new department, she will end up reporting to a person with the same title and much less job experience than she has. More important, while our manager has a long history of good performance appraisals, she is told that the person she would be reporting to in the new department has a reputation of being extremely political and overambitious, with a management style that borders on insensitivity.

Our manager, if she decides to join the new department, could quite possibly be heading into real trouble. Over the years, executives have been known to go from a very favorable image in one department to an image in another department of being a "loser." This is done simply by changing departments and not realizing that the new reporting executive simply does not like you.

What Do You Think?

• Do you share the feeling that the manager is under a company attack, and that she needs to do something about her situation?

• What, if anything, would you do about the situation the manager appears to be faced with?

• Suppose the manager decided not to do anything about the reassignment, what do you think will happen to her job security in the new department, and why?

Corporate Attack Counteraction

As soon as our publications manager gets the full story on this reassignment and the person she would be reporting to, she realizes that she has to make some fast countermoves or risk losing her career investment in the company—an investment of many years. So she quickly schedules a series of one-on-one meetings with a few of her high-ranking corporate friends and asks for guidance in making her decision. She wants to remain in her present position, without giving top management the impression that she resents or disapproves of their plans.

After meeting with her friends, she then schedules meetings with each top-management person involved in the decision-making process. She makes a well-rehearsed presentation to them that says, in effect, "I thank you for the opportunity to join the new unit in the new department, but I believe that my career objectives will best be met by remaining with my existing department, where I have initiated some important programs that I would like to see completed." She also reminds them that she has selected the best people in her department to fulfill the company's needs, that she is confident that the plans for realignment will accomplish some positive goals, and that she will be available to assist the newly formed department for as long as they might need her.

IV

Networking: Laying Your Corporate Foundation

Networking is a process that can enable you to gain support from friends, relatives, business associates, acquaintances, and even strangers, to achieve a goal or an objective—personal or otherwise.

Networking can help you to meet important people and make valuable friendships; it can give you opportunities to influence some people and win favors from still others.

Networking can also provide you with the opportunity to develop important contacts with people at various levels of society who may later support your ideas, interests, or personal concerns (political aspirations, job opportunities, and social ambitions).

Networking is the process of developing and exploiting a large number of professional and social relationships for the purpose of achieving some unspecified future advantage. Networking can help you gain:

- Needed information
- Job promotions
- Favorable business deals

- Political support
- Introductions to people you want to meet
- Help and guidance from experts
- The best medical advice available
- The best legal counsel possible
- Your child's admission to a good college
- A good table in a fine New York restaurant
- A loan from a major bank at favorable rates
- Clothing at discount rates... and the list goes on and on.

Finally, networking in its most sophisticated form represents real power in society. If used wisely, networking can even help you to benefit substantially from the socioeconomic system of the United States.

Networking, as you may well imagine, is not a new concept in our society, or any other society, for that matter. The term itself may have been popularized in recent years, but the concept in its most basic form probably dates back to the early beginning of human beings' tribal activity and their need to relate to other people on a competitive basis for food, shelter, weapons, protection, and the selection of a mate.

Anyone who really wants to learn the skill of networking must first be willing to put forth considerable effort. Few people can master this skill without really working at it. Nevertheless, because of the relative speed that it takes to develop some *contacts*, some people think that they can simply make a career of networking without effort, risks, and disappointments. Believe me, nothing could be further from the truth. You are going to have to pay some dues along the way if you want to build strong contacts with people who can help you when you need help. Dues in the form of courtesy, flattery, tolerance, loyalty, good deeds, errands run, or favors done. Please don't be naive and think that because you meet someone at a party, he or she is your personal contact. In fact, people with power protect their power very carefully and do not permit just anyone to have access to their influence without great scrutiny.

THE POWER BROKER

People who work at networking on a full-time basis and are successful at it are known as power brokers. They move among the movers and shakers. They have strong contacts in every part of society—religious, civic, social—and every part of the business and financial community. They have contacts in the private sector and the public sector and at every level of politics and government. They have worked at it over the years step by step, greeting, meeting, and getting to know the right people through the sharing, exchanging, and trading of ideas, information, contacts, favors, gifts, money... you name it. To put it another way, they know the rich and the poor, the big and the small. It is their business to know people and they work at it!

LEARNING TO NETWORK

Why are some people *so* successful at networking? The answer is simply that they have in abundance certain essential, very basic personal characteristics.

TWELVE TOP NETWORKING CHARACTERISTICS

1. *Desire:* moved by a strong need to be successful at networking and the ability to persevere

2. *Good personality:* approachable and pleasant to be around

3. *Intelligence:* displays depth of thought swiftly and clearly in conversation, is rational, and knows when to keep her or his mouth shut

4. *Conversational ability:* clever when necessary; able to carry on conversations with members of all socioeconomic and racial groups; wit and sensitivity

5. *Political skill:* clever, shrewd when necessary, knowledgeable about political affairs

6. *Good appearance:* dresses to suit the occasion, never offends target prospects

7. *Alertness:* always aware and always on to developing contacts

8. *Diplomacy:* skilled at saying the right thing to the right people at the right time

9. *Secretiveness, discretion:* strong ability to be secretive and to encourage confidence in handling secret information

10. *Reciprocation:* understands and fully respects the code of reciprocation

11. *Strength, energy:* constantly on the move, always at the right events at the right time with the right people present

12. *Financial resources:* has access to money or the monetary means to get the job done

Looking more closely at the concept, you will find that the *art of reciprocation* is the single most important element in keeping your network alive and well!

Those who consider networking to be an important part of their personal support system, or better yet, their survival system, must keep a running scorecard on whom they owe favors to and who owes them favors. It is all a matter of being able to help those who help you when the need arises. Sometimes, however, a contact may do a favor for you and he or she may not ask you for a favor in return for years. Exchanging favors really has no time limit, no statute of limitations, if you will. In fact, that same contact may not ever ask you for a favor in return, but instead may ask a favor for someone else he or she wants to help. It is like having money in a bank that you can withdraw whenever you need to. The bank where you have a credit line had better give you money when you need it. The point here is that if you want to be a serious networker, you cannot afford to forget the people who do favors for you and you cannot afford to let them down when they need you.

On the other hand, you may be in a position to do a contact a favor, and when you need that contact to reciprocate, you expect him or her to come through for you, or you will have to reconsider the person's status as a legitimate resource. In short, people who participate in the networking process are really obligated to respond favorably, if it is at all possible. Oh, yes, from time to time you may not be able to come through for people you owe the favor to, and depending on how you handle the situation, that may be all right. But you are still indebted to them, psychologically, morally, or otherwise. Therefore, it must be made clear to them that you have made a serious effort to help; otherwise, you run the risk of being eliminated from their list of dependable resources. (You may never know that such a person no longer considers you a reliable source—that is, until you attempt to use the contact for some other reason.) Remember, "networking" is just a newfangled word for the age-old practice of sharing, exchanging, and trading one good deed for another, among people who perceive each other as having the potential to help one another. Never forget this idea, or you will most certainly fail at effective networking.

Learning to Network—Phase One

Step I: Set up a good record-keeping and filing system. You need to have easy access to all names, addresses, and phone numbers. Two convenient methods are a business card file and a Rolodex file. You will need to keep records of all your contacts in easily retrievable form.

Always keep your special names and numbers under lock and key, unless they are in your own home. Some names and numbers can get you in a world of trouble if you are not careful. For example, if you are working in a corporate office, you must assume that if you get sick for a long period of time, someone other than your personal secretary can gain access to the files in your office. Even a personal locked file in your office will not stop a company security person, or a maintenance man, for that matter. So if your contact lists are really secret, keep them out of the office.

Step II: Learn to be a good socializer, but more important, don't view your activities as strictly a fun occasion. Remember, if your interest is networking, then you are actually "working" the event, not attending it socially. People who have a fun agenda attend various events for the fun of it all, but if you are a *networker,* you need to be about the business of networking.

Step III: Practice ways of concealing or disguising the element of calculation in your contacts with people. Never make your networking really apparent. Some really important people are turned off if you lack sophistication in your networking efforts. Some would-be networkers are downright sophomoric. Make sure you are not one of them.

Learning to Network—Phase Two

Step I: Always carry your business cards, but don't give them out at random. Be selective and place some value on your own name and address. Don't forget that you are working the event: concentrate on the people you need to meet and be instinctive when it comes to who should not get your number. This means that you have to develop ways and techniques for presenting yourself, your business card, and any personal information you may want to give to a target contact. And walking up to a person without an introduction from someone who knows the person may not be the best way to reach the individual. It could turn the person off immediately because he or she is uncertain about your intentions. So think about ways to approach people, and think about the timing and the best opportunity to make the greatest impact. In some cases, the direct approach may be the right approach. Each situation and every person require a tailor-made approach. If you don't make the "right" approach, you may lose the opportunity forever.

Step II: Practice methods of approaching people and learn to make strangers feel comfortable in your presence. Be sensitive to a person's title or status. Some people with important titles must be treated with deference. Therefore, try to find out if an introduction is the right approach.

Step III: Watch the professionals (public relations people, lobbyists, politicians, etc.) and see how they work an event. Study their techniques and their styles. If possible, try to get some of the professionals to give you some advice on how to network effectively. You will be amazed (and sometimes amused) to see all the different styles that can be effective.

Learning to Network—Phase Three

Step I: Build your contact list step by step and keep it up-to-date. All important names and addresses should always be updated.

Divide your contact list and classify your contacts by factors that are important to you. For example:

- Medical
- Legal
- Religious
- Social
- Political
- Financial
- Business
- Governmental (federal, state, and local)
- Communications (radio, television, print media)
- General

Step II: Develop a systematic follow-up procedure that enables you to keep in touch with the key people on your contact list. Here are various ways that might prove useful to you, depending upon your need and your financial means:

- Periodic telephone calls to say hello, etc.
- Birthday, anniversary, and other holiday greeting cards
- Personal letters and notes from time to time
- Reprints, articles, and clippings on subjects of interest, with covering note to make a point
- Informal breakfast meetings, luncheons, dinners, and after-work drinks
- Weekend houseguest
- Private parties for any and all occasions
- Tickets to special events, compliments of . . .
- Trips and vacations of all kinds
- Fund-raising events of all kinds
- Private dinners, dances, and theater parties of all types
- Special reception for VIPs and dignitaries of all kinds

- Weddings, christenings, bar mitzvahs
- Gifts of all prices and all kinds

Warning: The riskiest method of keeping in touch is the cold call, dropping in to see someone without warning. Do this only if you know the person very well and you are sure he or she will be happy to see you.

Learning to Network—Phase Four

Many minority management people (old and new) think that they are unable to develop friendly relationships with senior management (vice-presidents and above) because the executive's door is closed to them. However, thinking doesn't make it so. In this case, a perceived closed door may in reality be wide open. You would be surprised at the number of executives who would be very glad to have periodic informal luncheons and in-office meetings with lower-level corporate members. If nothing else, they would generally like to know what people in the company are thinking and feeling as it relates to the progress of the company and the business.

This is especially true if it is the executive's responsibility to know if minorities and women in the company are relatively satisfied with the corporate climate.

Corporate policies and practices for employees are important ingredients for planned growth and development. Management, for example, needs to know what its employees are thinking and how they feel about the existing work environment. Without this information, conditions of employment could decline rapidly.

A corporate "open door" policy offers considerable possibilities for employee networking, as well as a management information flow system, if handled tactfully and developed over a period of time.

Putting it in more specific networking terms, most minorities and women working in a corporate organization have an opportunity to bypass the chain of command from *time to time* and meet informally with a senior-level executive, *without threatening the system.* All you have to do is call the executive's secretary and say that you would appreciate it if Ms. or Mr. so-and-so would allow you a few minutes of her or his time on *an informal basis*, just so that you can get to know each other a little better. Explain that you have been with the company in the ABC department for *x* amount of time, and you have never had the opportunity to simply spend a few minutes with the senior vice-president (or whoever). I guarantee you that no matter how busy the executive might be, the secretary, if approached properly, will find a date when the two of you can meet, even if it is several weeks later. Tell the secretary that you would be perfectly willing to meet the executive for early morning coffee if that would be the most convenient time.

Now that you have gained the opportunity to meet informally with a member of your senior management, here are some pointers for the actual meeting:

If You Are Unknown to the Executive

1. Suggested length of meeting: approximately twenty to twenty-five minutes; no longer unless the executive wants to continue talking
2. Suggested information to give about yourself:
   a. Information to be given as you introduce yourself:
      - Your name, job title, and department
      - Brief description of your duties (twenty-five words or less)
      - Length of time with company
   b. Information to get across during the conversation:
      - Some personal immediate family data (single, married, number of children and ages)
      - Names of colleges you attended
      - Name of community where you live
      - Your hobbies and volunteer work outside of the company
      - Any corporate-supported employee activities or volunteer work you are involved in
      - Avoid any critical comments about your department or your department management. This is not the time to be critical about anything.

3. Suggested topics to ask the executive about:
   - Number of children and their ages
   - Names of colleges attended by the children
   - Name of community where the executive lives
   - Length of time executive has been with the company
   - His or her philosophy for corporate success
   - Any advice the executive could give relative to a successful career in the company

If You Are Known by the Executive

1. Suggested length of meeting: twenty to twenty-five minutes
2. Suggested course of conversation:
   - Mention any important personal information the executive has not learned at previous meetings.
   - Proceed directly to personal advice for success and the outlook for future minority and women's success.

Having elected to implement this exercise at your company, you might already have received a number of benefits. Among them:

1. Some personal corporate identification
2. The image of an established married family person, or
3. The image of a civic-minded, generous, spirited person
4. The perception that you are available and receptive to a mentorship (mentors and mentoring will be given special attention later in this chapter)
5. The perception that you are a hardworking, aggressive young executive, eager for advancement
6. An invitation to meet again

Based on your assessment of the exercise, how many of these benefits do you think you would have gained, and how would you apply them to your overall networking objectives?

CREATING YOUR IMAGE

Not too many years ago, if a businessman was unfortunate enough to develop a poor public image, he would more than likely have to live with that image for the remainder of his business career. Only a miracle could change that public mind-set, once the damage had been done. In other words, "Once a bad guy, always a bad guy," and that's the way it was.

But not so today. Today we have both the means and the know-how to change public attitudes and public perceptions about ourselves and our businesses.

How did this change come about? Did the public really become more fickle as the years passed by? Not at all. In fact, public opinion is probably more critical of the business community today than it has ever been. Rather, the difference lies in the growing sophistication of our channels of communication; the refinement of our communications technology; the expanding literacy rate; and finally the public's desire for more and more information. The practice of image building can be found in virtually every segment of our society. In addition, few institutions, organizations, or corporations of any size in the United States exist without some form of public relations support. Public relations is as much an integral part of our daily lives today as television. In fact, public relations (or image building) in its basic form can consist of knowing how to use the media and word of mouth to help create a desired image.

However, to be aware that this dynamic process does exist is really not enough. Why not learn how to tap into it and use it for your own corporate career purposes? Specifically, why not learn how to influence favorably the right corporate people with the aid of favorable word-of-mouth reports and internal and external media exposure? If you really want to do this, it is not an impossible task at all. And you don't have to wait until someone decides to give you recognition.

Favorable exposure or image building is for anyone and everyone who has the desire to learn the proven techniques and is willing to invest consistent effort over a long period of time. Most people don't get the exposure they want, because they are simply unwilling to take the time and effort to follow through after setting up an opportunity for good exposure.

The process of building your image is not a big mystery. It is not even costly. But you do have to understand how it is accomplished, and you have to take the time and effort to make it happen, unless you are fortunate enough to have the money to pay someone to do it for you.

Think about it for a moment. With this newly acquired awareness, you can begin to create some positive personal imagery. Not without some legitimate accomplishments on your part, of course, but the point is that you really don't have to wait until someone else decides to give you the exposure. You can actually trigger it yourself. Think about the added respect and goodwill you will gain from friends and business associates by their simply knowing about your good deeds and accomplishments. The goodwill is immeasurable, because everybody likes to hear about success stories, no matter how small they may be. In fact, there is so much negativity going on around us, on a daily basis, it is a blessing to hear about something pleasant and positive that someone has done; and when it happens to be someone you know, or who is associated with your organization, it becomes even more important and meaningful.

Your employers, for example, will see you in a very different light, because positive imagery adds to the character and personality of the business. They will start to feel that as a result of your good deeds and personal accomplishments, the business is benefiting by its association with you. Therefore, by making sure your good activities are mentioned in the channels of communication that management is familiar with, you give the people who make decisions in the organization a chance to be better informed about the kind of talent they have in the company.

Additionally, they will be getting the messages about you from a respected third party. You can imagine how much more effective this is than any effort you might make to convey the information yourself.

Most senior management people are extremely busy and have little time to spare for receiving information that is not directly related to the business or the welfare of the employees. Therefore, it makes good sense to know how to reach these people in such a way that they will welcome the information. And why not? Every successful business person knows that people need to know about not only the good skills and talents they may have but the good things they are doing on a regular basis. This is simply a matter of using good and effective communication skills in a highly competitive business environment.

With your new public relations sensitivity, you will know how to get your news items into the hands of the news media in a way somewhat like the way public figures and celebrities do. Remember, some people are in the public view because they make news and are considered opinion makers. Others are there because they know how to get information to the media in a useful format that is timely and suited for a particular audience.

The following suggestions for do-it-yourself P.R. projects are offered in the hope that you will be encouraged to research the public relations area more thoroughly—by reading and understanding a good introduction to the field. You can find this type of book in almost any library or bookstore. For example, there is *Lesly's Public Relations Handbook*, edited by Philip Lesly and published by Prentice-Hall, and there is also *The Practice of Public Relations*, written by Fraser P. Seitel and published by Merrill Publishing Company, a Bell & Howell Information Company.

Finally, talk with people who know how to do it right, and exchange ideas, tips, and techniques.

Working with Volunteer Organizations

By donating some of your time to a carefully selected volunteer activity, you can become associated with prestigious people and organizations that make news on an ongoing basis: noteworthy people and nationally known organizations that are involved in a positive way in major social issues that make good copy in the daily press, trade publications, and company house organs.

Corporations call this type of activity social responsibility, and what company in America, of any size and stature, does not want to be considered socially responsible? Your contribution to the corporation's image of social responsibility makes an excellent platform from which you can launch a solid personal recognition campaign. Every "concerned" and "committed" executive today personally supports some socially positive nonprofit effort. When you enhance your company's CSR (corporate social responsibility), as it is sometimes called, you are more valuable to your employer and have therefore enhanced your own career possibilities as well.

Although corporations generally encourage community-spirited activity among their management people, it is important to keep in mind the need to be very selective in your choice of people and organizations to identify with. In short, try to pick an organization that is well respected in the community and is known for its good works.

For very obvious reasons, any conspicuous involvement you have with controversial people and issues will tend to confuse management's understanding of your intent. Therefore, try to avoid such situations, if possible, because they can defeat your primary purpose, the development of your career. You have unlimited opportunities through other kinds of volunteer activities, to help people help themselves, while improving your own image.

There is nothing wrong with gaining a benefit from helping people. The fact is that this kind of community service is greatly needed, and your efforts rightly will be recognized by the community as well as by your employer.

Other opportunities to do good work and be recognized for it can come about by participating in the activities of important trade organizations or professional associations.

Working with Trade Organizations

Trade organizations play a major role in supporting an entire industry; they keep their members informed about developments in the industry and they also promote professionalism and high standards of production within the industry. Not least, they act as public relations and public affairs representatives for the industry. Therefore, to hold an office or play any other leadership role in a trade organization offers all kinds of possibilities for personal recognition. Again, be very careful when deciding whether to join a particular trade group. Make sure the organization is respected within the industry and by the various publics it seeks to communicate with.

Remember that trade groups have corporate members and often lobby for the special concerns and interests of their member companies. That is one of their chief functions, so it is simply good business for member companies to recognize and support employees of their own who are active in a trade group that serves the company. Companies, in fact, prefer to have some of their most talented employees actively involved in the principal trade organization of their industry, because the quality of those employees creates an impression of the high caliber of all the people employed by the company. What company executive in his right mind would want a mediocre or irresponsible person to represent the company?

Companies are sensitive about this sort of thing and they don't like to be embarrassed. So if you are not serious about your commitment to a special trade group assignment, don't get involved. The word-of-mouth publicity within your company, on assignments like this, can be enormous and you certainly don't want the president of the trade organization happening to mention to the president of your company over lunch that you're a nice person and then revealing, indirectly, that you don't seem to be interested in what you are doing.

Also remember that some of the issues the trade organization is working on may be sensitive enough to hold in the balance the continued existence of the *entire industry* as it is presently known. Therefore, you can be sure that the top management of your company is well aware of any of their employees who are involved in sensitive trade organization affairs. The contribution of these employees does not go unnoticed, and it need not go unrewarded.

Joining Professional Associations

Membership in a professional association, or association of people who do the same kind of work, but not necessarily in the same industry, can be a valuable asset from several points of view.

It keeps you up-to-date on important developments in your profession, is a ready-made networking resource, lets you know the condition of the job market in your field, and provides a listing of jobs available. It also can provide opportunities for positive recognition.

The organization must have *impeccable credentials* or the whole purpose of joining will be defeated.

When you finally decide on the group that reflects the kind of image you want to be identified with, seek out an opportunity to take on some responsibility in the organization. At first it may be just a minor assignment or two that the group will give you, until they see how you handle things, but over a period of time, you could end up holding a very important position in the organization and that could be a tremendous opportunity for positive exposure, both locally and in a larger context.

If the organization is truly an important asset to the professionalism of the field, people who work in that field will learn about you, and over a period of time you will become a recognized professional any company would be happy to have join their organization.

Don't Overdo Things

Don't go out and start joining every organization, group, and club you can find in order to get some added recognition. And please don't become a "corporate social responsibility butterfly." Moving from one volunteer group to the next, so that you appear to be everywhere but in the office conducting company business, is not what the whole idea of volunteerism is all about. Having too much exposure is just as bad as not having any exposure at all. So don't go overboard with your enthusiasm.

When you are *overexposed* in the corporate world, your business associates tend not to take you very seriously. They know roughly how much time it takes to do your job effectively, and if you are never at work, but out of the office working on various volunteer projects, they will more than likely begin to question your effectiveness on the job, and perhaps even your commitment to your profession. People who spend a lot of time out of the office working on volunteer matters either have a large staff of people they can delegate their work to or are "not taking care of business"! So don't go into this activity to the extent that you become overexposed. Seek to establish a good balance of time and effort, both in your paid position and in your volunteer work. Always remember that your paid job comes first.

If you establish a good balance of your time and effort, people will see you as a person with an exceptional talent for management, an executive type who is capable of handling a responsible paid position and concurrently finding the time to help others.

A final caution: Don't forget that you need a satisfying and relaxing life away from work if you want a personal life in the long run. If you are married and have children, you need to give a high priority to spending time with your family. If you are not married, you need to take time for friendships, recreation, and travel. Volunteer work must not be a negative item in your life. All the important elements in your life must work together—your job, your family commitments, and your volunteer efforts—or everything will certainly fall apart right in front of your eyes.

Writing Your Own Press Release

With few exceptions, volunteer organizations of any size have their own public relations staff people to publicize the newsworthy information about the organization and its members. However, if the volunteer organization that you are working with does not have a public relations person to see that the news story gets out to the press immediately, you could actually help them out in an emergency and write the news release or photo caption yourself. Then let the volunteer organization send the story out to the press. Remember, this is not something that I would recommend on a regular basis, but in an emergency you don't have to let a good news story go unseen or unread because there was no one around to write it.

The opening of your news release will look like this:

NEWS RELEASE

CONTACT: (Name, address, and
phone number)

DATE:

FOR IMMEDIATE RELEASE

Summary headline goes here.
Should be limited to two lines.

In a conspicuous place, give the source of the release (your name, business address, and phone number). This not only identifies you but also tells the editor where additional information can be obtained.

The release should be dated on the upper right-hand portion of the first page. Give an instruction to the editor specifying when the story can be used. This can be for *IMMEDIATE RELEASE, RELEASE AT WILL,* or for release on a specific date: *FOR RELEASE THURSDAY, OCTOBER 10.*

The headline is for the purpose of quickly summarizing the contents of the release. Near the page number on subsequent pages, always show a shortened version of the headline. This is an important precaution: If pages get separated at any point, they can easily be identified.

Begin the release with all pertinent information in the first or lead paragraph. Include who, what, where, when, and how. Be sure no details are left out. Include exact time and place of event.

All paragraphs and sentences should be short. Double-space between lines. Maintain wide margins. Leave plenty of space at the top of page 1. This space is not wasted. It is used by editors to make corrections and notations.

At the bottom of page 1, the word "More" should always appear if there is an additional page. This applies to all pages except the final one, on which the end of the release is indicated by using the designation -30-, ###, or -0-, or the word "End."

In writing the release, remember that its purpose is to provide complete, accurate, and factual information.

*   *   *

To prepare a photo caption, double-space all pertinent information and affix the photograph above it:

New York, N.Y., March 4, 1989: John Doe, Vice-President of the Safety Engineers of America (left), presents a plaque designating XYZ Products, Inc., as the safest manufacturer of the year to the cosmetic company's General Manager, Mary Johnson (center), as XYZ's Chief Safety Engineer, Darrell Twiford, looks on. The award was made last night at the Safety Engineers Annual Dinner in the Grand Ballroom of New York's Waldorf-Astoria Hotel.

XYZ Products, Inc.
11 East 12th Street
New York, N.Y. 10000
(212) 000-0000
Contact: Mary Johnson

MENTORS AND MENTORING

What is a corporate mentor?

A corporate mentor is a wise and trusted advisor who is willing to demonstrate *some degree* of commitment to your career.

Are corporate mentors important?

Show me a successful executive and I will show you a person who has been helped along the way by a mentor. In fact, if the executive has been around his company for ten or more years, it is quite possible that he or she has received mentoring support from more than one person within the organization. The whole idea here is that few people make it to the top jobs of a corporation of any size and stature without some mentoring support along the way.

Why are mentors so important?

Mentors are very important because they can often help you take advantage of opportunities within the company that you would not normally know about. A mentor can also help you avoid pitfalls that might negatively affect your career, which is another important reason to have one.

Politically astute mentors are of particular value to entry-level executives, because few entry-level people are really aware of the internal politics of their organization in the beginning. In most companies it takes time and strong networking efforts at the upper levels of management before you can be considered a politically astute executive. As a matter of fact, you have to be a corporate "insider" to really be in the best political circles of management. Therefore, becoming a politically astute executive in a company is no small feat to accomplish. You have to work at it!

Is it absolutely necessary to have a mentor in order to be successful?

The answer is no. It is not absolutely necessary to have a mentor in order to succeed in the corporate world, but it sure does help—if you have a good one. You see, more often than not, executives must be recommended for the better jobs in a company, and if you don't have anyone who is willing to stick his neck out for you, it makes your efforts to fight your way to the top a little more difficult. Remember, to get the big jobs, one generally has to participate in some sort of selection process to begin with, and if your name is never mentioned, it obviously will not come up in the selection process. However, you certainly *do not* have to have a mentor to get a promotion.

Let's make that very clear. There are many other ways to get a promotion. For example, earning it on the basis of some outstanding work or coming up with some great idea for the company to either make more money or save some of it.

Some high-ranking mentors may be willing to go so far as to push for the appointment of a protégé to some important job if they really feel strongly about it. This, of course, is always left totally up to the discretion of the mentor, because after all, the mentor is to some extent putting his reputation on the line if the protégé fails miserably in the new assignment.

In any event, you should know that there are all kinds of

mentors, some good and some not so good. A lot depends on the degree of experience, authority, and willingness to help in time of need.

Should an entry-level executive try to get a mentor?

If you want to, why not? First, look over the field of potential mentors available and see if there is someone in the organization that you think has the insight, experience, and influence to make a good candidate for you. It helps if you and the prospective mentor can identify with each other in some way. If not, the person you choose should at least be someone you respect who seems to be receptive to your apparent interest in growing within the company.

Once you have decided, slowly but surely try to develop a positive relationship with him, perhaps using a positive networking of tips and techniques that we have discussed in this book—for example, one-on-one meetings to get acquainted. The point is that you have to develop a good relationship, based upon mutual respect and friendliness. This does not come quickly or easily; it takes time. Sometimes it takes a few years for people to really get to know each other and develop mutual respect and admiration. Good relationships in this instance tend to grow out of friendly contact over a period of time and the need to exchange favors or advice. The ingredients of trust, sincerity, and respect must be present in the relationship, or it will not last very long.

In most cases, however, the relationship develops because of the outstanding work that you have done in the company and the pleasant and enthusiastic personality that you have. Remember, everybody likes a winner, and most people enjoy people with pleasant or *impressive* personalities.

Will a mentor guarantee a free trip to the top jobs?

The answer to that is *definitely not*! Having a mentor will not guarantee you anything. There are no guarantees in corporate life, and your "luck" can change overnight. You won't get a free trip to the top, so don't plan on one. A mentor is just what we said, a wise and trusted advisor who is willing to demonstrate some degree of commitment to your career.

Are there any risks involved in having a mentor?

Yes, there are some risks involved. It is like anything else in business: You simply must take your chances. For example, you could select a poor mentor and end up getting poor advice and poor results. You could also select someone who is on his way out of the company, or worse yet, about to lose his influence in the company. Therefore, he may not be able or willing to help you, because now he suddenly cannot even help himself.

The one thing you can do to minimize the risk is to make sure, as far as you can, that your selection of a mentor is a good one. This takes time and research, so don't be in a hurry to jump in the water (at least check the temperature of the water and see if you can withstand the heat or the chill if you have to).

What should I do if some big executive offers to be my mentor?

Obviously, no one can force you into a mentoring relationship. That is just not done in the business world, so you almost don't have to worry about a forced situation. However, it is quite possible that some senior management person might attempt to extend a hand of friendship for some reason, and that "friendship" could evolve into a mentoring relationship very naturally. This, I might add, happens quite a bit in corporate life. Therefore, you should not be surprised if it happens to you. These situations are almost always very positive in the life of a young corporate executive trying to move up the line. So don't fight it if the president of the company happens to like you, or the chairman of the board, for that matter.

Should mentoring be a part of my basic survival plan?

It is really up to you. However, even if a mentor, by giving some sound advice, does nothing but help you to protect your job, the relationship can be worthwhile for you. Additionally, if a company layoff comes about, and your mentor is able to help you save your job, then the experience has really paid off for you in large dividends.

Should every executive seek to become a mentor?

No. Mentors are very special people and mentoring is an important responsibility. Let's face it, everyone is not cut out for taking on that kind of responsibility. If someone is going to try the experience, he should be very clear about the commitment he is making to another person and very sure of his own sincerity. The mentoring relationship is not just practical but spiritual as well, and a mentor should be worthy of the responsibility of helping to direct another person's career and giving trusted advice.

To put it another way, you must be capable of advising someone who trusts you and must make yourself available to that person, whenever there is a real need. It should also be pointed out that mentoring can be a wonderful and rewarding experience, one in which the mentor actually helps someone to help himself. This is a very self-fulfilling undertaking.

Should capable, committed, and experienced minority executives become mentors?

Yes, yes, yes! It is very important for sincere and experienced upper-level executives to try to help a *deserving* inexperienced management person who is trying to make it in the corporate world. Realizing that entry-level minority management people have so few minority role models available in corporations to identify with, the minority executive's contribution to this all-important area is greatly needed. I might add that the mentor relationship need not be *confined* to people in the same company. Again, we are basically talking about mentors who can fulfill the role of a wise and trusted advisor. Therefore, mentor relationships may be extended well beyond the mentor's immediate organization.

Let me repeat that it is quite possible for an experienced upper-level manager to meet some deserving young person and extend his or her hand in friendship, and for the initial contact to evolve into a mentoring relationship. This has happened many times, over the years, and has proven to be a very healthy and rewarding experience for all.

THE NEED TO BE FRIENDLY

Friendliness is a very subjective quality. Like beauty, it is in the eyes of the beholder. When a candidate for employment or promotion is interviewed, it is the opinion of the interviewer that will establish whether the candidate is a friendly type of person or not. And the interviewer's opinion is formulated, of necessity, on the basis of a first meeting. Therefore, if the candidate appears to be unfriendly, it is unlikely that there will ever be another meeting.

This issue is of particular significance when it comes to black and Hispanic male candidates. For reasons that have yet to be fully explained, some black males, for example, just by their mere presence as a candidate for a management-oriented position, tend to make some personnel interviewers feel threatened during an interview. This is particularly true in the case of young corporate interviewers who simply lack experience and sophistication in good interview techniques, and corporate personnel people who have personal problems about race relations.

Corporate interviewers who fall into one of these two categories often tend to mistake a minority person's stern businesslike manner or ultraserious manner for "angry behavior," or perhaps "overly sensitive behavior." The result is that they will not look favorably upon the candidate because they believe the candidate to be unfriendly toward the power structure, generally, and potentially, toward their company.

A likely corporate personnel comment in a subsequent report on the interview might read: "The interviewee tended to lack friendliness as evidenced in the candidate's reluctance to smile." This superficial observation, when written in a personnel evaluation report, is interpreted to mean that the candidate may, in fact, have some unresolved hostile feelings that would have a negative effect on the company if he were hired. Unfortunately, comments like these can be made despite the fact that the candidate never actually said anything negative or unfriendly. It is a simple case of how the interviewer perceived the candidate, based upon his own value system, plus the human chemistry that might have been generated between two people during the course of the meeting. To put it another way, if the interviewer is uncertain about how he really feels about blacks and other minorities working on a management level in "his" company, chances are that he will really believe that his observations justify his evaluation.

Therefore, in the give-and-take process aimed at reaching a successful corporate interview experience, minority candidates must be aware of the subtle pitfalls and be prepared to react positively to a possible negative situation. This can be accomplished by changing the direction of the interview. Go from a passive posture to an active posture. Ask questions that show your real interest in and knowledge of the company. This is particularly important if it is your first meeting; if you don't do well now, you will never make it to the second (follow-up) interview. Remember, first impressions are important and all you have to do is get past the interview stage and you know that you will do well at the company. You just have to get around, over, or past the "palace guard" who has taken it upon himself to decide what type of people are good for the company and what type are not; all based on preconceived ideas.

Now, getting past the initial interviewer may take some good observation skills and some definite positivity, but it can be done if you pay attention to the finer points of the interview and read all of the signposts along the way. For example, be aware of the interviewer's voice tone and his line of questioning: Was his tone of voice pleasant or sharp? Did you respond in a like manner, perhaps keying off of some rather sharp tones? Did you decide that because you really want the job, you are going to be pleasant, friendly, and assertive, despite any personal "hang-ups" the interviewer might have?

In addition, are you watching his body language to see if he is rigid and unrelaxed, and thereby sending you more negative messages, or are you properly avoiding his negative body language and responding with positive messages, perhaps even sitting in a relaxed manner and using pleasant hand gestures to make a point, and most important, giving him ongoing eye contact with a friendly voice tone?

Finally, don't underestimate the power of a smile or a pleasant expression on your face. A friendly smile can communicate very positive messages in an interview, and in situations where the first meeting could be the last meeting, it will not hurt you to be as professionally alert and charming as you can be. This means that you need to display a pleasant personality, ask good questions, give good answers to the interviewer's questions, and don't be reluctant to smile when it is *natural* to do so. The point here is that you can influence people and their reaction to you through the power of friendliness.

The art of winning friends and influencing people is an important one that can be developed and applied from the initial interview stage, right through your entire corporate career. But always remember that there is a difference between being friends and being friendly. You don't have to be friends with everyone in the company, or anyone in the company, for that matter, but the corporation really pays you not to be unfriendly, because the effective communication channels in the business depend on friendly cooperation.

Being friendly is an important communication tool in the corporation. Most corporate people will never openly admit to being unfriendly with anyone, even when they don't really like half of the people in the company.

It's all a big game in the corporate world. Consequently, why make the art of friendliness a negative issue? If you don't have the skill, learn it quickly. And when you learn it, use it effectively. Play the game and play to win!

JOB HUNTING

Preparing for a Job Search

Whether you are contemplating a job change due to some new personal insights, or are faced with the challenge of graduating from school and looking for your first job, the road may not be easy. Often, it takes a lot of time, hard work, self-confidence, and resistance to disappointment. To be successful, you need to be prepared for some rejections and you need to have some clear direction as to how you can get started on the right road.

Talk to any two people working in the private sector and they will probably give you different opinions on the best way to go about finding a job in the corporate world. But they both probably will give you some good, sound advice, and that, coupled with a little luck, could get you the ideal job you are looking for. The point is that there is no single way to search effectively for a good corporate job. The only thing that really matters is, did your efforts pay off, did you get what you were looking for?

In fact, there must be at least a half dozen or more effective ways to search for a corporate job. This chapter describes one approach that can be used as a basic foundation in the art of job hunting. But remember, the ideas, suggestions, and exercises are only intended to help you develop your own approach to the often difficult challenge of finding the right job.

You must begin your job-search activities with a well-planned strategy. The last thing that you want to do is to react to a lot of stimuli without a clear sense of direction, effort, follow-through, and follow-up.

Building Self-confidence

Any plan of action worth its salt should allow for time to build self-confidence. Self-confidence is one of the main ingredients in a successful job search. In fact, there is really no way to get around the need to believe in yourself. Without this all-important asset, finding a job in today's market could be a devastating experience.

The question of how to build self-confidence is not a difficult one to answer. Building self-confidence starts with your desire to do just that. You really have to want to do it in order to be successful at it. No one can give you the desire that can only come from you.

Once you establish the commitment that comes from real desire, the next thing you have to do is have a good long talk with yourself. *Tell yourself that you know that there is a job out there somewhere, just waiting for you—all you have to do is find it. Also tell yourself that no matter how long it takes to find that job, you are not going to give up or give in.* You must tell yourself, and believe, that rejection is of no concern to you and that no matter how long and how many times you experience job rejection, it will have absolutely no negative impact on your spirit, self-confidence, and determination. You must say that you will not be "turned around" no matter what happens!

The next step is to go out and find someone who is successful in his or her field of endeavor, any field of endeavor—some friendly person you respect who, in your opinion, demonstrates self-confidence—and ask that person's help and guidance. Tell that person, in a way that is comfortable for you, that you are new in the art of building and maintaining confidence and that you may need to call on him or her for moral support from time to time; that you are going out to find a good corporate job and that you are just preparing yourself for any possible negative experience that may set you back.

Believe me, once you explain yourself, the person will certainly understand what you are talking about.

Okay, now you are on your way. The next thing you are going to have to do is create a daily exercise regimen, if you will, that enables you to look in a mirror and say to yourself, in effect and several times with conviction, "I am good, I have something to offer my employer, I know there is a corporate job out there waiting for me and all I have to do is find it—no matter how much time it takes!" You must do this every day and really believe it, or your confidence will not be able to sustain itself. At best, it will rise and fall with the results of each job interview, and that is not demonstrating confidence and building belief in yourself.

Your opportunity to measure your confidence level and your belief in yourself will come after each interview. The true test is how you feel about yourself after you review your experience: Was it positive, did you handle the interview well, did you learn something from it that can help you, or was it a bad experience and do you now dislike yourself for not handling the experience better?

Having the internal strength to persevere and improve with each job interview is a major step forward in the art of job hunting.

Understanding Job Interview Rejection

Job hunting is such an important personal experience because it deals with *rejection!* Any kind of personal rejection tends to get our psychological stability off center. Many people have a particularly hard time handling job interview rejections because our society seems to say that your value as a human being is measured, by and large, by the type of work you do.

For example, if you hold an important job, you are presumed to be an important person. The bigger the job, the bigger the person. Lose that job, and you are no longer an important person. Very interesting concept, isn't it? Now, tell me, is the person really important, or is it the job that is really important? No matter who holds the job, that person would be deemed important even if he were a perfect idiot with no redeeming qualities. Let any person holding some important job in our society die, and see how quickly that person is forgotten. However, the job does not die; someone else takes it over and then he or she becomes "important."

What are we saying here? We are saying that none of this is really *personal,* and, therefore, rejection should not affect us, because we know we are not our jobs. In fact, we are more than our jobs, much more than most of us can imagine.

Let's look at it another way. When you go to a cocktail party and meet someone, you are almost invariably introduced by your name and then your occupation ("This is Ms. Jane Doe; she is a doctor"), even though traditional etiquette says that this is not a polite way of introducing someone, unless there is a special reason for mentioning the person's occupation. A job title may tell you something about a person's status or income, but nothing about the person's character or how well she does her job.

What does the emphasis on occupational status do for the unemployed person who is having great difficulty in finding a suitable job? Unfortunately, over a period of time, it tends to erode that person's confidence. When you are unemployed, it is hard to believe you are a valuable member of society.

This is true for just about anyone. Think about a former President of the United States who is still young enough to hold a job. How does he handle the "out-of-work syndrome"? What kind of work would he look for after the presidency? How much money would he ask for? How well would he handle the classical interview process and how would he handle job rejection?

The rejection aspect of job hunting says nothing about the financial pressure that is created by being out of work. This is another dimension of the problem that can easily undermine confidence, if you are not careful. Over a period of time of being out of work, some people become desperate, and this desperation shows up in a negative way in the interview and negotiation process. That is why it is better to look for a job when you *have* a job, if you possibly can. You never appear to be hungry or desperate, because you can still eat and pay the rent.

Corporate interviewers do not consider overaggressive people or desperate people good candidates for employment. Oh, yes, it is true, they do want you to show interest, but showing too much interest puts you in a vulnerable position. The idea that you want a job so badly that you will do anything to get it puts prospective employers in a position to take advantage of you in the level of job they offer you or the starting salary. And, again, if you appear to be desperate for work, they more than likely will not hire you at all.

Therefore, be prepared to try to maintain that delicate balance of showing interest in the job, but not desperation; enthusiasm for the job, but not hunger for it. Corporate interviewers generally look for a pleasant disposition, supported by lots of professionalism. Try to remember that no matter how much actual job experience you have, you can be an experienced person, but if you don't have the proper disposition, you are out!

The Self-critique Process

To get the most out of your interviewing experiences, and improve on your interviewing technique, you will need to review your own performance by conducting a self-critique after each interview. By using the following exercise, you can refine many of your interviewing skills without the need to consult an employment interviewing specialist:

	Just Right	Improving	Can Do Better
Being on time for interview	————	————	————
Personal appearance	————	————	————
Friendliness	————	————	————
Knowledge about company you are applying to	————	————	————
Quality of questions you asked the interviewer	————	————	————
Frequency of eye contact	————	————	————
Relaxed appearance, level of confidence shown	————	————	————
Level of vocabulary	————	————	————
Quality of presentation of yourself (who you are, what you can do, why the prospective employer should hire you)	————	————	————
Quality of salary phase of the interview	————	————	————

Then add a brief summary of how you feel about yourself and what you can do to improve on the next interview.

Now, if you do this exercise and you find that things are not going well for you, sit down and review this report card, point by point, with your friendly advisor. Together, you should be able to devise strategies to help you avoid future mistakes. With your spirits lifted, you'll be ready to move on to the next challenge.

On the other hand, should your advisor be unable to help you get through the crisis periods, you can simply try to find someone else who can play this role for you. In any case, you are going to need ongoing positive feedback and positive reinforcement to help you sustain your level of confidence, until you establish a genuine belief in yourself and what you can accomplish.

The Interview Process

People with good job-interviewing skills are not born with them; they developed them through training, practice, and trial and error. If you find that you are lacking in this important skill, you owe it to yourself to take the time to research the subject. The time and effort you invest in improving your understanding of the interview process will unquestionably pay off for you in large dividends.

Dressing for an Interview

There are many important personnel tips and techniques that you should be aware of in this regard, so many that we could not possibly cover them all in this book. However, a few of the more significant tips come to mind at this point and they are presented for your enlightenment:

How does the candidate's personal appearance come across? Was he or she sensitive to business standards or ignorant relative to corporate codes of dress? It may be true that we should never judge a book by its cover, but when it comes to your success in a particular corporation, the way you dress on the job is very important to your employer. It tends to suggest how you feel about yourself (your self-esteem) and how you approach your work (how well organized you are, and so on). So why not invest a little money in good standard corporate interviewing attire, and make a good first impression on your prospective employer?

A good basic outfit for men is the classic dark suit, a white or blue shirt, a conservative tie, dark socks, and plain shined shoes. For women, the standard outfit is a business suit and a complementary blouse, natural daytime makeup, and well-groomed hair that is not distractingly styled. Plain, skin-toned stockings and plain, medium high heels complete the expected picture.

While running the risk of redundancy, the importance of looking the part must be stressed. Corporate dress codes are quite inflexible and they must be observed if you want to get on first base. Someone who walks into a corporate interview for a management-level job wearing a garment that makes a strong sexual statement or a flamboyantly styled suit is out of the running before getting started.

The unavoidable fact is that a person's appearance communicates a strong message in a typical interview. Therefore, why make the corporate dress code an issue? If you are uncertain about the dress code of an organization, go and visit the company before you have your interview; without making direct contact with the employees, observe the executives as they arrive in the morning or go out to lunch. In many cases you can observe a great deal about the male and female dress codes even from outside of the building.

Being on Time for the Interview

For the most part, business and industry equate time with money. So candidates who are late for an interview can expect this error to be held against them in the overall competitive scoring process. The assumption is that if a prospect is late for the interview, chances are that he or she will be a tardy employee and the company will lose money.

Companies want a full day's work for a full day's pay during the regular scheduled work hours. In a competitive race for a good job, why keep the interviewer waiting? The race between you and your competition could be very close, and a single point in the interviewer's judgment, one way or the other, could make the difference between success and failure.

Speaking Successfully

When you are a job candidate, what comes out of your mouth during an interview is just as important as your physical appearance. It can enhance a good impression or cause you to lose out altogether.

After the interview, the interviewer will consider a number of questions about you: Did you express yourself well? Are your thoughts well organized? Do you have good voice projection and frequency of eye contact? Are you knowledgeable about the job and the company? How many good questions did you ask about the job and the company during the course of the interview? And, finally, how did you handle yourself on the questions of salary and benefits?

Remember, candidates who take the time to conduct advance research on the company they are going to interview with generally ask good questions and otherwise present themselves as being interested, informed, and self-confident.

A Screening Process

In reality, the interview process is something like an obstacle course, in which the interviewer has the opportunity to make the course difficult or easy for the interviewee in whatever way happens to suit the temperament and objectives of the interviewer. In some cases, minority and female candidates go through a *screening-out* process instead of a *screening-in* process.

This simply means that if an employer does intend to hire a minority or female candidate, chances are that far more prospects will go through the process before someone is hired than would be the case if they were all white males. It also means that in many cases the minority male or female candidate must have superior credentials for the job in order to be seriously considered.

Therefore, it often occurs that the minority or female person hired for middle-management jobs is, in fact, overqualified from the very start, and among the lowest paid persons performing the same job in the department.

Injustice in corporate pay scales for minorities and females is more widespread than you might imagine. The problem is that it varies from industry to industry and company to company. In addition, it is also extremely difficult to prevent this kind of injustice, or even to redress it after the fact. Certainly no corporation is going to invite you in to examine their books, and it is not in the best interest of the corporation to make public statements about executives in the business who make a personal practice of this. Often, when salary injustices are committed, senior management is not even aware of it. Generally, a company would have to audit its payroll to get trends, patterns, and historical data before it is clear what some of its management people are doing to minorities and females.

The only meaningful protection you have is to be aware of the salary range for your field in general and, if possible, for the specific job you are seeking.

Salary and Benefits Negotiations

Salary and benefits negotiations for management-level positions in the corporate world present an excellent opportunity for the candidate and the potential employer to determine just how much interest the parties really have in each other. After the initial interviewing phase has been covered, what generally remains to be agreed upon is the total dollar amount of compensation for the candidate, which should include salary and benefits.

To better understand how one can improve his/her approach to negotiating a compensation package, take a close look at the process itself and see if there are some basic concepts to be identified that will help strengthen your position. By understanding certain basic ideas, the candidate will stand a much better chance of knowing when to be aggressive, when to stand hard and fast on the asking price, and when to retreat to a lesser figure with a more flexible posture. In any event, here are four basic issues that the candidate should be at least familiar with because they are important concepts in the normal negotiation experience:

1. The sum of money and benefits the candidate would ideally like to receive
2. The sum of money and benefits the potential employer is prepared to pay the candidate based on the company's salary guidelines
3. The sum of money and benefits the candidate will actually settle for
4. The sum of money and benefits the employer is prepared to pay the candidate over and above the company's salary guidelines to make sure that the desired candidate accepts the job

Corporate job-seeking candidates who are about to enter into salary negotiations should always remember that the experience offers an opportunity for some creative thinking if the bargaining parties are willing to be imaginative. The only things that are required are desire and flexibility in the many combinations of cash and benefits a company can put together as a total package. However, because neither the candidate nor the potential employer knows exactly what the other is prepared to accept, they both make it necessary to test each other's thinking.

This test should not be viewed as a negative move, but rather a necessary part of any serious negotiation. Remember, every employer has a right to try to stay within his salary guidelines to protect profits. Exceeding salary guidelines on a continuous basis can have a negative impact on profit margins. At the same time, however, the employer does want to recognize the prospective employee's potential value to his organization. This attitude will generally make the employer want to be fair but not overly generous, at least not until the candidate for employment has had the opportunity to prove himself on the job. That is why the use of benefits to supplement the compensation package can work for both the candidate and the employer if they are willing to think creatively. On the other hand, if the two negotiating parties are not sincere and not thinking creatively, the whole experience will be a mere exercise in futility. All of this, however, will reveal itself once the negotiations begin.

The important point for the job applicant to remember is that he or she must attempt to use whatever leverage he/she has during this process. This includes the candidate's formal education, expertise or skills level, job-related experience, specialized training, successful competitive work experience, and past business-related success stories. The best leverage, however, for most job applicants is the extent to which the employer is pursuing the candidate. If the employer is actively pursuing the candidate, then it is up to the employer to try to persuade the candidate to accept the job by making a good offer. This situation gives the candidate a definite advantage, because at some point the employer will have to demonstrate just how much he wants the candidate by making his best possible offer.

Guidelines to Remember

• It pays to negotiate from strength. Therefore, it is better to have a job or some other means of income so that you do not appear anxious during the discussion of money. Signs of high anxiety during the salary negotiation phase tend to put the candidate at a disadvantage. However, if you do find yourself unemployed at the bargaining table, you should have determined prior to the meeting the minimum salary and benefits for which you are willing to work. Always remain calm and under control of your emotions. Speak with confidence in your voice and make eye contact. Your display of confidence will show to your prospective employer that you are sure about your worth.

• Make sure that you have researched your asking price so that it is a realistic salary package. A totally unrealistic salary request could mean a lost opportunity. Therefore, the two key questions you want to research in preparation for salary negotiations are: What is the salary range within the industry for the particular job you are seeking? And where does the company rank within the industry for salaries? The answer to the first question along with your own perceptions as to how much the company wants you will help you come to a realistic asking price.

• Consider your total life-style and decide if it is better to cover it in cash or cash and benefits. Your needs assessment should be tied to the life-style you want to live and may include such benefits as travel, expense accounts, flexible working hours, use of a company car, company charge cards, allowance for membership dues in professional groups, tuition reimbursement, and so on.

• Candidates for new job opportunities should also keep in mind that the career potential of a management-level person is a very important asset to a company's future growth. If the company is to survive and thrive, it will need people who can manage the business well. Therefore, if you have demonstrated ability in running a business or key profit-center departments within a business successfully, you can factor this skill into your salary negotiations with prospective employers.

• Suggested resources to keep current on salary and benefit information are:

Industry trade groups
Industry trade magazines
Search firms and employment agencies
Human resource specialists
American Management Association

National Conference Board
National Association of Marketing Developers
U.S. Department of Labor
U.S. Chamber of Commerce
College placement offices
Black MBA Association
Association of MBA Executives of New York

Again, your protection in salary negotiations is to be aware of the salary range for your field and your specific job. Methods of salary negotiation and compensation change according to occupational specialty, industry, company, and economic conditions for the country.

• The following are some corporate "perks" you may want to consider when negotiating with a prospective employer:

Bonus plan
Stock option plan
Matching investment program
Profit-sharing plan
Life insurance
Disability insurance
Medical insurance
Annual health examination
Pension plan
Expense account
Financial planning assistance
Tuition reimbursement
Annual seminar training and development
Severance pay and outplacement service if terminated

Checklist for the Job-Research Process

Looking for work can be a traumatic experience, but it need not be a devastating one, if you plan effectively. All too often, people who are faced with the challenge of looking for a job find themselves reacting *to* their circumstances instead of acting *on* their circumstances. Reacting *to* circumstances suggests that you are disorganized and lack the necessary preparation time. Acting on your circumstances, on the other hand, suggests a more orderly, efficient, and realistic approach to the job search.

To help you get started in the right direction as quickly and as painlessly as possible, here is a checklist of things you will need to consider to be successful.

Step I: Preparation Time

- Establish self-confidence
- Reassess career goals and objectives
- Define career goals and objectives
- Critique career goals and objectives (professional opinion)
- Redefine and finalize career goals and objectives
- Investigate career-path options
- Select multi-career-path strategy (professional opinion)
- Confirm career-path strategy (professional opinion)
- Assess and define job skills
- Overlay job skills on career-path options by industry and by job classification
- Relate job skills to strategy and produce a set of options (one and two)
- Research résumé writing (professional opinion)
- Develop résumé incorporating options (one and two)

Step II. Target Market Research

- Domestic approach: Research available job markets.
  1. Private sector (profit)
     a. By industry
     b. By company
  2. Public sector
     a. Federal
     b. State
     c. Local
  3. Nonprofit sector
     a. Agencies
     b. Trade groups and associations

- International approach: Research available job markets.
  1. English-speaking country
     a. By industry
     b. By company
  2. Multilanguage countries (English plus others)
     a. By industry
     b. By company
  3. Overseas companies doing business in the United States
     a. By industry
     b. By company

Step III: Action Plan

- Develop direct corporate approach.
  1. Résumé and cover letter
  2. Referral via networking
  3. Cold calls from ads
- Research and select good search firm via:
  1. Newspaper ads
  2. Networking
  3. College or university placement office
- Refine interview skills and techniques.
  1. Background data on target audience
  2. Your projection quality—i.e., style
  3. Your knowledge base—i.e., profession
  4. Your personal appearance
  5. Friendliness
  6. Articulation quality—i.e., Q & A's
  7. Salary and benefits negotiation strategy

Step IV: Evaluation Process

- Establish feedback process and time.
  1. Checklist (self-critique)
  2. Networking (professional contacts)
  3. Family/friends support

- Begin search for employment.
  1. Work from established game plan.
  2. Develop contingency plan if necessary.
  3. Reaffirm self-confidence at every opportunity.

V

Managing Your Personal Life

WHY DRINKING CAN HURT YOUR CAREER

Drinking intoxicating beverages in a social setting in the corporate world is certainly nothing new; in fact, so many business people indulge in the practice of drinking socially at lunch and after work that the restaurant business in many cities around the country probably could not exist without these daily loyal patrons.

Despite the rather high incidence of drinking problems among middle and upper management in a number of corporations, social drinking in corporate America is still a very popular and accepted practice. This social phenomenon, however, despite its popularity, does create a great deal of conflict among top executives in corporations today, because excessive drinking is counterproductive.

For example, on the one hand, top management knows that many productive business hours are being lost to the company because some of its key people drink too much. On the other hand, these same executives also know that the social drinking is such an accepted practice that they dare not attempt to stop or curtail it. This does not mean that they are unaware of potential drinking problems among younger executives.

If you are an aspiring younger member of management, you must constantly practice self-control during the frequent social drinking opportunities. You must always ask yourself, at the business luncheons and other company-sponsored events, how much is too much. Because too much is dangerous for your career, the bottom line is that you must never let your drinking get out of hand. Most people who have had too much to drink do and say things that they would never do or say if they were not under the influence of alcohol. Good judgment is an important management characteristic, so why let a few extra drinks change your image within the company?

People who drink excessively have a tendency to send out confusing and conflicting messages to their associates all the time. They end up saying the wrong things to the wrong people at the wrong time. Don't be misled by what other people do in your department; your career path is separate and apart from any other persons. One effective way to deal with this issue is simply to make it your own policy not to drink during business hours.

There is no crime in drinking soft drinks or other nonalcoholic beverages when others order alcoholic drinks. Making sure that you remain alert during the workday is a sensible practice, particularly if your boss has a habit of getting his focus blurred at lunch.

Never be deluded into thinking that excessive drinking is an admirable quality, just because a number of corporate people are heavy drinkers. It is certainly not a quality for you to emulate at any time in your career. Don't be fooled by the amount of drinking or the availability of alcohol that is present at company-sponsored events.

While more-established business associates may in fact drink quite frequently during business hours, that is still no signal for you to follow their lead. You never really know just how top management feels about the drinking habits of your associates, and you don't want to develop the negative habits of people who may not be going anywhere in the company.

DATING ON THE JOB

If you are a single person, the subject of dating people who work in your department or in the company is perhaps one of the most sensitive areas of corporate life you need to look at.

While it is not really uncommon to see people dating people they meet at work and having no negative experience, my years of observation tell me that the possibility of a bad experience from dating in the workplace is real. Nevertheless, the bad experiences can be avoided if a couple are serious about their careers and willing to talk about the issue in the context of corporate survival—that is, how best to protect the image of one another at work.

Let me emphasize that dating people on the job can be a perfectly good approach to a healthy social life, ·if handled with sensitivity. Just think about it for a moment: The American corporate environment really presents an excellent opportunity for mature young men and women to meet each other, and, subsequently, to socialize off the job and otherwise have a most enjoyable time together. Where else could you find so many bright young people who are career-minded?

These young people, for the most part, have many things in common, socially, educationally, intellectually, and culturally. And, in addition, perhaps the one thing that they can really share with one another, and that will be a great source of help as they grow managerially, is their career challenges and aspirations. This process of sharing almost always develops into a valuable networking relationship, if they are sincere people and willing to help each other, even though they may no longer see each other socially.

On the other hand, some people have been forced to leave their jobs because of their lack of discretion and their insensitivity to the fact that their social life (love life, in particular) should not interfere with their performance on the job. It should also not be a source of entertainment for co-workers in and around the office or the surrounding community.

Finally, here are some practical points to help you avoid what might otherwise be a painful and costly experience in the maze of corporate stumbling blocks.

Things to Consider When Dating on the Job

• Be selective in your choice of dating companions. Some associates have a poor reputation because of drug use or sexual promiscuity, or a "poor" attitude, or simply for incompetence or stupidity. This type of association will damage your image in a traditional corporate environment if you are a serious career person. Some people may question your judgment ability and use your social life as a valid confirmation of their doubts about you.

• Always be extremely discreet in your relationships with an associate on the job, and never display anything but professionalism while you are both on company time.

• Never assume that a company-sponsored function is an opportunity to display your affection for anyone, least of all a fellow employee. Displaying affection at a company function could spell disaster for your image at the company.

• Always be on guard for people who want to get "into your business." Chances are that they are primarily interested in getting information about you and your associate that they can use on the gossip exchange. Remember that any story, even one not originally intended to injure you, can damage your reputation.

• If you confide in someone in the company about a relationship that you have with an associate, you must assume that you will hear the story again from someone else in the company, someone you did not tell the story to. The moral of this is *don't tell anyone anything that you or your associate would not like to hear again someday*, and perhaps from someone you don't happen to want to have known your business.

• Try to frequent places with your date that are not "company hangouts." Not that you should try to hide, but being seen a lot in restaurants and bars that are frequented by company people only increases the opportunity for some people to make negative remarks, which are usually directed toward the female employee, as opposed to the male employee. (This is because of the double standard that exists for male and female behavior. For example, if a man is seen dating several women from the company, he may be viewed as a smooth, charming, attractive person. However, if a woman is seen dating more than one man from the company, she may be viewed as being sexually promiscuous.)

USING SEX TO GET A PROMOTION

People who use their bodies in the corporate world for the express purpose of getting promoted or gaining other personal benefits really do a great disservice to themselves. What they end up doing, eventually, is creating some personal psychological problems that will surface later on in their career and cause them to fail. They know that they have, in effect, sold their bodies in order to get ahead. This type of self-defeating experience results in low self-esteem and is likely to come back to haunt them when they least expect it.

No one can deny that sexual favors are sometimes used in the corporate world in exchange for personal gain, but it is an exception rather than a rule. While some might argue, privately, that selling oneself is not so bad if the "price" is right, most people will agree that selling oneself is not a psychologically rewarding practice in the business world, or in most other professional fields of endeavor. You get used up fast! It is really too great a price to pay.

Training and education are readily available now that people can compete for jobs and opportunities without losing their self-respect. More important, there is really no substitute for earning promotions through hard work and fair and open competition. This is the most rewarding experience anyone can have in the corporate world.

People in the corporate world, today, do not have to use their bodies in order to get ahead in corporations, particularly when they know that profitability in business is derived from people who make intelligent contributions to the business, and not sexual contributions to the personal gratification of someone who is in a position to promote them. While it cannot be said that everyone who gets promoted earns that promotion based upon hard work, businesses could not function efficiently if sex were a requisite for advancement. Most of the people in a business must be qualified for their jobs, or the business will not be able to operate and make a profit.

As a manager, it is almost impossible to say that you have promoted a qualified candidate that is the best person for the job if you are having a love affair with the person, or have had sexual relations. Most people are generally not that objective in their relationships with other people. Chances are that some subjective thinking or sense of personal commitment will influence the manager's decision to promote the candidate for the job.

Also remember that people who work together in an office or plant environment eventually find out when a co-worker is engaged in some sexual activity in exchange for job benefits. Things like this are hard to hide from people who work closely with you. Then the rumors start to fly around the company and your reputation is put in serious question. Sexual activity in exchange for personal advancement creates all kinds of credibility problems for the person involved, and for obvious reasons, people on the job tend not to trust people who appear to be unprincipled in their business ethics.

Women, in particular, have to be aware of and very sensitive to this type of situation, because it is so easy for people on the job to say that a woman in competition did not really earn the promotion, but was promoted because of her intimacy with the boss.

Over a period of time, if you exchange sexual favors for personal gain in the corporate world, you will end up being disrespected by your co-workers. They will also resent you, and your leadership will always be in question. Try to supervise or manage people in a job situation where the employees have no respect for you, and see just how effective you can be! It is not an easy thing to endure and you end up with a no-win situation. In addition, should the management people in higher authority learn that your staff disrespects you and disregards your leadership, you can be sure that they will not allow you to remain in the job, because they cannot afford it. Business will suffer due to your inability to lead, and that is unacceptable.

So please take this important advice very seriously. Save yourself a lot of pain and personal problems, feelings of low self-esteem, and being disliked by your associates on the job. Don't even appear to engage in the game of sexual favors in exchange for personal gain.

MARRIED AND WORKING TOGETHER

Should a couple of *management-level* people who work for the same company decide to get married at some reasonable but not distant time, one of the two people would do well to consider leaving the organization for a career elsewhere.

Why? Well, the reason is this: My observations have shown me that where married couples work on a managerial level at the same company, there is an ongoing battle for the couple to establish and maintain separate identities on the job. This merging of individual identification can present sensitive issues for management, as well as for the employees involved.

For example, should one of the married partners suddenly fall into disfavor with management, it tends to reflect poorly on the other partner's career. In fact, one spouse is held indirectly responsible for the other spouse's performance on the job. Management also likes to feel that its decision to affect a manager's career will not have a negative impact on other managers in the company. Morale is very important, and it is hard to see your spouse treated one way while you are being treated another way.

In addition, if you happen to be working closely with your spouse, there are always questions about your judgment calls, objectivity, and influence. What about the whole male versus female parity issue relative to raises, bonuses, and other fringe benefits? After all, it is common knowledge that men have traditionally received higher levels of compensation than females performing comparable work.

Corporations also have a way of limiting the amount of influence any one person, aside from the CEO, can have in the company. Therefore, the chance that both spouses might hold senior management jobs of significant power and influence, at the same publicly held company, is highly unlikely. (Family-owned and -operated companies are another matter altogether. In such companies, the more power kept within the family structure, the easier it is to control the company.)

Mind you, no one is suggesting that a married couple *cannot* make it to the top at a Fortune 500 company, or even a Fortune 1000 company, but the fact of the matter is that the chances are really not that great. Do you remember the now famous couple of William Agee and Mary Cunningham? They met on a professional basis, but subsequently became involved on a close personal basis after Mary Cunningham joined Bendix Corporation. William Agee happened to be the chief executive officer of Bendix at the time, and attempted to promote Mary Cunningham up the corporate ladder at an incredible rate, passing over many long-established executives in powerful positions. This, of course, set off a negative management reaction and a general outcry among Bendix employees. It also drew national media attention to the company on an issue that had little to do with improving the company's bottom line. The rest of the story is all history now and one that Bendix, its shareholders, and customers would rather forget about.

Looking at this issue more objectively, there are obviously a number of young married people working in the same company today. As long as we are talking about low-level jobs, there is not much to be concerned about. However, once the couple attempts to move up into more senior management jobs, look out! Things can get difficult. For example, what does the young couple do when the company decides that it wants to assign one of the two people overseas? Should the spouse ask the husband or wife to give up his or her job and come along? What about the company? Is it a smart thing to ask management to move your spouse every time they want to relocate you? I wonder!

ON "DOING DRUGS"

A young professional football player, who had recently been suspended from playing professional football for using drugs, confessed on a well-known national television talk show that his chief motivation for using drugs came from his desire to be more attractive to young women at various parties and social events.

He explained that cocaine is so popular and so desirable among some young people that women would welcome his company whenever they found out that he could "turn them on to some free coke." He went on to say that the use of cocaine as a recreational support system became so important to his social life that he always carried some cocaine with him on social occasions. Despite the fact that he was spending thousands of dollars to maintain this practice, his use of drugs as a means of attracting female companionship proved to be "highly successful."

Eventually, the young man admitted that over a period of time, his fascination with and dependency on cocaine actually extended far beyond the social events and female companionship. He began using the drug during working hours. According to this professional athlete, he went from taking cocaine during weekend house parties to taking it in the locker room before practice, and before each and every football game, without the slightest hesitation.

If this story sounds familiar to you, it is probably because you have either read about a similar case or actually know of some young person who is caught up in "doing drugs."

Whatever the case may be, most mature people who are serious about their health and their career will agree that drugs and good health, and drugs and the world of work, simply do not mix well at all. While it is true that the use of drugs in the United States has reached epidemic proportions, drugs and the world of work really do not complement each other.

Doing drugs on the job is a social phenomenon that has taken hold of many young people today. Some young people seem to think that it is fashionable to go to work and "get high." For very obvious reasons, drug users and pushers alike are trying to make a legitimate case for doing drugs in the workplace. Some young workers even say that they function better when they are under the influence of drugs. They also say things like, "Drugs are good for relieving stress on the job" and "Drugs give you greater creative insight" and "Drugs make you feel more sociable."

But who are we really trying to fool when we boastfully use this type of rationalization to justify an act? Drugs may in fact be a social phenomenon in this country and drugs may even momentarily relieve someone's stressful feelings on a job, but drugs certainly have no legitimate place in our work environment, or in our social environment, for that matter. What we are really talking about is a multibillion-dollar parasitical industry that has the potential to destroy an entire society if we let it.

Life, itself, is the only narcotic that man needs, and it affords the greatest "high" that man can ever imagine. So if he must get high, let him get high off living. Life is on the side of health, life gives forth and sustains so that we can thrive and be productive. What more could we possibly need or even want?

There is not one single piece of evidence to prove that any society in the history of man on earth has ever been healthy, efficient, and productive under a drug culture.

The promotion and rapidly spreading use of cocaine and other narcotics among minority young people is equivalent to genocide.

Think what life will be like if and when drugs are widely used among surgeons, airline pilots, flight controllers, scientists and technicians of all kinds, not to mention military personnel who control the computers that operate the atomic missile defense systems. Think of these people using cocaine on their jobs because it makes them feel better or more creative and insightful.

Yes, it is true that these people all have very important jobs that the rest of us are depending upon for our survival. But are they not entitled to sedate themselves on the job, just as thousands of office workers, secretaries, and managers now do?

I will wager that not one legitimate company in this country today would knowingly hire a person who subscribed to getting high on the job. Yet, when you see the increasing number of office and plant workers rush to the rest rooms, parks, and playgrounds at lunchtime to get high, you really have to wonder how effectively and how efficiently our businesses are being run right now, and where all of this is going to lead us.

If you have not been told, let me be the first to tell you that no young aspiring person can afford to be sedated in the corporate world. And if that person happens to be a member of a minority group, his or her chances of surviving in the business world while constantly under the influence of drugs are nil!

Moreover, should the word get out to management that you are a drug user, you can forget about any opportunities for advancement in the company. What you may find, however, is that the company security department has suddenly taken an interest in you. Once the rumors start to get around the company, it is the security department's job to try to document the rumors so that the company can get rid of you fast.

Drug testing

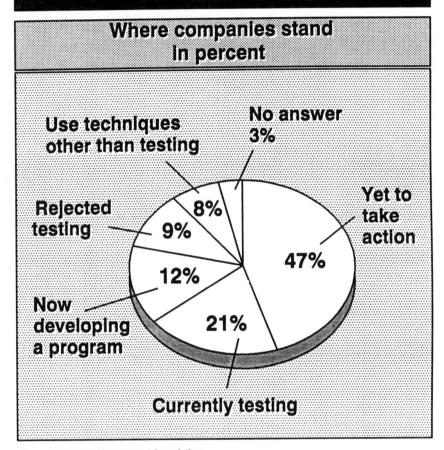

Where companies stand
In percent

Use techniques other than testing

No answer 3%

Rejected testing

Yet to take action

8%

9%

47%

12%

Now developing a program

21%

Currently testing

Source: American Management Association
Chicago Tribune Graphic

Norman Siegel, executive director of the New York chapter
of the American Civil Liberties Union, said there is a
"drug-testing craze" in the country and that it is a "very
alarming trend... it makes *1984* seem wimpy." Siegel said
the "impetus" to drug-test employees began in March 1986
when it was recommended by the President's Commission
on Organized Crime.

THE WEEKLY PAYCHECK SYNDROME

Let no one tell you that you cannot achieve financial independence, because you can achieve it if you want to. Let me repeat that. *You can be financially independent if you want to be.* The only important questions that you need to deal with are, do you really want that independence, and what are you prepared to do to see that it happens?

It is for certain that you already have the God-given power to determine your own economic destiny, living in this land of relative prosperity. Your success may not happen according to your present timetable, but it can and will happen if you want it badly enough.

For example, if your plans do not materialize through your efforts and hard work at one company, or in one line of business, then try another, and another, if need be. With each new venture, learn and refine your skills, ideas, and plans, and most important, rededicate your will to win. No matter how much inner strength it takes to make positive things happen for you, don't be afraid to go deep within yourself and bring forward whatever strength you need to accomplish the task. You will find that all of the inner resources that you need are inside of you, waiting to be used, when you need them.

There are literally thousands of different jobs, industries, businesses, and ideas that you can take advantage of to protect your psychological and financial independence. Admittedly, you may have to make some great personal sacrifices to achieve your objectives, but no one ever said that success comes easy.

Remember, you make the difference between success and failure and you, not your immediate supervisor or your present employer, determine if you are going to eat and generally live well. You may elect to live relatively well, or you may choose to starve to death; the decision, my friend, is yours. This is a land of abundance—let no one tell you differently—and it will yield to your wishes if you are aggressive and unyielding in your efforts and desires.

Oh, yes, it is quite possible for you to experience temporary setbacks during your sojourn; most people do. But the setbacks are, after all, only temporary! Again, this is a land of "economic opportunity" and "free enterprise." The only challenge to you is that the land and the system may not be aware that you have come to claim your share of it. Therefore, the extent of your determination will have a direct correlation with the degree of your success. Chances are that no one will readily give you a break in your pursuit; you may have to create your own ideas and opportunities, despite all odds.

However, the chance for success is in your favor, because the free enterprise system requires that a certain number of people succeed in this country, or the system itself will fail. It's all about competition, and the system thrives on competition—all kinds of competition. Therefore, in order to have "healthy competition," the system must have people who are willing to play the game, and that can mean you, if you want to be a player. Now, we know the system is not perfect, and it tends to have certain built-in biases toward some more-privileged groups of people, but that in no way should prevent you from getting into the game.

So if for some reason you encounter a serious obstacle to succeeding at one job, or in one line of business, rethink your approach. Perhaps you need to take a new direction, or a new approach in the same direction.

All too often, people make the mistake of conditioning themselves to believe that life can only be lived one way. That in order to live, for example, one must be tied to a weekly paycheck from a particular employer that happens not to be meeting your needs. And nothing could be further from the truth! There is life beyond your present employer; he or she is not the only game in town. If your present employer does not appreciate your efforts, and makes no attempt to see that you have at least a reasonable chance to meet your financial needs and career aspirations, change your job. Who knows, you may be able to just walk across the street and find work at your employer's competition, some organization that will appreciate your efforts and talent and therefore appropriately reward you for them.

Remember, our system is based on a free enterprise concept that entitles you to be as free and as enterprising as you care to be. In fact, if you happen not to like the weekly paycheck syndrome, you can become an employer yourself and make weekly paychecks to someone else. There is no secret in knowing how to set up your own business in this country, and as a point of consideration, your government at the federal, state, and local levels, in many areas, can actually help you start one of your own. Again, it may not be easy, but it can be done. People are doing it every day, somewhere in these United States.

Also remember that there are even some banks, corporations, private money-lending institutions, and individual people who will help you set up a business if your ideas are good. Perhaps not a lot of banks and people are available for lending opportunities, but you don't need a lot, you only need one! Private investors who are willing to make a loan or invest in a good business opportunity are all over the place. These people generally make lots of money in their primary business interest and they have to find creative and imaginative ways to invest their profits so that they can grow financially. These investors also look for good tax shelters, so why not invest in you?

In any event, having a full-time job is no justifiable excuse for not going into your own business. Many people in this country have more than one source of income; why not you? There is always your own personal time to run a separate business, if time seems to be an issue. And, as long as you are not in competition with your employer, or endangering his business, why should it matter? You, of course, will always give your employer an honest day's work, as a matter of professional commitment, but the remaining time is yours to be free and enterprising. You are, in reality, free—just see it that way and it will be a fact. The enterprise is up to you.

Coincidentally, you will in many cases find that your supervisor, and his boss, and the owner of the entire company, all have other (outside) business interests, separate and apart from the company... that is, if they are really smart business people. Few smart business people today put all of their eggs in one basket. Interesting concept, isn't it? This is the way the free enterprise system really works, so wake up—get on board the "gravy train." If you don't, you may find you are sitting on the tracks and that train will either run around or over you.

Having to depend *totally* on your weekly paycheck to make ends meet is not a nice way to live. However, this syndrome of dependency is as much a psychological predisposition as it is anything. Therefore, you can break that cycle of fear, custom, inaction, by doing something about it. If, unfortunately, your parents or relatives had to live that way, so be it, but you don't, and you are dealing with yourself, not your parents or other relatives or anyone else.

Now, here is an exercise you may want to try, to get yourself started in making the personal commitment to dedicate your energies to a concept called "pay yourself first." This means that each and every time your employer pays you, pay yourself. In fact, you pay yourself before you pay your creditors. Maybe, at first, it is just a small amount taken out of your regular paycheck each and every week, and put away in a separate account earmarked "my financial-independence account." Perhaps the first year the amount is, say, $20 per week. Twenty dollars per week times 52 weeks gives you $1,040 at the end of the year, plus interest. Take that money and continue to build on it during the second year, using the same system, only the second year you are going to raise your paycheck to, say, $40. In fact, as your employer raises your pay, you increase your saving.

Think how this independence account will start to grow and grow. Repeat the exercise year in and year out and you will have a nice fat nest egg. When your resources become significant, you will find that the psychological tie to your regular paycheck changes. Because your attitude about financial lack will change, the cycle of fear will be broken. While you may continue to look to your regular paychecks for some support to run your affairs, they will not be your sole source of survival.

In addition, should you need to look for a new job, you know you will not starve to death in the interim period. You will be free to get the best possible job for the best possible salary, or even start your own business.

Now you will have some time off from immediate financial dependency. Make the commitment if you dare! Don't be afraid to start small; just make sure that you get started and stick with it.

Financial lack and the appearance of lack are two different things altogether. While you may not have any money in your possession at the moment, that does not mean that you cannot reverse the situation. What you will need to do is first confirm that the condition does exist and that it is temporary. Then, believing that you have the necessary spiritual power and creative energy and presence of mind, move quickly to change your temporary condition. Remember, poverty of the pocket is a temporary situation, but poverty of the spirit can be a lifelong experience if you allow it to persist.

UNDERSTANDING AND COPING WITH CORPORATE STRESS

Few corporate people today can expect to go through their corporate career free from the experience of stress. Depending on the type of job you have and your level of responsibility, you can expect some degree of stress on an ongoing basis. The important matters to consider, however, are just how much stress you have to be exposed to on the job, how long those stress periods last, and what you personally can do to avoid unnecessary stress or effectively manage unavoidable stress.

On top of all of this, many black executives will find that they will encounter a special kind of stress that comes from the fact that they represent a minority group in a largely white-majority group environment. Moreover, their efforts to protect their existing jobs in a corporate setting and move up the corporate ladder of success present another real source of constant tension and stress. Few black executives can expect to make it to top jobs in the corporate world without paying some heavy stress-related dues.

The point that we want to drive home here is that while the struggle for upward mobility is by far not the only thing that can and will create stress for black corporate people, few will be able to avoid continual exposure to stress and stressful situations if they are aspiring corporate types.

Authorities such as Dr. E. M. Gherman define stress as "the nonspecific response of the body to any demand placed upon it." Others, such as Dr. J. P. Spradley and R. L. Venings, have said that stress is "anything that places an extra demand upon you." All of the authorities seem to agree that workers in people-oriented jobs are constantly under stress, which can be both short-lived or continuing.

Everyone is subject to some form of stress. Some individuals are more sensitive to stress than others, and some are better able to deal with it than others. People who are most subject to stress are classified as Type A personalities, according to Dr. Gherman. Characteristics of Type A personalities include intense drive and ambition, aggressiveness, competitiveness, a need to get things done (meetings, deadlines), visible restlessness, and impatience. Type B personalities have an easygoing manner, are patient, able to take time to appreciate leisure and beauty, are not preoccupied with social achievement, do not feel driven by the clock, and are less competitive.

No matter what type of stress you are exposed to (short-lived or continuing), you can develop a regimen that will help you effectively manage your stress and stressful situations. Here are several helpful tips on ways to manage your stress:

1. Get regular physical checkups from your doctor. If you are forty years old or older, you should consult your doctor about the benefits of a cardiac stress evaluation. This is a procedure designed to evaluate the state of the cardiovascular system under stress, by subjecting an individual to a measured amount of physical exertion under carefully controlled conditions. Stress testing and other studies are combined with a careful interview and physical examination by the internist in order to provide the examinee:

• Specific evaluation of present cardiovascular fitness
• Predictive information as to future expectations of cardiac performance
• Specific advice on exercise and general life-style for maximum longevity and cardiovascular health

In addition, feel free to seek stress-relieving medical advice on a regular basis should you have the need.

2. Make sure that you eat a well-balanced diet daily to maintain high energy levels and avoid food that could cause stomach disorders during stressful periods.

3. Make sure that you get a full night of uninterrupted sleep every night.

4. Try to avoid people as much as possible who tend to irritate you during stressful periods. Do not permit friends or family to call you on the telephone and spend hours "dumping" their negative stress on you while you are under stress yourself.

5. If your boss or supervisor tends to irritate you during stressful work situations, try shorter periods of effective contact without noticeably avoiding her or him. For example, try to plan what you need to discuss with your boss, be pleasant but to the point, and make an exit. Make regular but shorter visits to his office, never letting him know how you really feel.

6. Develop a regular physical fitness regimen, one that helps you to relieve stress while building a sound body. When confronted with stressful situations on the job, don't be afraid to use your exercise regimen to counter the mental and emotional strain. Activities like running, swimming, walking, and tennis are all good stress-relieving measures. So develop the regimen that is best for you, while learning to manage challenging business situations.

7. Deep-breathing exercises are another method for relieving stress, particularly on the job. Breathing exercises are easy to do and quite effective for getting some immediate relief. If you don't know how to conduct the exercises properly, consult your doctor or a qualified physical fitness instructor.

8. One of the best on-the-job stress-relieving things that you can do is establish a friendly relationship of trust with a co-worker with whom you can share your frustrations.

9. Using the same concept, but going beyond your immediate company, try identifying a friend that you can reach out to by telephone and share your frustrations with.

10. Some people have a great respect for the power of meditation. If you are interested in the concept of meditation, seek some professional instruction to be sure that you have a technique that works for you. Some people practice yoga and believe that it is an ideal stress reliever.

11. If things really get bad for you on the job, try rearranging your vacation schedule and take some time off away from the job. While on vacation, employ whatever stress-relieving measure

HYPERTENSION

Percent of Population 25–74 Years of Age with Hypertension* by Race and Sex in the United States: 1971–75 and 1976–80

1971–75

Sex	Total	Black	White	Black/White Ratio
Both Sexes	18.2	33.6	16.4	2/1
Male	20.1	36.5	18.5	2/1
Female	16.4	31.4	14.5	2.2/1

1976–80

Sex	Total	Black	White	Black/White Ratio
Both Sexes	14.8	24.6	13.8	1.8/1
Male	16.9	23.6	16.3	1.4/1
Female	12.9	25.5	11.3	2.3/1

*Systolic blood pressure of at least 160 mm Hg or diastolic blood pressure of at least 95 mm or both; based on three measurements.

Source: National Center for Health Statistics: Health U.S., 1983.

that you can to turn things around for yourself. This may include going to a vacation health spa or seeking some professional help. Excessive alcoholic drinking and the use of illegal drugs are certainly not the thing to get involved in.

12. One of the best ways to deal with a job that exposes you to prolonged stress and stressful situations may be to simply get another job. If that means leaving your present organization, then so be it! The important thing to remember is that your health and well-being come first. Stress kills!

A FAMILY DILEMMA

Some black and Hispanic families have seriously questioned the wisdom of continuing to encourage their bright children to pursue a career in corporate America. They suggest that the private sector has not kept faith with minorities during the recent cyclical changes in our economy, and that without an aggressive federal equal employment opportunity policy there is little hope for minority upward mobility in the corporate world at this time.

Armed with some logical rationale, these concerned families cite the combined presence of racism, hostile corporate mergers, takeovers, and middle-management downsizing as ample justification for their fears and unhappiness. Morever, they make the case that corporate America's intent on raising shareholders' wealth by reducing costs or increasing revenues has translated into an unfavorable employment climate for minority professional and managerial types.

Recognizing that black people in America have historically been the last ethnic group of people hired during an economic upturn and the first group fired in an economic downturn, these minority families seem to be saying that there must be a better career path for their sons and daughters to travel at this time in our country. Perhaps the legal or medical professions might offer a more rewarding future for well-educated minorities now. Some even suggest the nonprofit area, or the public sector, where presumably more job security can be found.

In any event, it is pretty clear that some minority families are not entirely happy with the prospects of a career in corporate America for their children if it means that the career will be short-lived, particularly when you consider the size of the investment they have made in educating their young people at some of the nation's finest colleges and universities.

Despite all of the seemingly logical rationale that minority families might have for dissuading their children from pursuing a career in corporate America, it would not serve the best interest of these bright young people to eliminate such a career without a definite viable alternative.

While corporate managers have a responsibility to increase shareholders' wealth in the near term, they also have a responsibility to strive for long-term profits. To do that takes an ability to recruit and train talented young people to carry on the corporate legacy, and let's face it, there are not that many talented people around to systematically overlook all of the available minority candidates. The truth is that corporations today cannot exist without talented people to run them. In short, they need talented minorities whether they seriously want them or not.

Finally, it is not unreasonable to suggest that minority families, corporate leaders, educators, and national minority leadership sit down and discuss creative ways that insensitive companies can be reminded about this talented pool of available people in a way that would have meaning.

HOW TO MAKE A FIVE-YEAR CAREER
FORECAST THAT WORKS FOR YOU

To make a good five-year forecast that is both meaningful and rewarding, you have to make a personal commitment to draft and refine your projections until they fit your personality perfectly. When it comes to forecasting, there is no substitute for realistic thought and an honest effort. In addition, don't be surprised if you invite your friends or business associates to join you in a forecast exercise of their own and they do not give you a positive response. It takes emotional maturity to craft a document that accurately reflects your career conditions, dreams, and aspirations in a constructive self-evaluation format. And let's face it, a lot of people are not ready to ask themselves penetrating questions that may cause their insecurities and self-doubts to surface. In all probability, they would rather confine their activities to more immediate concerns, and deal with their career challenges as they come up on a daily basis.

Here are some examples of typical comments and questions that some professionals, particularly those that have a lot of insecurities, might concern themselves with when discussing the merits of forecasting:

• Five years is such a long time to plan for anything. I'm young and having a good time in my present life-style. Why do I need to be concerned about the future?

• I'm not sure that I want to know about my future. Suppose it doesn't look good for me—then what?

• How can you forecast your dreams and aspirations? After all, they are merely dreams and aspirations—not reality.

• Forecasting to me sounds like an imperfect exercise. How can you benefit from something that is as uncertain as a forecast?

While these comments and questions are clearly legitimate, you should know that forecasting is not some supernatural exercise that is unexplainable and emotionally threatening. Forecasting a five-year career path is created by making a written record of your present conditions, plus an appropriate interpretation of your own desires and aspirations. Once you have documented your condition, projected new thoughts and conditions, you can disregard the unimportant and factor in the important.

Forecasting exercises provide an opportunity to identify, review, and evaluate facets of your career experience and personality to include things that you actually need to be successful versus the things that you simply fantasize about. When the important facets are associated, properly aligned, and brought together, ideas about your personal self and career path emerge, ideas that can be accurately plotted on paper like a road map and give you guidance all along the way. With a few days of honest self-reflection and self-evaluation, you can produce a good forecast that works for you—one that can be easily updated on a year-to-year basis to include new career developments, greater skill refinement, or changes in your personal life.

You don't have to wait until your boss calls you into her office one day and offers you an opportunity to work in the company's South American office for the next three years, before you decide to plot your next career move. Remember, you can't take too long to make a career decision when management makes you a good offer. Indecisiveness can create negative impressions about aspiring young executives if it is apparent that you can't make up your mind. On the other hand, it is your life, and you should be able to make an intelligent decision as to whether you wish to spend the next three years of it in South America or in your own hometown. After all, you have friends, relatives, social commitments (a boyfriend), and housing cost to think about. What happens when you come back? It's not that easy to just pick up and go, or is it?

Let's take a few minutes right now and review some of the basic components that go into the development of a five-year forecast. Consider your life-style/career as it presently exists and see if these guidelines will not help you establish a step-by-step approach to your career over the next several years.

Guidelines for a Five-Year Forecast: A Look at the Future

1. *Data Collection:*

- Résumé
- Present job description
- Company organizational chart showing positions you might want to aspire to
- General information identifying jobs you might want to aspire to outside your company
- Occupational trend data if available. This should include average income by state and average salary by job title or job classification, e.g., first-year (entry-level) accountant, etc.

2. *Personal and Career Data:*

• Create a personal format for your five-year forecast.
• Project your age in the next five years.
• Identify the level of educational attainment you will reach in the next five years.
• Anticipate your marital status. Add to that the number of children you plan to have, if any.
• Give your career goals and objectives and be very specific. Now identify the position that you plan to have in five years.
• After you identify the job you plan to hold, be sure that you give the job title and your responsibilities as you perceive them to be. Your job information should also include the number of staff people you envision reporting to you at the five-year point.
• Don't forget to note the size of the budget you will be personally responsible for. These details all reflect the speed and upward mobility of your career and the level of confidence that management will have in you in five years.
• Now identify your projected annual income and your total approximate net worth in five years: assets minus liabilities.
• If for some reason any one of these points does not apply to you, simply ignore it.

3. *Social and Professional Data:*

• Anticipate opportunities in your community that reflect your social status. List all information you believe to be pertinent in this area. Start with identifying the actual social, business, and professional organizations that you will hold memberships in in five years. Don't be general; name the actual organizations. Remember, professional people usually join organizations to enhance their status in some way or to create networking opportunities and share their skill and talents.
• Indicate any special vacation and travel plans you will have in five years.

4. *Major Challenges Encountered:*

• While it is difficult to anticipate experiences that are less than positive, make a list of the major challenges you anticipate in your career five years from now. This list should include things like:

Personal health
Social (male and female) relations
Educational
Occupational
Financial
Housing
Marital
Family (your parents due to age or health conditions or your own children)

• Next to each item on your major challenges list, make a notation identifying the reasons why this is a major challenge and what you plan to do about it, if anything. For example, occupational major challenge—promotion to director was denied. Reason—lacked master's degree. To offset/overcome—complete master's degree program within the next four years; use company tuition-reimbursement program to pay for education.

5. *Priorities:*

• Now let's identify your priorities in the next five years as you see them. *Items to list in this area should be made in order of their importance to you.* For example:

1. Spiritual life
2. Family life
3. Business and professional life
4. Social life

1. Personal development
2. Emotional development
3. Spiritual development

Guidelines for a Five-Year Forecast:
A Look at the Present

Now that you have had the opportunity to look five years into the future, it is time to return to your present status. This exercise will establish a bridge between your five-year projection and your present circumstances.

1. *Personal and Career Data:*

- Current age
- Current level of education
- Marital status
- Number of children, if any
- Career goals and objectives as they presently exist
- Present job title
- Job description and responsibilities
- Number of people now reporting to you, if any
- Size of the budget you are personally responsible for
- Annual income from your current full-time position only
- Your approximate total net worth: assets minus liabilities

2. *Social and Professional Data:*

- Identify current business and professional organizational memberships, and state reasons for joining.
- Also identify all current social organizational memberships, and give your reasons for joining.
- Give your vacation and travel plans for the current year. If you don't have any, state why you don't have any.

3. *Priorities:*

- Identify all current priorities, and list them in order of their importance to you.
- Make notations next to these items indicating what your plan of action for these priorities are. For example:
     Intellectual development
     Professional development
     Hobbies
     Career contingency plans
- Feel free to be very imaginative in this area and don't forget to make notations next to these items indicating what plan of action you will take during this period to implement your priorities. This is very important, so remember to include a timetable with your plan of action.

4. *Your Forecast Update:*

• As you update your forecast, review your priorities from year to year and make notations indicating the progress that you have made in each priority area.

• In those areas where you have not made progress, so indicate, and explain why. When you have identified the reason or reasons that you have not made progress in your priority areas, indicate what you plan to do about that situation and when.

• Remember, you must be honest and realistic with your updates, or your forecast will not help you very much. For example, if you lack money to manage your affairs and deal with your priorities, state the fact, but also show how you plan to raise the money that you need to manage your affairs and deal with your priorities.

5. *Major Accomplishments:*

• Within your professional environment, list your major accomplishments. Examples: awards, citations, and all forms of personal recognition.

• Within your social environment, list your major accomplishments. Examples: awards, citations, and all forms of personal recognition.

• Within your intellectual/academic environment, list your major accomplishments. Examples: books and articles, inventions and discoveries, awards and citations, all forms of personal recognition.

6. *Strengths:*

• Identify your perceived professional strengths, and list them as part of your forecast data.
• Identify and list your social strengths.
• Identify and list your professional weaknesses.
• Identify and list your social weaknesses.

7. *Goals, Objectives, and Strategy:*

• Utilizing your current career plan, identify and list your career goals, objectives, and strategy within your forecast. (If you do not have a career plan with goals, objectives, and strategy, it is suggested that you develop one.)

8. *Final Note:*

• Now that you have identified your present and future life-style/career path, be prepared to update each segment on a yearly basis to build the bridge between your life as it presently exists and the life you have forecast.

• Remember, you should see a step-by-step line of progression in many areas of your five-year forecast if you regularly update the forecast charts, work hard at building your career, and make planned career-path changes when necessary.

VI

Issues and Answers

As we noted earlier, there are rules, regulations, and outside influences that corporate people are guided by when seeking job security, upward mobility, financial success, and power. These rules, regulations, and influences are not easily accessible, because the information and insight are not openly discussed anywhere in the corporation, or published, for that matter.

STRAIGHTFORWARD TALK

Should minorities seek career opportunities in the corporate world?

Yes, despite all of the events that have recently served to impede or retard the progress of minorities in the corporate world, minorities should continue to actively and aggressively pursue career opportunities in the corporate world. While downsizing, reorganization, mergers, hostile takeovers, and racism have had a significant impact on job stability and progress for minorities, these things still do not constitute a reason to totally avoid or abandon the career experience altogether.

Instead of avoiding the corporate world, minorities should come together now more than ever before and help each other through networking and mentoring activities. The collective will of minority professionals can have a significant impact on the corporate world with all of the planning and implementation skills that exist. Moreover, minorities need to protect the gains that have been made by actively supporting each other. They should push for their fair share of the corporate job opportunities, particularly in the nontraditional areas, with or without the federal government's EEO support.

Minority professionals have a constitutional right to share in the good fortunes of this country, because they have earned it. As college-trained people, voters, taxpayers, and veterans of the armed forces, minorities cannot be legitimately excluded from participation in the business community at any level.

America has a great need for people who can contribute to the nation's economy and help to make it more competitive in the world marketplace. For this reason, minorities must constantly remind the private sector in a variety of creative ways why progress for minorities means a stronger industrial complex for all of America.

Is it difficult to find a good job in private industry today?

Despite all of the downsizing and restructuring activities of the 1980s, corporations continue to need new talent to run their businesses. The difference in the climate today as opposed to a decade ago is that companies are more selective in their hiring practices. While top management realizes that it must hire new people, it still plans to retain its lean and aggressive posture. This means that the gatekeepers of the corporations, the human resource people, will continue to employ stringent tactics in their recruiting and selection process. For example, some companies may elect to use the new video interview technique that allows an outside consultant or search firm to screen candidates and show the video film results to the company before the candidate is interviewed at the company. Other human resource techniques may involve the use of job simulation exercises for technical-oriented candidates and IQ tests. Drug testing and polygraph tests may be used also, depending on the type of job being considered.

In the final analysis, it is more difficult today to find work in the private sector, but it is by no means impossible. People are finding good jobs every day.

Can you suggest any new industries that college graduates might consider for career planning and development?

It is important to realize that industries, like many facets of the business world, are not constant. Industries are born, reach a level of maturity, and often die and make room for new industries. Industries have a life cycle of their own, and being aware of their birth, growth, and maturity can help you in your career planning.

One of the lesser-known industries that promises to provide career opportunities for a variety of college graduates is the trade association industry. The trade association industry uses accountants, lawyers, marketing people, graphic artists, information services specialists, communications people, government relations specialists, human resource specialists, and managers and administrators. According to R. William Taylor, head of the American Society of Association Executives, the trade association industry is growing at the rate of about 5 percent a year. There were about 20,000 workers in 1986 compared to 19,000 the previous year. Overall, Taylor estimates that there are currently about 500,000 associations in all, including trade, professional, local, and charitable. It is an industry worth investigating because of its growth potential.

What are some of the things that human resource people look for in an interview situation?

Every interviewer really has his or her own special set of guidelines to go by; however, the things that many human resource people tend to look for during the initial interview are:

- Physical appearance
- Ability to articulate
- General interviewing skills (eye contact, sense of humor, level of confidence, voice projection, etc.)

- Résumé quality
- Knowledge about the organization you are interviewing with
- Your professional skill level
- Your salary level
- Previous work experience
- Educational background
- Type and quality of references

What preparations do you consider to be important when looking for a corporate job?

There are a number of things you need to do that have all been outlined in this book. However, if you stick to the basics, you should do well:

1. Prepare yourself for the challenge spiritually, emotionally, and physically. Refuse to be defeated no matter what you experience.

2. Get a good mentor for guidance and positive feedback. If possible, try to get someone who has years of experience in the corporate world or the business world in general.

3. Do as much networking as you possibly can. Networking and mentoring are very important elements in the search for a corporate job.

4. Develop a good written career plan and make sure that your current job-search activities fit well within the scope and timetable of your overall plan.

5. Take the time to research the companies that you are interested in. You can never know too much about a potential employer.

6. Practice your interviewing skills and check your references.

Will minorities be able to find financial help if additional corporate training and development are needed?

If the federal government has lost its appetite for subsidizing national training and education programs, many people, minorities included, will have to look for more creative ways to finance their educational needs. For example, minorities can look for jobs that provide training and education as a condition for employment or a fringe benefit package. Many companies, today, make a substantial effort to encourage employees to further their education if it is job-related. In addition, corporate history has demonstrated that a well-trained and -educated employee ultimately makes a more rounded and productive employee.

This important idea of supporting job-related training and education should serve as a real incentive for people who want to get ahead in business. It is one of the best ways to fulfill your developmental needs, impress your employer as an aggressive employee, and pay for an otherwise expensive learning experience.

What corporate departments offer the greatest promise for job security and upward mobility today?

There are no safe havens in corporate America and no guarantees for job security and upward mobility. Your career experience to some degree involves a certain amount of risk no matter where you work. So always keep an open mind, be alert, and be prepared to take your chances on success.

On the other hand, there are some jobs in corporate life that appear to receive more attention than others and consequently may, in fact, promise greater job security and upward mobility. It really depends on the company and infrastructure of the organization. You would do well, however, to consider the managerial style and the avenues traditionally available for upward mobility if you want to get ahead.

DEPARTMENTS WITH TRADITIONAL HIGH VISIBILITY

1. U.S. marketing
2. Finance (corporate level)
3. Sales management (U.S.)
4. International marketing
5. Operations/manufacturing
6. Research and development (managerial level)
7. Mergers and acquisitions
8. Information services (managerial level)

Of these departments, marketing and finance tend to produce the greatest number of presidents and chief executive officers.

Which departments in the corporate world currently provide some promise for upward mobility, but perhaps not as much as the more visible departments identified above?

DEPARTMENTS WITH SOME PROMISE OF OPPORTUNITY

1. Personnel (human resources)
2. Legal (corporate level)
3. Advertising
4. Public relations (corporate level)
5. Government relations
6. Market research and development

How long does it take before you can realistically expect to be promoted in the private sector?

Actually, there is no set amount of time that you can rely on. Promotions in the corporate world are generally based on a combination of things:

1. The company's need to fill an open position or to create a new position
2. Your record of performance at the company
3. A respected member of management that would like to recommend you for promotion
4. Your length of service at the company and your current salary level
5. Your potential for success in the new job
6. The willingness of the person you would be reporting to in the new position to support your candidacy for the job
7. Finally, your desire to accept the new job if and when it is offered to you

Is it important to have a written job description when working in the private sector?

It doesn't matter where you are working—public, private, or nonprofit—you should always have a written description of your job. And you should refer to it from time to time to be sure that you are doing your job as far as you can tell from the written document.

If for some reason a written job description does not exist for your position, don't be afraid to ask your boss for one. It protects you and your boss from misunderstanding what it is that you are expected to accomplish. The written job description also is an important reference source when it is time for your performance appraisal, which involves a formal written document that goes into your personnel file.

Are performance appraisals/reviews all that important, and what could happen if your boss does not give you a review and you don't ask for one?

Performance appraisals/reviews are very important because they document your performance on the job, and that document becomes a record in your personnel file for as long as you are a member of the organization. In addition, the performance appraisal process at most organizations provides an opportunity for you and your boss to agree or disagree on a point-by-point basis. In fact, you do not have to accept your boss's evaluation of your performance if you believe that he has not been fair. You can ask your boss for a meeting to discuss his evaluation of you and you can challenge it issue by issue. You can also inform your boss that you wish to make a written response to his evaluation and that you would like that response to be a part of your permanent record as well. It is your right to do this if you so desire.

On the other hand, if your boss neglects to give you a performance review and you do not ask for one, you may find that you have no written proof of your good work at the company. Quite often, performance appraisals/reviews over the years become the best form of job security you can have. Remember, supervisors come and go over the years, but your company personnel file is a permanent record for management to judge your value to the organization if a decision about your future has to be made. Finally, your written record of performance will be of enormous help to you when you are making a bid for promotion.

If you are faced with sexual harassment from your boss, what steps can you take to protect yourself?

Realistically, you have to decide what practical alternatives you have and which ones you should take to save yourself as much personal pain and discomfort as possible.

One possible first step might be for you to share the problem with someone in the company, like the vice-president of personnel, and seek his or her advice as to how you should handle such a situation. If the situation cannot be resolved to your satisfaction, it may be necessary for you to get the vice-president's help to transfer out of the present department without letting your boss or supervisor know your plans until it is too late for him to stop you. By sharing the problem with the vice-president of personnel, you create an opportunity to gain support from a high-ranking executive who should be sympathetic to your problem of sexual harassment and who also does not want the company to get the bad publicity that would result from a lawsuit by the Human Rights Commission.

Always document every incident that suggested sexual harassment in any way. Write letters to your own personnel file and indicate names, dates, and places where you believe sexual harassment took place. But keep your records at home until you have a need to produce them.

Generally speaking, the Equal Employment Opportunity Commission (EEOC) states that in deciding whether alleged conduct constitutes sexual harassment, the commission will review the record in its entirety, and then the totality of the circumstances, such as the nature of the sexual advances and the context in which the alleged incidents occurred.

Should a person who wants to succeed in a company have a personal plan for success?

Yes, every person who wants to be successful in corporate America should have his or her own personal marketing plan, and that plan should be tied into the company's plans for the future. For example, you need to be sure that your skills and personality are consistent with what your company will need to reach its goals and objectives. Remember, companies that are serious about their goals and objectives must have skilled people to carry out their plans, or those plans will not work. Make sure that you have the talent and skills that your company needs, according to their plan, or you may find that your company will not need you in the future.

Do all who pursue a career in private industry aspire to the same goals?

Some people in private industry have a need for achievement, some have a need for power, and some have a need for affiliation. A person's goals and aspirations in private industry really vary from person to person, and a lot has to do with their age, skill level, and experience. What many people seem to have in common, however, is a need for a sense of security, personal recognition, and incremental stages of financial compensation that keeps them ahead of the cost-of-living index. The important thing to remember is, don't be too concerned about what other people are doing. You should be aware and generally informed, but not too involved. Keeping up with what other people are doing with their career path can be a very time-consuming thing, so concentrate on your own career path. Networking, business-related reading materials, and seminar training can tell you a lot.

What should you do if you suddenly find that someone in the company plans to take over your job for his or her own career advancement?

It really depends upon how serious the corporate attack is. In some cases, such threats are not to be taken seriously. On the other hand, a corporate attack from an associate in the company could be very dangerous for your career, and you need to deal with the threat before it gets out of hand.

However, always remember that no two situations are alike; therefore, you really need specific information before you make your move to deal with the crisis. For example, consider some of the following fact-gathering steps as a general means of protecting yourself in a job crisis:

• Get all of the facts and get them as fast as you can. Try not to react to a job crisis without the facts. Reacting to a job crisis based purely on imaginary conditions or hear-say information can create *serious problems*.

• Quickly assess the political strength of your foe. Also determine the direction in which the attack is likely to come, and the ability of your opponent to win in a corporate fight.

• Once your research has been completed and confirmed, prepare to take positive and aggressive action designed to defeat your enemy.

• Protect your territory by making sure that your work is up-to-date, your performance is good, and your staff is willing to support you. If, for example, you identify people in your department or group that will not support you during your crisis, you need to try to minimize the impact that they can have on the outcome of the battle.

• Don't be afraid to use your corporate mentors both inside and outside of the company. Also ask your mentors if they have any networking opportunities that you can take advantage of.

• Reinforce your position in the crisis by conducting serious networking activity early in the fight. But remember that a tactful networking approach is vital in a major political fight. You may not know just how much management support your opponent really has until the fight is over. Be careful in selecting the people you take into your confidence. Corporate people talk a lot and sometimes to your opponent's friends.

• Don't run away from a good corporate fight. Do all that you can to defeat your enemy, but do it with intelligence, faith, and determination to win.

• Finally, should you be defeated for reasons beyond your control, never lose your composure and your dignity. Be a professional to the bitter end. Your associates and friends will respect you for it.

At what point should a career-minded person decide to make a career change?

It all depends on the career goals and objectives of the individual involved. Generally, career changes should be seriously considered when it is clear that opportunities for advancement no longer exist. To make that determination, however, you need to have a good career plan that provides reliable "feedback" data to make an intelligent decision. In addition, it would be advantageous to have professional career counseling before making a decision about a career change. Since career changes tend to be final, you really don't want to do anything you may regret later on in life.

Do all roads to success lead to corporate America?

Absolutely not. There are many different directions you can take to find success and a rewarding career. However, it should be recognized that more and more nonprofit institutions and public organizations are reorganizing to reflect a bottom-line mentality. With an overall decline in federal funding for many domestic programs, nonprofit and public sector agencies are demanding greater management accountability and fiscal restraint than ever before. They have also reviewed other corporate reorganization initiatives and found them to be quite compatible with their own goals and objectives. Consequently, many of the attitudes, perceptions, and value systems found in the corporate world will find their way into nonprofit and public organizations.

So you might conclude that while not all roads to success lead to a career in corporate America, and never will, corporate America is having an increasing influence on how people manage organizations in the country. If you are a person that strongly disagrees with the bottom-line mentality of business and industry, you may find your choice of career opportunities to be somewhat limited.

Is it devastating to be terminated as a result of corporate reorganization?

A lot depends on whether you are mentally and emotionally strong. A lot also depends on your financial status and your will to survive and thrive.

If your job is eliminated, it certainly does not mean that you will automatically become devastated. While termination or forced early retirement due to reorganization can be a very traumatic experience, people respond to it differently and some even see it as a blessing in disguise. In other words, they perceive the situation as a chance to move on to bigger and better things career-wise. Such people suddenly see opportunities for advancement in areas that they would not normally consider, because they were very comfortable in their old jobs. Now they suddenly have a chance to move on with their lives and fulfill some of their lifelong dreams and aspirations.

In addition, happiness and a general sense of well-being for some who have been excessed are not always directly connected with their job status. Their lives actually transcend their professional status. Therefore, termination from any job would simply not be the end of the world for them, but the beginning of something new and exciting. As a matter of fact, in a number of instances, victims of excess employment or corporate downsizing have gone on to excel far beyond anyone's imagination. Basically, they use the adverse or negative condition as a vehicle for self-motivation. Moreover, they pick themselves up after the initial shock of separation and go right on with the business of surviving and thriving.

That all sounds well and good, but how do these survivors actually survive the shock of losing their job, and what steps do they take to get themselves going again?

Well, the first thing that they do is to quickly accept the reality of what has happened to them and then avoid any danger of wasting valuable time and energy engaged in self-pity and resentment. Self-pity and resentment, if left unchecked, can lead to emotional problems of a very serious nature. Following the acceptance phase, they put their job crises in total perspective and see the situation as it should be seen—a temporary condition that requires faith, a good career contingency action plan, and a strong desire to live a full and productive life. Having taken these steps, the exercise becomes a matter of setting their career plans in motion with total commitment and a will to win. As an aside, no professional should ever be so comfortable on the job that he or she does not have a good and workable set of career contingency plans that can be implemented at any time. To function in today's business world without a set of career contingency plans is to leave oneself wide open for potential problems and perhaps a major career setback at some point.

But suppose an excessed person simply doesn't have a plan, and suppose that person also happens not to have a strong positive mental attitude about himself. What type of experience could he have?

For a number of people, few adverse conditions in their lives will have a greater negative impact on their sense of well-being than the sudden loss of a job, particularly a good job. Unfortunately, some people in America attach more importance to their jobs than they should—so much so that they end up putting job above their family and their own regard for personal health and safety. Therefore, it is not uncommon for some people to experience a major setback in the loss of a job. And while they may fully recognize that it is a poor business person that neglects to plan for the future, they will tell you that they just never took the time to plan for career changes of any kind. Consequently, when they do become the victim of downsizing or forced early retirement, life for them can become unbearable. Excess drinking, drug abuse, and depression are only some of the problems that can occur when people neglect to protect themselves and plan for their future. To be more specific, it may take a lot of time and effort to find the job you really want, but good career planning will allow for that possibility. In some cases, landing another good job can take as much as six months to a year and even longer, depending upon the availability of work in the industry that you are interested in and the title and salary you want. However, a good career contingency plan that includes cash reserves of some amount, resources for short-term loans if needed, employment contacts, networking opportunities, consultant work, and so forth can make all the difference in the world during a job crisis.

Finally, people who place less importance on themselves than they do on a single job tend to be very insecure employees in a company and that usually shows at the management level. These people tend to have little professional integrity, and at the appropriate time, it is not uncommon for management to use that personality weakness against them. On the other hand, employees that are secure and enjoy high professional integrity and self-esteem make better management material for the company, and the senior management of the organization usually knows that as well.

JOB TERMINATION:
A SEQUENCE OF EMOTIONAL EXPERIENCES

Termination:
1. Shock and stress
2. Rage and revenge
3. Anxiety and self-pity
4. Mild depression
5. Self-doubt and fear
6. Low self-esteem
7. Depression
8. Physical illness due to stress

A Recovery Cycle:
1. Recognized vulnerability
2. A creative wellness program:
   Spiritual awareness
   Daily meditation
   Daily physical exercise
   Daily balanced diet
   Rest and relaxation
   Paid or volunteer work in your field of interest

What is the greatest challenge for females who seek senior management positions in the corporate world?

There are many challenges that women encounter when they decide to seek senior management positions in the corporate world, but the greatest one of all is dealing with the extensive male dominance that exists in corporations. When a woman moves up among the ranks of corporate senior management, she quickly learns that male bonding, leadership, and dominance are omnipresent in the business world.

Unfortunately, this condition often serves to reinforce the female minority status and her feeling of being the low person in the corporate pecking order. Despite the long history of male dominance in the business world, women still continue to experience the unsettling magnitude of it throughout their careers.

Iris Randall, president of New Beginnings, a successful career training and development firm in New York City, spent many years in a major corporation as a senior member of management. She says, "I think the most challenging experience of my career in corporate America was to accept the feeling of always having to prove myself and to be seen as a decisive and assertive executive without being considered brash and aggressive."

If you're in a job that doesn't fit your career strategy, what immediate adjustments can you make?

You may want to consider making a lateral career move within the company as part of a plan to increase your chances of getting the job responsibilities, title, and benefits you want. Lateral moves open up a variety of career possibilities, and you should never overlook such an important career move that is so readily available to you.

What this job opportunity requires, however, is that you apply the same job-search skills that you would apply to any other job search. Making lateral moves within the company can be quite demanding, and prospective employers in new departments will apply practically the same rules for lateral candidates as they do for the people they hire from outside the company. The fact that you have worked for the organization for some period of time and now wish to transfer to another department, division, or plant operation does not automatically qualify you for a job. If you want to take advantage of a job opportunity in another area of your company's business, you have to prepare for it just as you would prepare for any other job opportunity. In other words, you have to shop for a job inside the company. So the first thing you would need to do is develop an action plan for a lateral move.

This plan should include, among other things, extensive internal research regarding the future growth of each department you are considering and a clear understanding of their goals and objectives. In addition, make sure that your interview skills are in good shape and that you can get a good reference from your present department head should one be needed. A favorable reference from your boss will go a long way when a lateral is being made. Qualifications and capability are important issues as well, so make sure that your résumé fits the job you are applying for.

Remember, your company does not want to lose anything in

your transfer/lateral move, particularly when it comes to employee productivity. Therefore, senior management, including the new receiving department, must perceive that your lateral move is a plus for all concerned, or they may not approve of it. While it is true that we are discussing ways to enhance your career path, you must not forget that we are also discussing the needs of the company. Every personnel move in this regard should be designed to help the company improve its productivity and maximize the use of its human resources, or the company is really losing out on the move. There are also no free rides in lateral moves, so don't expect any! A bad lateral move in a new department could spell disaster for your job security in a company in which you have spent years building a good work record for yourself. Being an old employee in a new department doesn't mean much if you can't do the job. Every lateral move that an employee makes in his company is in effect a brand-new job with a brand-new company. You must prove your worth to the new boss in the new job situation.

For people interested in utilizing the lateral/transfer career path, follow these basic guide points:

- Be careful in your planning process.
- Be very serious about your opportunity to move laterally.
- Be confident that you can do the job if given a chance.

From a positive point of view, if you know what the new job challenge is all about, work hard at it, and contribute as a "team player" toward the goals and objectives of the new department, chances are your future in the company will be very bright, because you, the company, and the new department made the right career decision. After all, having knowledge, a proven track record, and friends in the company that will support you can go a long way in helping you move up in the business.

If you think about it, getting your employer to give you a lateral job change that builds and enhances your future can often be a lot easier than trying to get that same employer to give you a promotion when you want it. Promotions as a rule are not easy to come by when you want them, because they tend to create an unplanned increase in your employer's overhead cost. In addition, they also tend to create the need for your employer to reorganize his corporate chart at a time when he or she may not want to do that. On the other hand, lateral moves require less reorganization, the employee continues with basically the same benefits and salary package, and the new-employee orientation period developed by the company is not required, thereby creating another time-saving expense.

Theoretically, an internal lateral move could prove to be a good thing for you, your employer, and the new department head, if the fit is right. It can remove the pressure from your company to give you an unscheduled promotion, particularly if they were really not ready to promote you. The move also provides increased movement and motivation for you, because you have taken positive action and found a new job on your own, with company approval, of course. Finally, your benefits continue without a break, and the new department gets an experienced, motivated person ready to help it meet its goals and objectives.

How do you feel about making a lateral to another city—relocation?

While it is true that some lateral moves may require geographic relocations and possibly a cost-of-living salary cut, you may find that your career potential is better served by making a relocation lateral move. Sometimes you have to take one step back in order to go two steps forward on your career path. In many cases, people have actually welcomed a pay cut in exchange for an opportunity with a smaller company that offered greater responsibilities and real decision-making powers. Although salary is an important consideration in the career planning process, it should by no means represent the only consideration. If you live in New York City or Los Angeles, the cost of living actually dictates the minimum salary you can accept and still maintain a certain life-style. However, in cities like Atlanta, Dallas, Hartford, and Memphis, the cost of living is significantly less than in New York, which means that you can live as well if not better for less money. The quality of housing and health care is good, and social amenities are considerable and improving all the time. In addition, stress levels of city life for professionals with good jobs living in less populated and less costly areas are generally lower.

So don't be afraid to explore lateral job opportunities that require relocation as a means of career enhancement and advancement long-term. It could be the best way to move ahead without fighting your boss for a promotion in your existing company.

There are some factors that you may want to consider when exploring lateral/relocation opportunities:

- Cost-of-living comparisons in:

Food, shelter, and clothing

Transportation, education, and entertainment

- Available support systems in:

Religious services

Medical services

Social services

Training and development

- Available social activities for:

Single adults (to include educational, racial, and religious preferences)

Married couples

Family life

- Access to national and international ground and air transportation
- Business and industry growth-and-development trends
- Employment patterns and salary data—history and forecast
- Racial climate—history and forecast
- Intellectual climate—history and forecast

Informational resources for relocation research include:

- Department of Commerce
- Public libraries
- Regional Office, Bureau of Labor Statistics
- Local Chamber of Commerce
- State Board of Education
- Local churches
- Urban League
- Opportunity industrialization centers
- NAACP

Do you consider entrepreneurship to be a viable alternative to a career in the corporate world?

Absolutely. You live in a capitalist society and the United States is totally committed to the preservation and advancement of the entrepreneurial spirit. Not a day goes by when a newspaper, magazine, radio station, or television program does not recognize and publicize the merits and success of the business community. Remember, business people reinforce the validity of the American way of life; therefore, the country must recognize and support the people who help make it what it is today.

If you think that you can make a positive contribution by developing a business and providing goods or services, don't be afraid to join the ranks of the entrepreneurs. However, knowing that there is risk involved, you should not approach this field in a casual way. A lot of careful planning is needed if you are to be successful. While it is true that there is great financial risk in business, it is also true that the rewards of business are greater.

Instead of helping a corporation to grow and develop, you can grow your own company. After all, that's what free enterprise is all about. Don't sit back and indulge yourself in wishful thinking; wishful thinking alone does not build successful businesses. Conceive your idea and take advantage of one of the single most powerful formulas for success available—find a need and fill it.

You should also be aware that you don't have to leave your present job to become an entrepreneur. As long as your business does not conflict with your employer, and you don't use company time to grow your own business, there is no reason why you cannot work at a corporation and create a business of your own. A lot of very successful executives work for corporations and own their own businesses on the side. It's not something that executives generally talk about publicly, but it is also not unusual at all. Should you decide to do this, it may take some creative thinking, help from friends, relatives, and partnerships, but it can be done.

Check your company's policy about personal business sidelines and see if they have any problems with it. *If they do, try investing your corporate earnings in a reliable friend's or relative's business as a hedge against a downturn in your corporate career at some future date.* Just be sure that the business you invest in is sound and the people are completely reliable.

THOUGHTS FOR CAREER WISDOM AND SUCCESS

There are really no guarantees for success in any field, no easy way, no shortcuts, and no free rides. You are going to have to prepare yourself for success if you want it, and do it with the same enthusiasm that a professional athlete uses when he or she prepares for a championship contest. You must be ready mentally, spiritually, and physically to accept any challenge and defeat any foe. To do this, you will have to examine closely your credentials and make sure that they match up well against the best competition in your field of endeavor. Next, build a strong foundation for your spiritualness. No one should be allowed to disrupt, challenge, or kill your spirit. You have a God-given right to be successful and you should claim that right. Let no one turn you around, and let no one deny you the opportunity to make a positive contribution to society. Finally, you must be true to your dreams and aspirations. There is no substitute for complete dedication to what you believe in and what you want out of life in the form of a career.

While mentors, family, and friends may advise you and open doors of opportunity for you, the ultimate responsibility for your success and failure rests with you. No matter how much someone else may want you to succeed, you and only you can make that determination.

Learn to accept your mistakes and failures without punishing yourself and learn to use your mistakes and failures to improve your learning curve. If viewed properly, mistakes can serve as a guidepost and as a source of inspiration for a brighter future. Remember, mistakes and failures merely present some temporary diversion that can be corrected or changed in some way, shape, or form. Mistakes and failures provide an opportunity for profound insight into those areas of your mental, emotional, and physical self that need attention. And if they did not need attention, you would not have made the mistake or created a failure in the first place. So don't hesitate to analyze and evaluate carefully your mistakes and failures. In retrospect, it is perhaps the best way to learn.

While it is true that your career in any field can be lost by a single act of poor judgment, nothing is final with respect to new and different career opportunities unless you decide to make it final. There is always tomorrow, and what a difference twenty-four hours can make in your life. Learn to keep your faith! In maintaining your faith, you will find that all things are possible. Remember, you can only live one day at a time, so why not simply take each day as it comes, one day at a time, and see what life has in store for you—success is a God-given right and you can claim that right if you only persevere.

Don't be impatient for life's good fortunes. While you may want success when you want it, success does not work on your own personal timetable. Success can come at any time or stage in your developing career. However, you must be ready when it comes or you will not have it to enjoy for very long. Receiving success is one thing, but being ready for it is something altogether different. One really doesn't have a lot to do with the other; that is why so many people struggle for years to gain success, only to lose it in a very short period of time. Impatience will no doubt be one of the greatest challenges you will have to face and overcome if you are to be successful. Learn to prepare while you wait, build a strong intellectual base, and learn to understand the meaning of success so that you can manage it properly. If you do this, you will never regret it—after all, success may only come once in your lifetime.

You Always Have a Choice

There are no predetermined career paths to follow. You may have a plan to guide you but you will need a set of contingencies, because every path has its own special set of circumstances that make it unique. With the proper contingency plans you can make course alterations without wasting time. The beauty in all of this, however, is that you do have a choice. If, for example, you decide that you don't like the direction that you are traveling in, change it. You always have a choice in the selection of routes and alternative routes available to you all along the way of any career path.

Again, don't be afraid to change your career if you are

thoroughly convinced that that is what you need to do. You can have as many legitimate career changes in your lifetime as you desire. There are no rules that say you can't pursue a new and different career experience if you want to. It would be wise, however, to examine fully your motives for making a career change, and be sure that they can withstand great scrutiny. It would not be good to find subsequently that you made a complete career change merely to avoid a difficult assignment or because your coping skills were a little weak. An inability to handle a difficult assignment may not be a legitimate reason for making a major change in your life. It may simply mean that you need more training or career counseling.

On the other hand, if you are thoroughly convinced (after research, counseling, and proper evaluation) that what you need to do is change your career path—change it! Just think of all the wonderful options open to you in life, and don't attach any more importance to your career disappointments than you absolutely have to. If you give importance to your career disappointments, you are likely to feel defeated and you should never feel that way, because there are just too many opportunities available. So remember to "keep the faith," plan well, and act aggressively. Never let any grass grow under your feet.

Don't be quick to give up on your dreams and aspirations. Take a world view of opportunity and pursue it whenever and wherever you can find it. If not in America, then some other country perhaps. Think about the third world countries, think about Europe, Asia, Africa, and South America, where your talents and skills are needed. What difference does it really make where you find success geographically? The important thing is that you find it at all. Is it better to be among the homeless in New York City because you have experienced failure, or to be a needed and respected professional in some other country? If one company, city, town, or state in America says no to your skills and talents, sell your skills and talents to the next company, city, town, state, or country.

Take a Calculated Risk

Don't be afraid to relocate if a career opportunity comes your way; take a calculated risk. Research the career opportunity to be sure that the relocation offer is worth your effort, but don't be afraid to take a chance. Be sure to research all of the social, religious, educational, and business support services that you might anticipate needing in a move to a new location, but don't reject a real opportunity simply because it requires a change in your environment.

Historically, black and Hispanic professionals in the United States were reluctant to move to communities where they were not well represented. Discrimination in housing, education, and the basic social services were so severe that the risk in a job opportunity involving relocation was often not worth the effort. But times are changing every day in the United States and throughout the world, and while discrimination still exists in many areas, you cannot let that stop you. No doubt, there will come a time in your career when you will have to fight for your right to sit at the table of opportunity, but you should not be afraid to do that if and when your time comes.

The downsizing of corporate America, particularly at the middle-management level, is expected to continue through the 1990s and beyond. This means that competition for available middle managerial and professional jobs will be keen.

So remember, carefully research all of the job opportunities that come your way, but don't be afraid to take a calculated risk on the job that offers real possibilities. If for some unforeseen reason, however, things don't go well for you after you have relocated, you can always return home and start over again, or you can simply move on to another town, city, state, or country. The world is your field of competition; make your unyielding demand on it and fulfill your aspirations.

Motivation Plays a Vital Role

The motivation that it takes to achieve success no matter where you are working cannot be given to you. While some would have you believe that they can provide you with all the motivation you will ever need to succeed, don't be fooled by them. Motivation is always self-generated, and it comes from within you, or it will not develop at all. The best that anyone can do to help you become motivated is to create an environment in which you can motivate yourself. They cannot give you a "handout," but they can give you a "hand-up." Motivation is that inner urge that calls you to action with a sense of purpose. Motivation fuels the drive that makes you stop at nothing to achieve your ultimate goal. This can come only from within you and nowhere else.

Finally, always remember that you can be whatever you want to be and be successful at it. Scientist, master builder, professional dancer, or business person—if you can conceive of it, you can achieve it. *The secret of achieving success is inherent in your faith, your belief in yourself, your motivation, and your total commitment.*

VII

Outlook for the 1990s

SOCIOECONOMIC ISSUES
AND EXPECTATIONS

• It is expected that over 12 million jobs will be created in
the United States during the 1990s. Ninety percent of these jobs
will be in service-related industries.

• Up to 80 percent of the jobs created in the service-related
industries will be filled by females, minorities, and immigrants.

• According to the Bureau of Labor Statistics, GNP is projected
to range between $3.0 and $3.6 trillion by 1995. With disposable
personal income expected to be between $2.0 and $2.1 trillion,
civilian employment is expected to range between 116 and 126
million jobs.

• The Bureau of Labor Statistics also projects that civilian
unemployment will decline, from 7.5 percent in 1984 to 6.3
percent in 1990 and 6.0 percent in 1995.

• While manufacturing has declined in the United States over
the years it will continue to make a sizable contribution to
America's gross national product in the nineties.

• A growing number of foreign companies will have manufacturing facilities in the United States. These foreign companies will also bring new management values and systems to America, and American university textbook management theory will be challenged by foreign management values and foreign management concepts of business. Moreover, foreign-owned companies doing business in the United States will have difficulty in accepting the aggressive business behavior of American employees. This will be particularly true of union-supported employees and executive-level men and women. Finally, the American executive's drive for corporate status, upward mobility, and profit sharing will not be encouraged by foreign-owned companies.

• American corporations of the 1990s will maintain a small middle-management work force. Emphasis will be placed on greater productivity and fewer middle managers. College graduates seeking upward mobility in corporate America will find formidable competition for a limited number of middle-manager jobs.

• Managers employed in line positions in American companies will enjoy greater job security than managers who are employed in staff positions.

• Profit-center departments in American companies will provide more job security than nonprofit-center departments during this period of declining middle management (marketing and sales departments versus public relations and personnel departments).

• The employment of farm operators and managers is projected to continue to decline well into the 1990s.

• An industry that is expected to do very well in the 1990s is health care. Home health care in particular should grow rapidly. Physical therapists, psychiatrists, chiropractors, and other health professionals should be in great demand. Recreational therapist positions will also grow in the 1990s with the expanding elderly population.

• The growing use of laser technology in the health services field will create new jobs.

• Another fast-growing business in the next decade should be the financial services industry. While salaries in this field will be very attractive, the big six-figure salaries of the 1980s will not be available to the extent that they were.

• The industrial robot is expected to create some new job opportunities in the next decade, and the robotic industry, should create career development opportunities in research and development, design, manufacturing and installation, marketing, sales, public relations, and service and maintenance work.

• With automation, robotics, and the like, fewer workers will be needed to run America's manufacturing plants.

• Temporary work offers new opportunities for professional workers. Marketing specialists, accountants, attorneys, physicians, and information systems specialists will receive more freedom and autonomy working on a temporary basis or special assignment than ever before. This practice is expected to extend well into the 1990s.

• As some companies eliminate in-house marketing, communications, training specialists, and legal operations they will increase the demand for consultants and outside specialists. This approach allows companies to receive needed services without profit sharing, bearing the costs of health insurance benefits, and other overhead cost.

• A demand for nursing professionals will continue well into the next decade. By the year 2000 the industry is expected to expand to 2 million workers. This is up from 1.5 million in 1985, according to the Bureau of Health Professionals in the Department of Health and Human Services.

Prospects for Employment
in the Mid-1990s

Actuaries. Employment opportunities for actuaries are expected to be favorable in the mid-1990s. College graduates who have passed at least two actuarial examinations while in school and have a good mathematical and statistical background should do very well as entry-level professionals. The volume of insurance sold and the volume of pension plan business will influence job opportunities in the field.

Mechanical engineers. The demand for machinery and machine tools will increase the need for mechanical engineers well into the 1990s. Employment opportunities are expected to grow as industrial machinery and its developmental processes become increasingly complex. The need for new energy developments and defense systems should also help the employment picture in the 1990s.

Nuclear engineers. Nuclear engineers may not enjoy a fast growth rate relative to new employment opportunities through the mid-1990s. It is expected that most job openings will result from the need to replace nuclear engineers who retire or leave the field for one reason or another. Less demand for electric power because of energy conservation will have an impact on the number of available jobs. In addition, few nuclear power plants are expected to be developed in the early 1990s because of the public's concern for nuclear power plant safety.

Petroleum engineers. The employment of petroleum engineers should grow as fast as the average for all occupations through the mid-1990s. The demand for petroleum and natural gas is expected to increase. This should influence job opportunities of petroleum engineers.

Computer systems analysts. The U.S. information-oriented society will increase its need for computer systems analysts. Job opportunities in this field should be very favorable in the mid-1990s and beyond. Advances in technology will lead to new applications for computers. Factory and office automation, telecommunications, and scientific research are just a few areas where use of computer systems will expand. College graduates who have computer programming course work (systems analysis, data processing, and applied study) should do well in the job market.

Mathematicians. The demand for mathematicians is expected to increase in the next decade. Many job opportunities will become available due to the number of people retiring and leaving the field of mathematics. In addition, the demand for Ph.D.'s in mathematics is expected to increase over the next decade. People with doctorate degrees in applied mathematics may enjoy greater employment opportunities than people with a theoretical mathematics background. The need for mathematical modeling, operations research, numerical analysis, computer systems design, programming, data processing, applied mathematical physics, robotics, market research, commercial surveys, and consultants are some of the many areas that will stimulate the job market.

Hotel managers and assistants. Job opportunities in the hotel industry for managers are expected to be favorable in the years ahead. A continued growth in business travel and domestic and foreign tourism should create the demand for qualified hotel managers through the mid-1990s. Interested candidates in hotel managerial positions during this period would do well to have a degree in hotel administration to maintain a competitive advantage. The willingness to relocate will be another advantage for people interested in working in this field.

Health services managers. The number of hospitals may decline into the mid-1990s. This could mean that hospitals will experience a slower growth rate than some of the other areas in the health field. For example, those facilities that provide outpatient care are expected to provide new jobs for health professionals and managers. Specifically, organizations like HMOs, group medical practices, urgent-care centers, surgicenters, cardiac rehabilitation centers, diagnostic imaging centers, and wellness centers should go a long way in providing job opportunities during the next decade.

Lawyers. The number of law school graduates has more than doubled in the last seventeen years. This rapidly growing supply of legal talent will make the competition for jobs in the field rather difficult in the years to come. Law firms and corporations will continue to compete for graduates from prestigious law schools and give preferential treatment to those who rank high in their graduation class. National interest, however, in consumer protection, the environment, and safety should create more job opportunities for lawyers than might be expected. An increase in legal services by middle-income people could produce an unexpected favorable impact on the job market for lawyers as well. This would include the use of legal clinics and prepaid legal service programs. Job opportunities will be better for those who are willing to relocate, although such relocation may result in the need to be licensed in a new state, which might require an additional bar examination.

Managers and administrators. The demand for managers and administrators should be influenced by the growth and development of certain industries. Job opportunities in the health care field, for example, are expected to be favorable for professionals. This includes managers and administrators in group medical practices, emergency centers, surgicenters, and rehabilitation centers for patients not requiring the full spectrum of medical services offered by hospitals. Other industries expected to create good job opportunities for managers in the next decade are robotics; wholesale trade in nondurable goods; food stores; equipment manufacturing; apparel and accessories stores; and state-owned and -operated facilities of all kinds, though not including education and hospitals.

Bank officers and managers. Employment opportunities for bank officers and managers are expected to grow into the mid-1990s. This growth should result from the banking industry's continuing interest in the financial services area as a viable business. Knowledge of insurance, securities, computers, telecommunications, telemarketing, and data processing systems should give interested candidates a competitive advantage. According to Dr. Walter V. Collier, a Martha's Vineyard–based research consultant, employment opportunities in banking will also grow in the 1990s due to deregulation of financial services and products. Competition will be high among banks, insurance, security, and investment companies. Because of this, there will be a greater demand for experts in marketing, selling, and management of financial services.

Biological scientists. Employment opportunities for biological scientists should improve from the late 1980s through the mid-1990s and beyond. The increased job opportunities will result from advances in genetic research that will spur developments in new and improved drugs, improved plants, and medical discoveries. New developments in biotechnology should also create job opportunities in this field. Scientists interested in the genetic, cellular, and biochemical areas of biology should experience good job opportunities in the years ahead.

Health professionals. A demand for health professionals into the mid-1990s is expected. The 1990s will witness a greater public sector concern for AIDS care than ever before. State health officials and insurers will be forced to try and set up a system that provides comprehensive AIDS care at the least possible cost. To deal with the AIDS epidemic, states may have to promise increased reimbursement to hospitals. This should encourage more effective management of health care for AIDS patients. With increased reimbursement, hospitals will be expected to arrange not only inpatient care but the less expensive alternative, home health care, hospices, counseling, and clinics.

Psychologists. Employment opportunities for psychologists are expected to improve considerably as the demand for health maintenance increases. This will include increased testing and counseling of children and the growing elderly population. Job opportunities in the health field, education, military, and law enforcement should be favorable. People with only a master's degree in psychology may find a limited number of job openings that they can qualify for in the 1990s.

Sociologists. Employment opportunities for sociologists in the mid-1990s may not be favorable. Job opportunities for this occupation are expected to result from the need to replace those professionals who are transferring to different jobs or retiring from the field altogether. A significant number of new jobs is not anticipated at this time.

WHAT ABOUT TOMORROW'S JOBS?

The Bureau of Labor Statistics gives a picture of job opportunities through the year 2005:

• Industries differ substantially in the kinds of workers they employ.

- Industries providing services will continue to employ many more people than those providing goods.
- Through the mid-1990s, some industries will grow much faster than others.
- Even though an occupation is expected to grow rapidly, it may provide fewer openings than a slower growing but larger occupation.

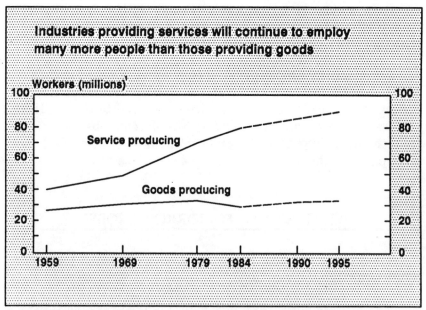

¹Includes wage and salary workers, the self-employed and unpaid family workers.
SOURCE: Bureau of Labor Statistics

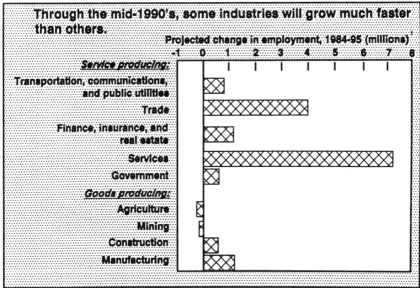

Through the mid-1990's, some industries will grow much faster than others.

Projected change in employment, 1984-95 (millions)[1]

SOURCE: Bureau of Labor Statistics

[1]Wage and salary employment except for agriculture, which includes self-employed and unpaid family workers.

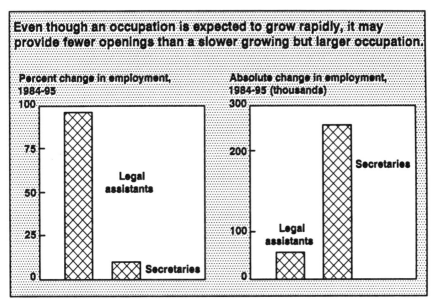

Even though an occupation is expected to grow rapidly, it may provide fewer openings than a slower growing but larger occupation.

Percent change in employment, 1984-95

Absolute change in employment, 1984-95 (thousands)

SOURCE: Bureau of Labor Statistics

Updated Reports on Employment and Economic Trends Expected Through 2005

Projections of key measures of employment and economic growth—the labor force, jobs, and gross national product—indicate continued expansion from 1900 to 2005, although the rate of growth for each measure will be slower than during the previous fifteen years.

Gross National Product

GNP—the measure of goods and services in demand— will increase by $1.7 trillion to $5.8 trillion in 2005.

GNP will grow slower than it did during the past 15 years.

GNP growth will slow because growth of the labor force, one of the major factors of production, will slow.

As in the past, however, GNP will grow faster than the labor force and employment due to increasing labor productivity.

Source for historical data: U.S. Department of Commerce

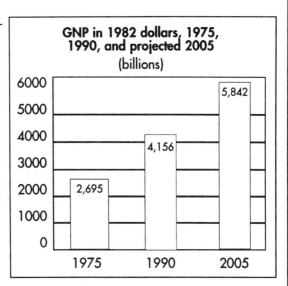

GNP in 1982 dollars, 1975, 1990, and projected 2005 (billions)

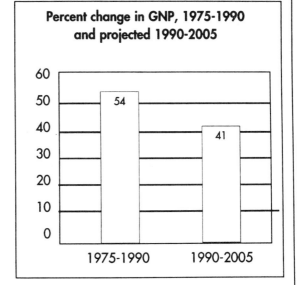

Percent change in GNP, 1975-1990 and projected 1990-2005

Source: Bureau of Labor Statistics

Employment

Employment will continue to shift from the goods-producing to the service-producing sector of the economy.

Within the goods-producing sector, agriculture and construction will increase and offset the decline in manufacturing and mining. All service sectors will increase, but most of the growth will be in two industry divisions—services and retail trade.

Non-farm wage and salary worker employment, projected 1975-2005
(millions)

Total

Service-producing sector

Goods-producing sector

1975 1980 1985 1990 1995 2000 2005

Employment by industry, 1975, 1990, and projected 2005
(millions)

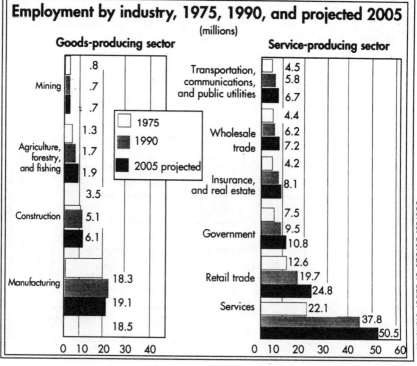

Goods-producing sector

Mining
- .8
- .7
- .7

1975
1990
2005 projected

Agriculture, forestry, and fishing
- 1.3
- 1.7
- 1.9

Construction
- 3.5
- 5.1
- 6.1

Manufacturing
- 18.3
- 19.1
- 18.5

0 10 20 30 40

Service-producing sector

Transportation, communications, and public utilities
- 4.5
- 5.8
- 6.7

Wholesale trade
- 4.4
- 6.2
- 7.2

Insurance, and real estate
- 4.2
- 8.1

Government
- 7.5
- 9.5
- 10.8

Retail trade
- 12.6
- 19.7
- 24.8

Services
- 22.1
- 37.8
- 50.5

0 10 20 30 40 50 60

Source: Bureau of Labor Statistics

Earnings by education and occupation

Education is important in getting higher paying jobs; people with more education have higher earnings within virtually all occupations.

In each occupational group, average earnings are higher at each higher level of education.

Annual earnings of workers by highest level of educational attainment, 1987

Occupation group	Total	Less than high school	High school	1 to 3 years of college	4 years of college and more
Average, all occupations	$21,543	$15,249	$18,902	$21,975	$31,029
Managerial	30,264	22,306	23,286	27,255	37,252
Professional speciality	30,116	19,177	23,233	27,485	31,311
Technicians	24,489	16,207	21,358	23,830	28,004
Marketing and sales	22,220	13,746	17,654	22,546	32,747
Administrative support	17,120	15,535	16,554	17,491	20,823
Service	13,443	10,764	13,093	16,937	21,381
Precision production	24,856	20,465	25,140	27,042	30,938
Operators	18,132	15,365	19,303	21,627	22,114
Agriculture-related	11,781	10,571	12,730	16,331	17,130

Source: Bureau of Labor Statistics

Labor Force Entrants

By sex, race, and Hispanic origin, 1990-2005

Hispanic entrants will number 8.7 million and account for 15.7 percent of all entrants. Asians, despite rapid growth, will only account for 6 percent of all entrants. Blacks, 13 percent of the total, will account for 7.2 million entrants, fewer than the number of Hispanic entrants.

Distribution of entrants to the labor force by sex, race, and Hispanic origin, projected 1990-2005 (percent)

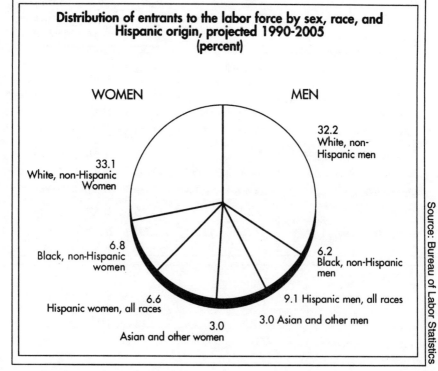

WOMEN

MEN

32.2
White, non-Hispanic men

33.1
White, non-Hispanic Women

6.8
Black, non-Hispanic women

6.2
Black, non-Hispanic men

6.6
Hispanic women, all races

9.1 Hispanic men, all races

3.0
Asian and other women

3.0 Asian and other men

Source: Bureau of Labor Statistics

Race and Hispanic origin

Blacks, Hispanics, Asians and others will continue to increase in numbers faster than the average growth of the labor force as a whole.

Hispanics and Asians and others races[1] will grow faster than other groups. For Asians and others, this is primarily due to immigration. The number of Hispanics will increase because of immigration and a higher historic birth rate.

Blacks will grow faster than whites because the birth rates for blacks declined more slowly than for whites during the 1970s.

Although minority groups will account for an increasing share of the labor force, the vast majority of workers will continue to be white non-Hispanics.

[1]The Asians and others group includes Asians, Pacific Islanders, American Indians, and Alaskan Natives.

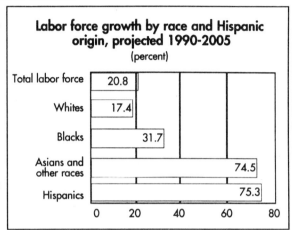

Labor force growth by race and Hispanic origin, projected 1990-2005
(percent)

Total labor force	20.8
Whites	17.4
Blacks	31.7
Asians and other races	74.5
Hispanics	75.3

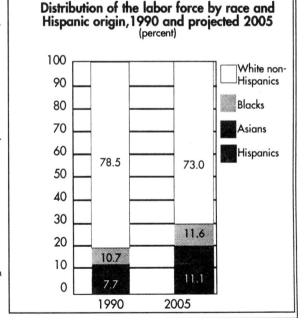

Distribution of the labor force by race and Hispanic origin, 1990 and projected 2005
(percent)

Legend: White non-Hispanics; Blacks; Asians; Hispanics

1990: 78.5, 10.7, 7.7
2005: 73.0, 11.6, 11.1

Source: Bureau of Labor Statistics

Sex

Women will continue to increase their share of the labor force through 2005.

The number of women in the labor force will continue to increase faster than the number of men as labor force participation rates for women increase, especially in the 35-44 year age group, and those for men decrease. However, the rate of increase will be slower over the 1990–2005 period than during the past 15 years as the rates for women approach those of men.

The labor force participation rate of women rose steeply during the 1960s and 1970s and now approaches that of men. The rate will continue to rise, though more slowly, while the rate for men declines.

During the past two decades, the labor force participation rate of women born during any 10-year period has generally been higher than that for women born in the previous 10-year period. The differences have gotten smaller, however, as shown by the rates for women age 25 to 34.

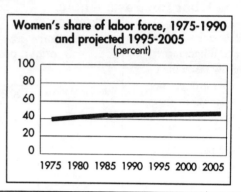

Women's share of labor force, 1975-1990 and projected 1995-2005
(percent)

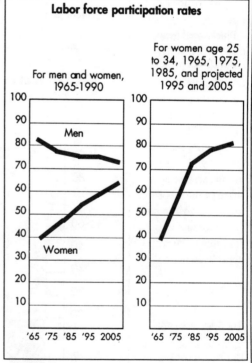

Labor force participation rates

For men and women, 1965-1990

For women age 25 to 34, 1965, 1975, 1985, and projected 1995 and 2005

Source: Bureau of Labor Statistics

Major occupational groups

On average, job growth will be faster in occupational groups requiring the most education.

Managerial, professional, and technician occupations have the highest proportion of workers with 4 years of college or 1-3 years of college; these occupations will grow faster than average. In contrast, precision production, operators, and agriculture occupations have the lowest proportion of workers with college training, and these occupations are projected to have the slowest employment growth.

Nevertheless, jobs will be available at all levels of education because of the large size of the occupation groups requiring less than college training and the need to replace workers who will leave their jobs from 1990 to 2005.

Projected occupational growth, 1990-2005, and distribution by educational attainment, 1990
(percent)

Occupational group	Projected change, 1990-2005	Educational attainment of workers,1990[1]			
		Less than high school	High school	1 to 3 years of college	4 years of college and more
All occupations	20	15	39	22	24
Managerial	27	4	27	24	45
Professional specialty	32	1	8	16	74
Technicians	37	3	28	37	33
Marketing and sales	24	12	39	25	24
Administrative support	13	6	51	31	13
Services	29	28	45	19	6
Precision production	13	21	53	20	6
Operators	4	31	52	13	3
Agriculture-related	5	35	41	14	8

Job openings by major occupational group, projected 1990-2005
(thousands)

Occupational group	Job openings due to replacement needs	Job openings due to employment increases	Total job openings
All occupations	38,851	26,892	65,743
Managerial	3,085	3,414	6,499
Professional specialty	4,281	5,107	9,388
Technicians	1,200	1,551	2,751
Marketing and sales	5,379	3,401	8,780
Administrative support	6,413	3,309	9,722
Service	7,403	5,830	13,233
Precision production	4,764	2,068	6,832
Operators	5,449	1,734	7,183
Agriculture-related	863	477	1,340

[1]Rows may not sum to 100 because of rounding.

Source: Bureau of Labor Statistics

Occupations gaining large numbers of jobs

Among the 500 occupations for which projections were developed, 30 will account for half of total employment growth over the 1990-2005 period.

Occupations with the largest numerical increases, projected 1990-2005
(thousands)

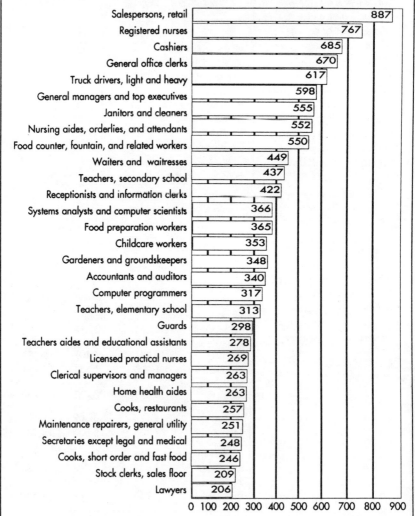

Salespersons, retail	887
Registered nurses	767
Cashiers	685
General office clerks	670
Truck drivers, light and heavy	617
General managers and top executives	598
Janitors and cleaners	555
Nursing aides, orderlies, and attendants	552
Food counter, fountain, and related workers	550
Waiters and waitresses	449
Teachers, secondary school	437
Receptionists and information clerks	422
Systems analysts and computer scientists	366
Food preparation workers	365
Childcare workers	353
Gardeners and groundskeepers	348
Accountants and auditors	340
Computer programmers	317
Teachers, elementary school	313
Guards	298
Teachers aides and educational assistants	278
Licensed practical nurses	269
Clerical supervisors and managers	263
Home health aides	263
Cooks, restaurants	257
Maintenance repairers, general utility	251
Secretaries except legal and medical	248
Cooks, short order and fast food	246
Stock clerks, sales floor	209
Lawyers	206

0 100 200 300 400 500 600 700 800 900

Source: Bureau of Labor Statistics

Fastest growing occupations

Growth of half of the 30 fastest increasing occupations stems from the demand for health services. Half of the fastest growing occupations are professional and technical occupations that require significant post-secondary education.

Fastest growing occupations, projected 1990-2005
(percent)

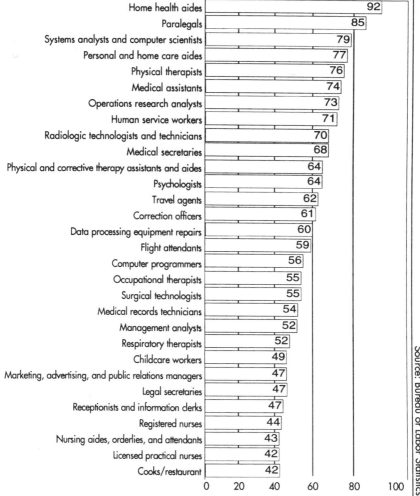

Home health aides — 92
Paralegals — 85
Systems analysts and computer scientists — 79
Personal and home care aides — 77
Physical therapists — 76
Medical assistants — 74
Operations research analysts — 73
Human service workers — 71
Radiologic technologists and technicians — 70
Medical secretaries — 68
Physical and corrective therapy assistants and aides — 64
Psychologists — 64
Travel agents — 62
Correction officers — 61
Data processing equipment repairs — 60
Flight attendants — 59
Computer programmers — 56
Occupational therapists — 55
Surgical technologists — 55
Medical records technicians — 54
Management analysts — 52
Respiratory therapists — 52
Childcare workers — 49
Marketing, advertising, and public relations managers — 47
Legal secretaries — 47
Receptionists and information clerks — 47
Registered nurses — 44
Nursing aides, orderlies, and attendants — 43
Licensed practical nurses — 42
Cooks/restaurant — 42

0   20   40   60   80   100

Source: Bureau of Labor Statistics

Declining Occupations

Occupations with the greatest declines in employment are concentrated in declining industries or affected by technological change. Some occupations are affected by both factors. About half the declining occupations are concentrated in manufacturing.

Occupations with the greatest declines, projected 1990-2005

(thousands)

224	Farmers
133	Bookkeeping, accounting, and auditing clerks
124	Childcare workers, private household
116	Sewing machine operators, garment
105	Electrical and electronic assemblers
103	Typists and word processors
101	Cleaners and servants, private household
92	Farm workers
81	Electrical and electronic equipment assembler
61	Textile draw-out and winding machine operators
57	Switchboard operators
43	Machine forming operators
42	Machine tool cutting operators
40	Telephone and cable TV line installers and repairers
34	Central office and PBX installers and repairers
31	Central office operators
31	Statistical clerks
27	Packaging and filling machine operators
26	Station installers and repairers, telephone
25	Bank tellers
20	Lathe turning machine tool setters
-19	Grinders and polishers, hand
-18	Electromechanical equipment assemblers
-18	Grinding machine setters
-17	Service station attendants
-16	Directory assistance operators
-14	Butchers and meatcutters
-14	Chemical equipment controllers
-13	Drilling and boring machine tool setters
-12	Meter readers, utilities

Axis: -250 -200 -150 -100 -50 0

Source: Bureau of Labor Statistics

Occupations requiring a bachelor's degree

Of the 20 fastest growing occupations requiring a bachelor's degree or more education, the top seven are tied to the health service industry or computer technology.

Fastest growing occupations requiring a college degree or more education, projected 1990-2005
(percent)

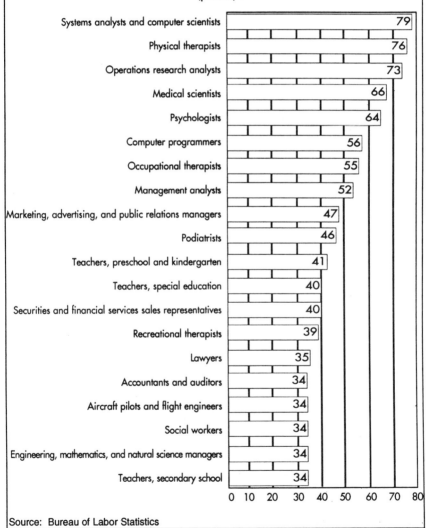

Occupation	Percent
Systems analysts and computer scientists	79
Physical therapists	76
Operations research analysts	73
Medical scientists	66
Psychologists	64
Computer programmers	56
Occupational therapists	55
Management analysts	52
Marketing, advertising, and public relations managers	47
Podiatrists	46
Teachers, preschool and kindergarten	41
Teachers, special education	40
Securities and financial services sales representatives	40
Recreational therapists	39
Lawyers	35
Accountants and auditors	34
Aircraft pilots and flight engineers	34
Social workers	34
Engineering, mathematics, and natural science managers	34
Teachers, secondary school	34

Source: Bureau of Labor Statistics

Occupations requiring high school education or less

Service occupations account for nearly half of the 20
fastest growing occupations requiring a high school
graduation or less education; these jobs often require
some on-the-job training.

**Fastest growing occupations requiring a high school diploma
or less education projected 1990-2005
(percent)**

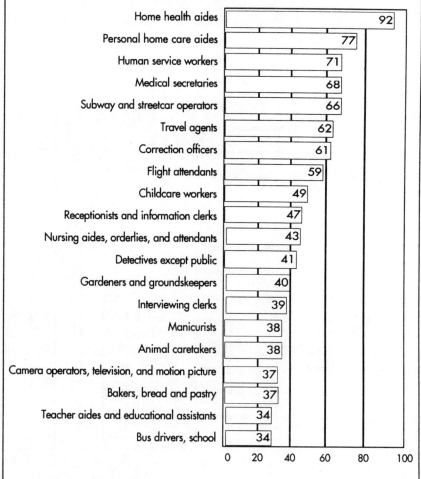

Occupation	Percent
Home health aides	92
Personal home care aides	77
Human service workers	71
Medical secretaries	68
Subway and streetcar operators	66
Travel agents	62
Correction officers	61
Flight attendants	59
Childcare workers	49
Receptionists and information clerks	47
Nursing aides, orderlies, and attendants	43
Detectives except public	41
Gardeners and groundskeepers	40
Interviewing clerks	39
Manicurists	38
Animal caretakers	38
Camera operators, television, and motion picture	37
Bakers, bread and pastry	37
Teacher aides and educational assistants	34
Bus drivers, school	34

Source: Bureau of Labor Statistics

VIII

Your Easy Reference Source for Mentoring, Networking, and Career Opportunities

Planning your career strategy for the future can be a major challenge if you do not have access to pertinent socioeconomic data that indicate the important national trends and developments. Domestic and international issues, for example, that ultimately influence the thinking of our legislators, government officials, and business leaders can escape your attention if you do not carefully monitor the socioeconomic pulse of the nation.

Fortunately, most of the information that you will need to plan, effectively, your career strategy can be obtained from personal research efforts and for little or no cost at all. The secret, however, is in knowing where to find this information, taking the time and effort to get the information, and putting it in a useful form.

Places like the Department of Commerce, Bureau of Labor Statistics, local Chambers of Commerce, and the public library (business division) are just a few of the many resources to obtain reliable information.

Why not begin your data collection efforts now? It could be one of the most important steps that you will ever take in planning your career strategy for the future.

Directories

American Manufacturers Directory 120,000 manufacturers with twenty-five-plus employees organized in three sections:
Alphabetical by company name
Alphabetical by SIC code
Alphabetical by City
American Business Directories, 5711 South 86th Circle, PO Box 27347, Omaha, Nebraska 68127. Copyright 1992.

America's Top-Rated Cities Statistical handbook includes statistical information and other data in one easy-to-use source—with helpful tables and charts—on the U.S. cities that have been cited in various magazine surveys as being the best places for business and living opportunities.
Volume I (Southern Region)
Volume II (Western Region)
Volume III (Central Region)
Volume IV (Eastern Region)
Volume V (Northeastern Region)
Edited by Rhoda Garoogian. Universal Reference Publications, 1355 W. Palmetto Park Rd., Suite 315, Boca Raton, FL 33486. Copyright 1992.

Black Americans Information Directory, 1990, 1991 A guide to over 4,500 organizations, agencies, institutions, programs, and publications concerned with Black American life and culture. Gale Research, Inc., 835 Penobscot Building, Detroit, MI 48226-4094. Copyright 1990.

Career Opportunities in the Music Industry—Second Edition Details on salaries, skill requirements, advancements, prospects, labor unions, and other things. Facts On File, Inc., 460 Park Avenue South, New York, NY 10016. Copyright 1990 by Shelly Field.

Careers in Medicine (Traditional and Alternative)—Revised Edition This volume has been prepared primarily for college juniors who are considering applying to medical school. The contents will also be valuable to medical students attempting to identify an appropriate specialty, as well as physicians in practice who wish to explore non-clinical positions for their training skills. Edited by T. Donald Rucker, Ph.D. and Martin D. Keller, MD, Ph.D. Garrett Park Press, Garrett Park, MD 20896. Copyright 1990.

Consumer Guide: Best-Rated Retirement Cities and Towns One hundred of the most attractive retirement locations across America. If you are planning to retire soon, you may be wondering which of the "Sunbelt's" 100 most popular retirement cities would be best for you. Publications International, Ltd., 7373 N. Cicero Avenue, Lincolnwood, IL 60646. Copyright 1988.

Directory of Public Interest Legal Internships, 1991–1992 Public interest internships provide committed students with the opportunity to put recently acquired skills to the test, while, at the same time, helping people in need and advancing worthy social causes. The directory offers information on more than one hundred fifty organizations. It includes perspectives from employers and students. The National Association for Public Interest Law, 1118 22nd Street NW, Washington, DC 20037. Copyright 1991.

Encyclopedia of Associations, 1992 (National Organizations of the United States) Copyright 1991.
Volume 1, Part 1: Trade, Business, and Commercial Organizations
  • Environmental and agricultural organizations
  • Legal, governmental, public administration and military organizations
  • Engineering, technological, and national and social science organizations
  • Educational organizations
  • Cultural organizations
Volume 1, Part 2: Social Welfare Organizations
  • Health and medical organizations

- Public affairs organizations
- Fraternal, foreign interest, nationality, and ethnic organizations
- Religious organizations
- Veteran, hereditary, and patriotic
- Hobby and avocational organizations
- Athletic and sports organizations
- Labor unions, associations, and federations
- Chambers of commerce and trade and tourism organizations
- Greek and Non-Greek letter societies, associations, and federations
- Fan clubs

Volume 1, Part 3: Name and Keyword Index
- Alphabetical index to organization names and keywords

The (Florida) Job Bank, 1992 Annual updated guide to finding a career in the Sunshine State. When considering employment elsewhere, review *Job Bank, 1992* for the cities and states that interest you.

The Atlanta Job Bank
The Boston Job Bank
The Chicago Job Bank
The Dallas–Ft. Worth Job Bank
The Denver Job Bank
The Detroit Job Bank
The Houston Job Bank
The Los Angeles Job Bank
The Minneapolis–St. Paul Job Bank
The New York Job Bank
The Ohio Job Bank
The Philadelphia Job Bank
The Phoenix Job Bank
The St. Louis Job Bank
The San Francisco Job Bank
The Seattle Job Bank
The Washington Job Bank

Bob Adams, Inc., 260 Center Street, Halbrook, MA 02343. Copyright 1992.

Hispanic Americans Information Directory, 1990, 1991 A guide to over 4,500 organizations, agencies, institutions, programs, and publications concerned with Hispanic American life and culture. Edited by Darren L. Smith, Associate Editor Donna L. Weyd. Gale Research, Inc., 835 Penobscot Building, Detroit, MI 4822-4094.

How To Get A Job In the New York Metro Area Each how-to book gives you 1,500 or more major employers, numbers to call, and people to contact. Other publications include: *How To Get A Job In* . . . Atlanta; Boston; Chicago; Dallas/Ft. Worth; Europe; Houston; The Pacific Rim; San Francisco; Seattle/Portland; Southern California; Washington, DC. Edited by Thomas M. Camden and Susan Fleming-Holland. Surrey Books, 230 East Ohio Street, Suite 120, Chicago, IL 60611.

International Internships and Volunteer Programs This book provides application procedures and program descriptions for organizations that sponsor internship and volunteer opportunities of international scope including: Businesses; non-profits; religious organizations; international institutions; government agencies. Edited by Will Cantrell and Francine Modderno. Distributed by Worldwise Books. Copyright 1992.

Internships, 1994—Fourteenth Edition Over 30,000 on-the-job training opportunities for today's job market. Complete listings tell you how to: get your foot in the door; gain valuable experience; and achieve your career objective. This book is a comprehensive directory of internship opportunities across the United States and abroad. Peterson's Guides. PO Box 2123, Princeton, NJ 08543-2123. Copyright 1993.

Internships (Volume 1)
Advertising, Marketing, Public Relations, and Sales Thousands of internships at hundreds of major advertising and public relations agencies, research firms, corporations, and associations throughout the United States and Canada. Edited by Ronald W. Fry. The Career Press, 62 Beverly Rd., PO Box 34, Hawthorne, NJ 07507. Copyright 1990.

Internships (Volume 2)

Newspapers, Magazines, and Book Publishing Thousands of internships at hundreds of major newspapers, magazines, and book publishers throughout the United States and Canada. Edited by Ronald W. Fry. The Career Press, 62 Beverly Rd., PO Box 34, Hawthorne, NJ 07507. Copyright 1990.

Internships (Volume 3)

Accounting, Banking, Brokerage, Finance, and Insurance Thousands of internships at hundreds of major accounting, brokerage and investment banking firms, banks, insurance companies, and a broad range of major corporations nationwide. Edited by Ronald W. Fry. The Career Press, 62 Beverly Rd., PO Box 34, Hawthorne, NJ 07507. Copyright 1989.

Internships (Volume 4)

The Travel and Hospitality Industries Thousands of internships at hundreds of major airlines, cruise lines, hotels and resorts, travel agencies, convention and visitors bureaus, tourist boards, car rental companies, and attractions nationwide. Edited by Ronald W. Fry. The Career Press, 62 Beverly Rd., PO Box 34, Hawthorne, NJ 07507. Copyright 1989.

Internships (Volume 5)

Radio and Television, Broadcasting and Production Thousands of internships at hundreds of radio and television stations throughout the United States and Canada. Edited by Ronald W. Fry. The Career Press, 62 Beverly Rd., PO Box 34, Hawthorne, NJ 07507. Copyright 1991.

Job Seeker's Guide to Private and Public Companies Detailed profiles on more than 15,000 U.S. companies, containing information critical to job seekers. Quick and easy access by geographic arrangement and company name and industry indexes. Edited by Charity Anne Dorgan and Jennifer Mast. Gale Research, Inc., 835 Penobscot Building, Detroit, MI, 48226-4094. Copyright 1992.

Jobs in Paradise A listing of more than 200,000 jobs in the U.S., Canada, South Pacific, and Caribbean. This book concentrates on jobs in great locations. A good resource for college students, part-timers, and adults of almost any age. Edited by Jeffery Maltzman. Perennial Library, HarperCollins, 10 East 53rd Street, New York, NY 10022. Copyright 1990.

Life In America's Small Cities This book provides the most up-to-date information available on the two hundred nineteen U.S. "Micropolitan" areas—cities with 15,000 to 50,000 residents within its limits and in the surrounding territories. Includes: climate; diversions; economics; education; environment; health care; housing; public safety; sophistication; transportation. Edited by G. Scott Thomas. Prometheus Books, 700 East Amherst Street, Buffalo, New York 14215. Copyright 1990.

National Directory of Arts Internships Over nine hundred host organizations offering more than 2,100 internship experience opportunities for art careers in arts management, dance, theatre, music, literature, art/design, film/video, photography, performing arts design technology, and interdisciplinary art fields. Edited by Warren Christensen, president, NNAP. The National Network for Artist Placement, NNAP, 935 West Ave 37, Los Angeles, CA 90065. Copyright 1991.

The National Directory of Internships TNDI is a source of internship data and information for students. They can find specific internships or seek to create one on their own by knowing what type of organization they are looking for. Edited by Amy S. Butterworth and Sally A. Migliore. National Society for Internships and Experiential Education, 3509 Haworth Drive, Suite 207, Raleigh, North Carolina. Copyright 1989.

National Directory of Minority-Owned Business Firms The information in this directory was compiled by the staff of Business Research Services, Inc., for the use of subscribers. Listings were edited from data received from federal and state governments. Business Research Services, Inc., 4201 Connecticut Ave., NW, Suite 610, Washington, DC 20008. Copyright 1992.

The National Job Bank, 1992: A Comprehensive Guide to Major Employers In the United States. Managing Editor Carter

Smith. Bob Adams, Inc., 260 Center Street, Halbrook, MA 02343. Copyright 1992.

New Careers: A Directory of Jobs and Internships In Technology and Society—Third Edition Provides a wide range of opportunities, which include employment information with state and federal governments—opportunities in over thirty states across the country. Edited by Rachel Helfand. Student Pugwash USA, 1638 R. Street, NW, Suite 32, Washington, DC 20009. Copyright 1990.

1991 Non-Profit Employer Directory This directory includes contact people and names and addresses of employers and their phone numbers. Access: Networking in the Public Interest. Copyright 1991.

The 100 Best Small Towns In America A national guide to the best in small-town living. Edited by Norman Crampton. Prentice Hall, 15 Columbus Circle, New York, NY 10023. Copyright 1993.

The Only Retirement Guide You'll Ever Need A step-by-step approach to retirement planning. Poseidon Press, Simon & Schuster, 1230 Avenue of the Americas, New York, NY 10020. Copyright 1991.

Standard Directory of Advertisers: (Guide to 25,000 Corporations) National Register Publishing Company, 3004 Glenview Rd., Wilmette, IL 60091. Copyright 1992.

Where to Look for Information, Referrals, and Placement Services

The College Campus

• Job openings listed in the campus placement office are a good source for leads if you get to the postings early.
• College recruiters from the public and private sectors are

paid to develop a working relationship with the campus placement officer and his or her staff. Volunteer work at the placement office over a period of time should produce favorable networking results for interested students.

• The campus alumni office can provide unlimited alumni networking possibilities. Don't be afraid to volunteer your services when you can, and build friendships with the staff.

• College professors and administrators can provide career counselling and networking opportunities for job seekers.

• Classmates can also provide job referrals and networking opportunities, particularly when their parents and relatives are well established professionally or socially.

Public Resources

• The United States Employment Service has over 2,500 offices around the country and provides counselling and job referral services for professional and non-professional people at no cost to the applicant.

• The State Employment Service has offices located in various cities throughout each state. Professional and non-professional job referrals and counselling is available at no cost to the applicant.

Private Resources

• Private employment agencies number in the thousands throughout the United States. They provide job placement and counselling of professional and non-professional workers. The fee arrangements for private employment agency services will vary from city-to-city and state-to-state. Job seekers who utilize the private agencies will find that some employers pay the agency fee and some do not. If the employer doesn't pay the agency fee, the job seeker can expect to pay the fee out of his or her weekly or monthly earnings.

• When doing business with a private employment agency, it is important to read the employment contract carefully and make sure that the agency you are doing business with is obligated to find you a job before you are obligated to pay them a fee for service.

Your Community As a Job Resource

• Don't underestimate the power of your local religious leaders and political leaders. Corporations and public agencies often communicate with them to reinforce their corporate image and solicit public support on a variety of issues.

• Family doctors, lawyers, and accountants may also have strong contacts in the public and private sector. For example, many serve on the board of non-profit agencies and serve as counsel to public and private organizations.

Magazines

The Black Collegian
New York, NY

Black Enterprise
New York, NY

The Black Scholar
Oakland, CA

Business Week
New York, NY

Ebony
Chicago, IL

Emerge
Arlington, VA

Essence
New York, NY

Fortune
New York, New York

Jet
Chicago, IL

National Black Monitor
(editorial supplement to
newspapers)

Temas
New York, NY

Tiempo Latino
San Francisco, CA

Working Woman
New York, NY

Newspapers (Fifty Leading U.S. Markets)

These newspapers are recommended for news and information relative to:

• National and Worldwide News
• Real Estate Information
• General Current Events

• Business News and Information
• Job Opportunities Information

Albany-Schenectady-Troy
   Times-Union
Atlanta
   Constitution
   Journal
Baltimore
   Sun
Birmingham
   News
   Post-Herald
Boston
   Globe
Buffalo
   News
Charleston-Huntington
   Gazette
   Mail
Charlotte
   Observer
Chicago
   Sun-Times
   Tribune
Cincinnati
   Enquirer
   Post
Cleveland
   Plain Dealer
Columbus
   Dispatch
Dallas
   Dallas Times-Herald
   Ft. Worth-Dallas News
Denver
   Rocky Mountain News
Detroit
   News
Grand Rapids-Kalamazoo
   Grand Rapids Press
   Kalamazoo Gazette
Greenboro-Winston-Salem
   News & Record
Greenville-Spar-Ash.-News-P.

Harrisburg-York
   Intel. Journal
   New Era
   News
   Patriot
Hartford-New Haven
   Hartford Courant
   New Haven Register
Houston
   Chronicle
   Post
Indianapoli
   Star, News
Kansas City
   Star
   Times
Los Angeles
   Los Angeles Times
Louisville
   Courier Journal
   Times
Memphis
   Commercial Appeal
Miami
   Herald
   News
Milwaukee
   Journal
   Sentinel
Minneapolis-St. Paul
   Minneapolis Star & Tribune
Nashville
   Tennessean Banner
New Orleans
   Times Picayune
New York City
   Daily News
   The New York Times
   Wall Street Journal
Norfolk-Newport News
   Ledger
   Star
   Virginian Pilot

Oklahoma City
   Oklahoman
Orlando-Daytona Beach
   Orlando Sentinel
Philadelphia
   Daily News
   Philadelphia Inquirer
Phoenix
   Gazette
   Republic
Pittsburgh
   Gazette
   Post
   Press
Portland
   Oregonian
Providence
   Bulletin
   Journal
Raleigh-Durham
   Raleigh News & Observer
   Times
Sacramento-Stockton
   Sacramento Bee
   Sacramento Union

Salt Lake City
   Deseret News
   Tribune
San Diego
   Tribune
   Union
San Francisco
   Chronicle
   Examiner
San Antonio
   Express News
   Light
Seattle-Tacoma
   Seattle Post Intelligencer
   Seattle Times
St. Louis
   Post-Dispatch
Tampa-St. Petersburg
   St. Petersburg Times
   Tampa Tribune
Washington
   Post

Black Oriented Newspapers I.*

Alabama
   Eutaw Green County Democrat
   Montgomery/Tuskegee Times
Arkansas
   Little Rock State Press
California
   Bakersfield Metro Star
   Fresno California Advocate
   Los Angeles TV Journal & News
      Magazine
   San Francisco New Bayview
      News

Connecticut
   Hartford North End Agent's
Florida
   Fort Myers Community Voice
   Fort Pierce Chronicle
   Jacksonville Advocate
   Jacksonville N.E. Free Press
   Tallahassee/Ocala N.E. Florida
      Group
   Tampa Dollar Stretcher
   West Palm Beach Florida Photo
      News

*For information on this group of newspapers, contact Black Resources, Inc., New York, NY.

Georgia
  Augusta Black Focus
  Columbus Times
  Cordele Southeastern News

Illinois
  E. St. Louis Monitor
  Tri-City Journal
  Voice Group:
    Bloomington Voice
    Decateur Voice
    Peoria Voice of the Valley
    Springfield Voice

Indiana
  Fort Wayne Frost Illustrated
  Indianapolis Indiana Herald

Louisiana
  Oklahoma City Ebony Tribune

Maryland
  Baltimore Times

Michigan
  Detroit/Escorse Telegram
  Grand Rapids Times
  Jackson Blazer

Missouri
  St. Louis Crusader

Nevada
  Las Vegas Sentinel

New Jersey
  New Jersey Greater News

New York
  Buffalo Criterion
  Buffalo Fine Print

Ohio
  The Akron-Cleveland Reporter

Oklahoma
  Oklahoma City Ebony Tribune

Pennsylvania
  Pittsburgh News

Rhode Island
  The Providence American

South Carolina
  Charleston Coastal Times
  Columbia Palmetto Post

Orangeburg View South News
The South Carolinian Group:
  The Aiken South Carolinian
  The Anderson South
    Carolinian
  The Charleston South
    Carolinian
  The Columbia South
    Carolinian
  The Darlington South
    Carolinian
  The Fairfield South
    Carolinian
  The Florence South
    Carolinian
  The Georgetown South
    Carolinian
  The Greenville South
    Carolinian
  The Myrtle Beach South
    Carolinian
  The Orangeburg South
    Carolinian
  The Rock Hill South
    Carolinian
  The Spartanburg South
    Carolinian
  The Sumter South
    Carolinian
The Carolina Tribune Group:
  Aiken Tribune
  Charleston Tribune
  Chester Tribune
  Columbia Tribune
  Fairfield Tribune
  Florence Tribune
  Greenville Tribune
  Myrtle Beach Tribune
  Orangeburg Tribune
  Rock Hill Tribune
  Spartanburg Tribune
  Sumter Tribune

Tennessee
  Chattanooga News Weekly
  Memphis Mid-South Express

Texas
  Houston Sun
  Lubbock Southwest Digest
  Tyler Smith County Herald

Virginia
    (Bowling Green) Caroline
        Times-Post
    Portsmouth Citizens Press
    American Newspaper
    Richmond Voice

Washington, DC
    Washington Informer
    Washington New Observer

Washington
    Seattle/Tacoma Facts

Black Oriented Newspapers II.*

Alabama
    Birmingham World
    Mobile Beacon & Alabama Citizen

California
    El Mundo
    Los Angeles Sentinel
    Post Newspaper Group:
        Berkeley Tri-City Post
        Oakland Post
        Richmond Post
        San Francisco Post
    Reporter Publications:
        Berkeley Metro Reporter
        California Voice (Oakland)
        Oakland Metro Reporter
        Peninsula Metro Reporter
            (San Jose)
        Richmond Metro Reporter
        San Francisco Metro
            Reporter
        San Joaquin Metro Reporter
        Sun Reporter
            (San Francisco)
        Vallejo Metro Reporter

Florida
    Daytona Times
    Florida Courier (Fort Pierce)
    Florida Sentinel Bulletin (Tampa)
    Florida Star (Jacksonville)
    Miami Times
    Westside Gazette (Ft.
        Lauderdale)

Georgia
    Atlanta Daily World
    Metro County Courier (Augusta)

Illinois
    Chicago Crusader

Indiana
    Gary Crusader
    Indianapolis Recorder

Kentucky
    Louisville Defender

Louisiana
    Alexandria News Weekly
    Baton Rouge Weekly Press
    Louisiana Weekly (New Orleans)
    Shreveport Sun

Maryland
    Baltimore Afro-American

Massachusetts
    Bay State Banner (Boston)

Michigan
    Michigan Chronicle
        (Detroit/Pontiac)

Minnesota
    Minneapolis Spokesman
    St. Paul Recorder

Missouri
    Kansas City Call
    St. Louis American
    St. Louis Argus
    St. Louis Sentinel

*For information on this group of newspapers, contact the Amalgamated Publishers, Inc.,
New York, NY.

New Jersey
  City News (Newark)

New York
  Amsterdam News (New York)
  Buffalo Challenger
  New York Beacon
  Westchester County Press

North Carolina
  Carolina Times (Durham)
  Carolinian (Raleigh)
  Charlotte Post
  Wilmington Journal
  Winston-Salem Chronicle

Ohio
  Cincinnati Call & Post
  Cincinnati Herald
  Cleveland Call & Post
  Columbus Call & Post

Oklahoma
  Black Chronicle (Oklahoma City)

Pennsylvania
  Philadelphia Tribune Group
  Pittsburgh Courier Group

Tennessee
  Tri-State Defender

Texas
  Dallas Examiner
  Forward Times Group (Houston)
  Houston Informer & Texas
    Freeman Group
  Post Tribune (Dallas)
  San Antonio Register
  Texas Times (Dallas, Fort Worth)

Virginia
  Norfolk Journal & Guide Group
  Richmond Afro-American
  Richmond Voice
  Roanoke Tribune

Washington, DC
  Washington Afro-American

West Virginia
  West Virginia Beacon Digest

Wisconsin
  Milwaukee Community Journal
  Milwaukee Courier
  Milwaukee Star

Black Oriented Newspapers III.*

Alabama
  Inner City News (Mobile)
  The New Times (Mobile)
  Speakin' Out News (Huntsville)

Connecticut
  Inner City News (New
    Haven-Waterbury)

California
  Los Voz Latina (San Jose)
  San Diego Voice & Viewpoint

Washington, DC
  Washington New Observer

Florida
  The Broward Times, Inc.
    (Pompano Beach)

Capital Outlook (Tallahassee)
The Community Voice (Fort
  Myers)
Florida Photo News (West Palm
  Beach)
Jacksonville Advocate
Jacksonville Free Press
New American Press (Pensacola)
Northeast Florida Advocate
  (Jacksonville)
Palm Beach Gazette
Pensacola Voice
The Times-Herald (New Smyrna
  Beach)

Georgia
  Atlanta Tribune
  Atlanta Voice

*For information on this group of newspapers, contact the Amalgamated Publishers, Inc.

Augusta Focus
The Champion (Decatur)
Columbus Times
Georgia Sentinel Bulletin

Illinois
Chicago Westside Journal
Tri-City Journal (Illinois)
The Voice (Decatur)

Indiana
Indiana Herald

Louisiana
The Drum (Ponchatoula)

Maryland
Baltimore Times Group:
The Annapolis Times
(Baltimore)
Baltimore Times
The Shore Times (Baltimore)

Michigan
Blazer News (Jackson)
Ecorse Telegram
Grand Rapids Times

New York
Buffalo Criterion
Hudson Valley Black Press
(Newburgh)
The Network Journal (Brooklyn)

North Carolina
Carolina Peacemaker
The Public Post (Raeford)

Ohio
The Communicator News
(Columbus)

Oklahoma
The Oklahoma Eagle
(Tulsa)

Pennsylvania
Pittsburgh Renaissance News

South Carolina
Charleston Chronicle
Pee Dee Times
South Carolina Media Group:
Black News (Columbia)
Black Post (Sumter)
Black Star (Greensville)
Black Sun (Florence)
Black Times (Charleston)
Black Views (Rock Hill)
Black Voice (Orangeburg)
View South News

Tennessee
Memphis Silver Star
Metro Forum (Jackson)
Nashville Pride

Texas
Houston Newspapers
La Vida News (Fort Worth)

Virginia
Richmond Free Press

Hispanic Newspapers

California
El Hispano
Sacramento

El Mundo
Oakland

La Opinion
Los Angeles

Colorado
La Voz Hispana
De Colorado
Denver

Florida
Diario Las Americas
Miami

Noticias Latinas
Miami

Illinois
El Informado
Chicago

El Manana Daily
Chicago

New Jersey
El Especial
Union City

La Tribuna de North Jersey
Newark

New Mexico
El Hispano
Albuquerque

New Mexico Independent—
The Trader
Santa Fe

Sandoval County
Times-Independent
Bernalillo

New York
El diario/La prensa
New York

Noticias del Mundo
New York

Texas
El Continental
El Paso

El Sol De Texas
Dallas

Hispanic Magazines, Directories, and Periodicals

Adelante
Orlando, FL

Caminos
Los Angeles, CA

Hispanic American Arts
New York, NY

Hispanic Review of Business
New York, NY

Hispanic Times Magazine
Westlake Village, CA

Hispano
Albuquerque, NM

Mexican American Sun
Los Angeles, CA

Noticias de Aztlan
Univ. of Calif.
Los Angeles, CA

Noticias de New York
New York, NY

Noticias Para Los
Californianos
Ripon, CA

Noticias del Serra
Chicago, IL

Spanish Today
Miami, FL

Temas
New York, NY

Tiempo Latino
San Francisco, CA

Westsider
(Chicano Times)
San Antonio, TX

Native American Directories and Periodicals

American Indian Culture and
   Research Journal
Campbell Hall–UCLA
Los Angeles, CA

American Indian Directory 1986
NAES College Press
Chicago, IL

American Indian Historical Society
San Francisco, CA

American Indian Libraries Newsletter
Chicago, IL

American Indian Review
San Francisco, CA

American Indian Society of
   Washington
SE. Washington, DC

Arizona Commission of Indian
   Affairs-Tribal Directory
Phoenix, AZ

Association of Indians in America
   Journal
New York, NY

Career Development
   Opportunities for Native
   Americans
Albuquerque, NM

Cherokee Times
Cherokee, NC

Cherokee One Feather
Cherokee, NC

Cherokee Advocate
Tahlequah, OK

Chickasaw Times
Ada, OK

Navajo Area Newsletter
Rock, AZ

Navajo Times Today
Window Rock, AZ

Asian Directories, Periodicals, and Broadcasting

Amerasia Journal (Articles on Asians
   in America)
University of California
Los Angeles, CA

American Chinese News
S. San Pedro, Los Angeles, CA

Apple Television
New York, NY

Asia Times
Toronto, Canada

Asianadian (Deals with concerns of
   Asian Canadians)
Toronto, ON

Asian Cine Vision
New York, NY

Asian Family Affair
Seattle, WA

Asian Tribune
Toronto, ON

Asian Week
San Francisco, CA

Bridge: Asian American Perspectives
New York, NY

Central News Agency of China
   (Wire Service for Paper in Taiwan
   & U.S.)
New York, NY

Cheng Yen Pao
San Francisco, CA

China Post
New York, NY

China Post Daily
New York, NY

Chinatown News
Vancouver, BC

China Tribune
New York, NY

Chinese American Association of
Greater New York Annual
New York, NY

Chinese American Citizens Alliance
Bulletin
Los Angeles, CA

Chinese American Citizens Alliance
Directory
Los Angeles, CA

Chinese American Progress
Chicago, IL

Chinese American Weekly
New York, NY

Chinese Canadian Bulletin
Vancouver, BC

Chinese Cultural Association Journal
Palo Alto, CA

Chinese Directory and Telephone
Book for Each Province of Canada
Vancouver, BC

Chinese Express Daily News
Toronto, ON

Chinese Intellectual
Rutgers State University
New Brunswick, NJ

Chinese Pacific Weekly
San Francisco, CA

Chinese Times
Vancouver, BC

Chinese Times
San Francisco, CA

Chosun Daily News
New York, NY

Chung Wha Commercial Broadcasting
Co.
New York, NY

Daehan Broadcasting
New York, NY

The Dong-A-Daily News
New York, NY

International Daily News
New York, NY

Japan-America Society Bulletin
Washington, DC

Japan Christian Quarterly
Brisbane, CA

Japan New York (Bi-Monthly
Magazine)
New York, NY

The Joong Ang Daily News
Long Island City, NY

The Korea Herald
New York, NY

Korea Monitor
Vancouver, BC

Korea News
Long Island City, NY

Korea Times
Toronto, ON

New York Nichibei
New York, NY

Nippon Television
New York, NY

OCS News
New York, NY

Overseas Broadcasting
Chinatown Community Television
Network
New York, NY

Peimei News
Long Island City, NY

Sankei Shimbun
New York, NY

Sing Tao Newspaper
New York, NY

Sino Cast Broadcasting
New York, NY

Sino Communications Group
New York, NY

Sino Daily Express
New York, NY

Vietnamese Association Newsletter
Toronto, ON

Viet Nam Hai Ngoai
San Diego, CA

World Journal
New York, NY

Minority Oriented Radio and Television Stations

Alabama
WBIL-AM/FM Radio Tuskegee
Black-oriented programming

WENN-FM and WAGG-AM
Birmingham
AM station is gospel music,
FM station has Black-oriented
programming

WEUP Radio Huntsville
Black-oriented programming

WTQX-AM Radio Selma
Black-oriented programming

WZZA Radio Tuscombia
Black-oriented programming

Arizona
KPHX Radio Phoenix
Spanish programming/
Mexican-American

KXEW Radio Tucson
Spanish Programming/
Mexican-American

Arkansas
KWTD Radio Lonoke
Dunn Broadcasting, Inc.
Black-oriented programming

California
Fuji Telecast and Production Co.
San Francisco
Japanese language TV station,
Channel 26

KACE-FM Radio Los Angeles
Black-oriented programming

KAZA Radio San Jose
Spanish language station

KCTY and KRAY Radio Salinas
Spanish language station

KFOX-FM Radio Redondo Beach
Black-oriented programming

KFTV-Television, Channel 21 Fresno
Spanish language station

KJLH-FM Radio Los Angeles
Black-oriented programming

KLIP Radio Fowler
Black-oriented programming

KMEX, Television, Channel 34
Hollywood
Spanish language station

KOFY Radio Burlingame
Spanish language programming

KRE-AM and KBLX-FM Berkeley
Black-oriented programming

KSTS, Television, Channel 48 San
Jose
Financial news network station and
minority entertainment channel

KGFT and KUTE Radio Los Angeles
Black-oriented programming

XPRS Radio Los Angeles
Spanish language programming

Colorado
KBNO Radio Denver
Spanish language programming

KRMX Radio Pueblo
Spanish language programming

Connecticut
WKND Radio Windsor
Black-oriented programming

WLVH Radio Hartford
Spanish language programming

Washington, DC
WHUR Radio DC
Black-oriented programming

WMJQ Radio DC
Black-oriented programming

WYCB Radio DC
Black-oriented programming

Florida
AMA, 86 Radio Tampa
Spanish language programming

WAMA Radio Tampa
Spanish language programming

WOCN Radio Miami
Spanish language programming

WRHC Radio Miami
Spanish language programming

WRXB Radio St. Petersburg
Black-oriented programming

WTMP-AM Radio Tampa
Black-oriented programming

WZAZ Radio Jacksonville
Black-oriented programming

Georgia
WAOK-AM Radio Atlanta
Black-oriented programming

WIGO Radio Atlanta
Black-oriented programming

WRDW-AM/FM Augusta
Black-oriented programming

WSOK Radio Savannah
Black-oriented programming

Illinois
WESL Radio East St. Louis
Black-oriented programming

WJPC Radio Chicago
Black-oriented programming

Indiana
WLTH-AM Radio Gary
Black-oriented programming

WTLC-FM Radio Indianapolis
Black-oriented programming

Louisiana
KBCE-FM Radio Boyce
Black-oriented programming

WYLD-AM/FM Radio New Orleans
Black-oriented programming

Maryland
WEBB Radio Baltimore
Black-oriented programming

Massachusetts
WILD Radio Boston
Black-oriented programming

Michigan
WCHB-AM Radio Inkster
Black-oriented programming

WGPR Radio and Television
  Stations
Channel 62 Detroit
Black-oriented programming

WJZZ-FM Radio Detroit
Black-oriented programming

WKWM Radio Kentwood
Black-oriented programming serving
  Grand Rapids area

WWWS-FM Radio Saginaw
Black-oriented programming

Minnesota
KXLI Television Minneapolis
General and Black-oriented
  programming

Mississippi
Channel 3 Television Inc. Jackson
General and Black-oriented
  programming

WBAD-FM Radio Jackson
Black-oriented programming

WORV-AM and WJMG-FM Radio
  Hattiesburg
General programming

Missouri
KPRS-FM Radio Kansas City
Black-oriented programming

Nebraska
KBWH-FM Radio Omaha
Black-oriented programming

New Jersey
WNJR Radio Union
(Black-oriented programming)

WXTV, Television Channel 41
Secaucus
Spanish language programming

WUSS-AM Radio Atlantic City
Black-oriented programming

New Mexico
KDCE Radio Espanola
(Spanish language)

KNAT, Television Channel 23
Albuquerque
Spanish language programming

KRDO Radio Roswell
Spanish language

New York
WDKX-FM Rochester
Black-oriented programming

WLIB-AM and WBLS-FM
New York
Black-oriented programming

WUFO Radio Buffalo
Black-oriented programming

WWRL Radio New York
Black-oriented programming

North Carolina
WGIV-AM Radio Charlotte
Black-oriented programming

WLLE-AM Radio Raleigh
Black-oriented programming

Ohio
WBLZ Radio Cincinnati
Black-oriented programming

WCIN-AM Cincinnati
Black-oriented programming

WCKX Radio Columbus
Black-oriented programming

Oklahoma
KPRW-FM Radio Oklahoma City
Black-oriented programming

Pennsylvania
WAMO-FM Radio Pittsburgh
Black-oriented programming

WDAS-AM and FM Radio
Philadelphia
Black-oriented programming

WYIS-AM Radio Phoenixville
Spanish language

South Carolina
WOIC Radio Columbia
Black-oriented programming

WPAL Radio Charleston
Black-oriented programming

WWWZ-FM Radio Charleston
Black-oriented programming

South Dakota
KILI-FM Radio Porcupine
Native American programming

Tennessee
WLOK-AM Radio Memphis
(Black-oriented programming)

WVOL-AM and WQQK-FM Radio
Nashville
Black-oriented programming

Texas
KEDA Radio San Antonio
Spanish language programming

KESS-FM Radio Fort Worth
Spanish language programming

KFHM-AM Radio San Antonio
Spanish language programming

KIRT-AM and KQXX-FM Radio
McAllen
Spanish language programming

KJJT Radio Odessa
Spanish language programming

KLFB Radio Lubbock
Spanish language programming

KLVL-AM Radio Houston
Spanish language programming

KORO, Television Channel 28
Corpus Christi
Spanish language programming

KRGT-FM Radio Austin
Spanish language programming

KWEX, Television Channel 41
San Antonio
Spanish language programming

Virginia
WOWI-FM Radio and WPCE-AM
Radio Norfolk
Black-oriented programming

WPCE-AM Radio Portsmouth
Black-oriented programming

Washington
KKFX Radio and Kfox Radio Seattle
Black-oriented programming

Wisconsin
WAEO-Television Rhinelander
Black-oriented programming

WLUM-FM Radio Elm Grove
(Black-oriented programming)

WNOV Radio Milwaukee
Black-oriented programming

Includes station formats/rhythm and blues and soul

Alabama
WAR(AM) Abbeville
WATV(AM) Birmingham
WRAG(AM) Carrollton
WJLD(AM) Fairfield
WAJO(AM) Marion
WBLX(FM) Mobile
WOOK(AM) Mobile
WXV(AM) Montgomery
WZMG(AM) Opelika
WORJ(FM) Ozark
WTQX(AM) Selma
WOXR(AM) Talladega
WZZA(AM) Tuscumbia
WBIL(AM) Tuskegee
WBIL-FM Tuskegee
WYLS(AM) York

Arizona
KCRI-FM Helena
KCAT(AM) Pine Bluff
KYDE(AM) Pine Bluff
KCLT(FM) West Helena

California
KLIP(AM) Fowler
KJOP(AM) Lemoore

KFJC(FM) Los Altos
KGFJ(AM) Los Angeles
KDAY(AM) Santa Monica

Colorado
KEPC(FM) Colorado Springs

Connecticut
WWCO(AM) Waterbury

Washington, DC
WDJY(FM)
WHUR (FM)
WOL(AM)

Florida
WPDO(AM) Jacksonville
WZAZ(AM) Jacksonville
WWAB(AM) Lakeland
WEDR(FM) Miami
WRBD(AM) Pompano Beach
WIQ(FM) Quincy
WWSD(AM) Quincy
WPGS(AM) Scottsmour
WRXB(AM) St. Petersburg Beach
WANM(AM) Tallahassee

WTMP(AM) Temple Terrace
WOKB(AM) Winter Garden

Georgia
WXAG(AM) Athens
WAOK(AM) Atlanta
WIGO(AM) Atlanta
WYZE(AM) Atlanta
WBAF(AM) Barnesville
WEAM(AM) Columbus
WOKS(AM) Columbus
WXLL(AM) Decatur
WTJH(AM) East Point
WXKO(AM) Fort Valley
WJGA-FM Jackson
WDDC(AM) Macon
WBB(AM) Macon
WFDR(AM) Manchester
WSNT(AM) Sandersville
WEAS(AM) Savannah
WSOK(AM) Savannah
WXRS(AM) Swainsboro
WGOV(AM) Valdosta
WTCO(FM) Vidalia
WAYX(AM) Waycross
WRDW-FM Wrens

Illinois
KATZ-FM Alton
WVON(AM) Cicero
WESL(AM) East St. Louis
WLUV-FM Loves Park
WBMX(AM) Oak Park

Indiana
WLTH(AM) Gary
WGRT(AM) Indianapolis
WDGS(AM) New Albany

Iowa
KOJC(FM) Cedar Rapids
KALA(FM) Davenport
KBBG(FM) Waterloo

Kentucky
WLOU(AM) Louisville

Louisiana
KTRY(AM) Bastrop
KTRY-FM Bastrop

KBCE(FM) Boyce
KGRM(FM) Grambling
KJCB(AM) Lafayette
KQXL-FM New Roads
KVGO(AM) Pineville
KXLA(AM) Rayville
KCIJ(AM) Shreveport
KOKA(AM) Shreveport
KEZM(AM) Sulphur
KZZM(AM) Tallulah

Maryland
WANN(AM) Annapolis
WEAA(FM) Baltimore
WWIN(AM) Baltimore
WJDY(AM) Salisbury

Massachusetts
WUMB-FM Boston
WAIC(FM) Springfield
WSCB(FM) Springfield
WACM(AM) West Springfield
WCUW(FM) Worcester

Michigan
WGPR(FM) Detroit
WJIB(FM) Detroit
WQBH(AM) Detroit
WEHB(FM) Grand Rapids
WHPR(FM) Highland Park
WTHS(FM) Holland
WCHB(AM) Inkster
WKWM(AM) Kentwood

Minnesota
KUMD-FM Duluth

Mississippi
WMGO(AM) Canton
WZFL(AM) Centreville
WAID(FM) Clarksdale
WCLD-FM Cleveland
WACR(AM) Columbus
WACR-FM Columbus
WCBI(AM) Columbus
WYKC(AM) Grenada
WTAM(AM) Gulfport
WORV(AM) Hattiesburg
WKRA-FM Holly Springs
WKXI(AM) Jackson

WOKJ(AM) Jackson
WBAD(FM) Leland
WESY(AM) Leland
WLTD(FM) Lexington
WALT(AM) Meridan
WOIC(AM) Meridan
WPMO(AM) Moss Point
WQBC(AM) Vicksburg
WABO(AM) Waynesboro
WROB(AM) West Point

Missouri
KRC(FM) Cape Girardeau
KPRS(FM) Kansas City
KPRT(AM) Kansas City
KATZ(AM) St. Louis

Nevada
KCEP(FM) Las Vegas

New Jersey
WUSS(AM) Atlantic City
WNJR(AM) Newark

New York
WUFO(AM) Amherst
WSIV(AM) East Syracuse
WLIB(AM) New York
WWRL(AM) New York
WBLS(FM) New York
WRP(FM) Troy

North Carolina
WKXR(AM) Asheboro
WVOE(AM) Chadbourn
WRTP(AM) Chapel Hill
WGIV(AM) Charlotte
WRRZ(AM) Clinton

WWCU(FM) Cullowhee
WDKC(FM) Dunn
WAFR(FM) Durham
WLOE(AM) Eden
WZBO(AM) Edenton
WRVS-FM Elizabeth City
WBLA(AM) Elizabeth Town
WFMO(AM) Fairmont
WFSS(FM) Fayetteville
WIDU(AM) Fayetteville
WHCH(AM) Forest City
WOKN(FM) Goldsboro
WEAL(AM) Greensboro
WOMG(FM) Greensboro
WZMB(FM) Greenville
WWIH(FM) High Point
WRFX(FM) Kannapolis
WRKB(AM) Kannapolis
WELS(AM) Kinston
WKML(FM) Lumberton
WHIP(AM) Mooresville
WDJS(AM) Mount Olive
WRSV(FM) Rocky Mount
WCPS(AM) Tarboro
WARR(AM) Warrenton
WFXI(FM) Washington
WDJB(FM) Windsor
WAAA(AM) Winston Salem
WAIR(AM) Winston Salem
WSMX(AM) Winston Salem

Ohio
WCIN(AM) Cincinnati
WJMO(AM) Cleveland Heights
WWSN(FM) Dayton
WCKX(FM) London
WVOI(AM) Toledo

NETWORKING OPPORTUNITIES
Some Selected Minority Organizations

Selected Native American

Arkansas
American Indian Center
Little Rock

California
American Indian Center (Bay Area)
San Francisco

American Indian Center West
Culver City

American Indian Community Coalition
Los Angeles

Iowa
American Indian Center
Sioux City

Illinois
American Indian Center
Chicago

Maryland
American Indian Center
Baltimore

Minnesota
American Indian Center
St. Paul

New York
American Indian Club of Rochester
Rochester

Ohio
American Indian Center
Akron

American Indian Center
Columbus

American Indian Center
Youngstown

Oklahoma
American Indian Census And
   Statistical Data Project
Oklahoma City

American Indian Center
Oklahoma City

Texas
American Indian Center
Dallas

American Indian Center
Fort Worth

Selected Asian

California
Asian American Bar Association of
   The Greater Bay Area
San Francisco

Asian American Bilingual Center
Berkeley

Asian American Community Mental
   Health Training Center
Los Angeles

Asian American Manufacturer's
   Association
San Francisco

Colorado
Asian American Educational
   Opportunity Program
Boulder

Washington, DC
The Asia Foundation

Asian American Chamber of
   Commerce Association

Asian American Free Labor
   Institute

Asian Benevolent Corporation

Illinois
Asian-American Community Legal
   Aid Clinic

Missouri
Asia Resource Center
St. Louis

New Jersey
Asian American Committee For
   Human Rights
Morristown

Asian American Legal Fund
Morristown

New York
Asia Society
New York

Asian/Pacific American Librarians
   Association
Brooklyn

Asian Speakers Bureau
New York

Selected Hispanic Organizations

American Association for Higher
   Education
Hispanic Caucus
Ypsilanti, MI

American GI Forum of The United
   States
El Paso, TX

Arizona Mexican-American Chamber
   of Commerce
Phoenix, AZ

Asociacion Nacional Pro-Personas
   Mayores
Los Angeles, CA

Aspira of America, Inc.
New York, NY

Association of Hispanic Arts
New York, NY

Association of Mexican American
   Educators
Los Angeles, CA

Bilingual Private Schools Association
Asociacion de Escuelas Privadas
   Bilingues
Miami, FL

Border Economic Council
Alexandria, VA

California Chicano News Media
   Association
Los Angeles, CA

Centor de Informacion Latino
   Americano
Reno, NV

Chicano Correctional Workers
   Association
Gonzales, CA

Chicanos Por La Causa
Phoenix, AZ

Coalition of Cuban Professionals
Miami, FL

Colorado Association for Bilingual
   Bicultural Education
Thornton, CO

Colorado Migrant Council
Henderson, CO

Comision Feminil Mexicana Nacional,
   Inc.
Los Angeles, CA

Committee of the Spanish-Speaking of
   Virginia
Falls Church, VA

Congreso Nacional de Asuntos
   Colegiales
Washington, DC

Congressional Hispanic Caucus
Washington, DC

Congressional Hispanic Caucus
   Institute, Inc.
Washington, DC

Consortium of National Hispanic
   Organizations
Washington, DC

Cuban American Committee
Washington, DC

Cuban American Legal Defense and
   Education Fund
Fort Wayne, IN

Cuban National Planning Council
Miami, FL

D.C. Commission on Latino
Community Development
Washington, DC

Delaware Governor's Council on
Hispanic Affairs
Wilmington, DE

Democratic National Committee
Hispanic Caucus
Washington, DC

Grand Council of Hispanic Societies in
Public Service
New York, NY

Greater Washington Ibero American
Chamber of Commerce
Washington, DC

Hispanic American Construction
Association
Washington, DC

Hispanic Business Alliance
Detroit, MI

Hispanic Chamber of Commerce of
Greater Kansas City
Kansas City, MO

Hispanic Chamber of Commerce of
Michigan, Inc.
Grand Rapids, MI

Hispanic Coalition for a Free Central
America
Washington, DC

Hispanic Coalition for Economic
Recovery
Washington, DC

Hispanic Higher Education Coalition
Washington, DC

Hispanic National Bar Association
Washington, DC

Hispanic Organization of Professionals
and Executives
Silver Spring, MD

Hispanic Policy Development Project
New York, NY

Hispanic Public Affairs Association
Washington, DC

Hispanic Public Relations Association
Los Angeles, CA

Hispanic Society of Engineers and
Scientists
Richland, WA

Illinois Hispanic Chamber of
Commerce
Chicago, IL

Institute for Puerto Rican Policy, Inc.
New York, NY

InterAmerican College of Physicians
and Surgeons
New York, NY

Iowa Spanish-Speaking Peoples
Commission
Des Moines, IA

Kansas Advisory Committee on
Mexican American Affairs
Topeka, KS

Labor Council for Latin American
Advancement
Washington, DC

Las Hermanas
Tucson, AZ

Latin American Educational
Foundation
Denver, CO

Latin American Manufacturers
Association
Washington, DC

Latin American Union for Civil Rights
Foundation
Milwaukee, WI

Latin Business Association
City of Commerce, CA

Latin Chamber of Commerce of
Nevada, Inc.
Las Vegas, NV

Latin Chamber of Commerce of U.S.A.
Miami, FL

Latino Institute
Chicago, IL

League of United Latin American
Citizens
Washington, DC

Maryland Governor's Commission on
Hispanic Affairs
Silver Spring, MD

Massachusetts Commission on
Hispanic Affairs
Boston, MA

Mexican-American Cultural Center
San Antonio, TX

Mexican-American Democrats of
Texas
Austin, TX

Mexican-American Engineering
Society
Fullerton, CA

Mexican-American Legal Defense and
Education Fund
San Francisco, CA

Mexican-American Opportunity
Foundation
Monterey Park, CA

Mexican-American Political
Association
Sacramento, CA

Mexican-American Republicans of
Texas
Dallas, TX

Mexican-American Women's National
Association
Washington, DC

Michigan Spanish-Speaking
Democrats
East Lansing, MI

Migrant Legal Action Program, Inc.
Washington, DC

National Alliance of Spanish Speaking
People for Equality
Washington, DC

National Association for Bilingual
Education
Washington, DC

National Association for Chicano
Studies
San Antonio, TX

National Association of Cuban
American Women and Men of the
United States, Inc.
Washington, DC

National Association of Cuban
American Women USA, Inc.
Fort Wayne, IN

National Association of Hispanic
Journalists
Los Angeles, CA

National Association of Hispanic
Nurses
Los Angeles, CA

National Association of Hispanic
Publications
Los Angeles, CA

National Association of Latino Elected
and Appointed Officials
Washington, DC

National Chicano Council on Higher
Education
Claremont, CA

National Coalition of Hispanic Mental
Health and Human Services
Organizations
Washington, DC

National Concilio of America
San Francisco, CA

National Conference of Puerto Rican
Women
Washington, DC

National Council of La Raza
Washington, DC

National Federation of Cuban
American Republican Women
Fort Wayne, IN

National Hispanic Association of
Construction Enterprises
Washington, DC

National Hispanic Council on Aging
Washington, DC

National Hispanic Institute of Public Policy
Los Angeles, CA

National Hispanic Leadership Conference
Corpus Christi, TX

National Hispanic Psychological Association
Los Angeles, CA

National Hispanic Scholarship Fund
San Francisco, CA

National Image, Inc.
Corvallis, OR

National Institute for Multi-Cultural Education
Albuquerque, NM

National Institute for Resources in Science and Engineering
Washington, DC

National League of Cuban American Community-Based Centers
Fort Wayne, IN

National Neighborhood Coalition
Washington, DC

National Puerto Rican Coalition, Inc.
Alexandria, VA

National Puerto Rican Forum, Inc.
New York, NY

Nevada Association of Latin Americans, Inc.
Las Vegas, NV

New Jersey Office of Hispanic Affairs
Trenton, NJ

New York Governor's Advisory Committee on Hispanic Affairs
New York, NY

New York State Black and Puerto Rican Legislative Caucus, Inc.
Albany, NY

Office of Hispanic Education, Michigan State Board of Education
Lansing, MI

Ohio Commission on Spanish Speaking Affairs
Columbus, OH

Oklahoma Governor's Advisory Committee on Hispanic Affairs
Oklahoma City, OK

Oregon Commission on Hispanic Affairs
Salem, OR

Padres Asociados para Derechos Religioso, Educativo y Social
Los Angeles, CA

Pennsylvania Governor's Council on the Hispanic Community
Philadelphia, PA

Personnel Management Association of Aztlan
Los Angeles, CA

Puerto Rican Congress of New Jersey
Trenton, NJ

Puerto Rican Legal Defense and Education Fund
New York, NY

Republican National Hispanic Assembly of Michigan, Inc.
Detroit, MI

Republican National Hispanic Assembly of the United States
Washington, DC

SER-Jobs for Progress, Inc.
Dallas, TX

Society for the Advancement of Chicanos and Native Americans in Science
Bethesda, MD

Society of Hispanic Professional Engineers
Los Angeles, CA

Society of Spanish Engineers, Planners and Architects
New York, NY

Spanish-American League Against Discrimination
Miami, FL

Spanish-Speaking Community of
Maryland, Inc.
Silver Spring, MD

State of Michigan Commission on
Spanish-Speaking Affairs
Lansing, MI

State of Minnesota Spanish-Speaking
Affairs Council
St. Paul, MN

State of Nebraska Mexican-American
Commission
Lincoln, NE

Texas Alliance for Minorities in
Engineering, Inc.
Arlington, TX

Texas Association Mexican American
Chambers of Commerce
Austin, TX

United Migrant Opportunity Services,
Inc.
Milwaukee, WI

U.S. Catholic Conference/Secretariat
for Hispanic Affairs
Washington, DC

U.S. Hispanic Chamber of Commerce
Kansas City, MO

Utah State Governor's Office on
Hispanic Affairs
Salt Lake City, UT

Valle del Sol, Inc.
Phoenix, AZ

Washington Commission on
Mexican-American Affairs
Olympia, WA

Wisconsin Governor's Council on
Hispanic Affairs
Madison, WI

State Political Caucuses

Alabama Legislative Black Caucus
Montgomery, AL

Alaska Black Caucus
Anchorage, AK

Arkansas Black Legislative Caucus
Little Rock, AR

Black and Puerto Rican Legislative
Caucus (NY)
Albany, NY

Black Elected Democrats of Ohio
(BEDO)
Columbus, OH

California Legislative Black Caucus
Sacramento, CA

Connecticut Legislative Black and
Puerto Rican Caucus
Hartford, CT

Florida Caucus of Black State
Legislators
Opa Locka, FL

Georgia Legislative Black Caucus
Atlanta, GA

Greater Fairbanks Black Caucus
(Alaska)
Fairbanks, AK

Illinois Legislative Black Caucus
Chicago, IL

Indiana Black Legislative Caucus
Indianapolis, IN

Iowa Legislative Black Caucus
Des Moines, IA

Kansas Black Legislative Caucus
Kansas City, KS

Louisiana Legislative Black Caucus
Baton Rouge, LA

Maryland Legislative Black Caucus
Hillcrest Heights, MD

Massachusetts Legislative Black
Caucus
Boston, MA

Michigan Legislative Black Caucus
Lansing, MI

Mississippi Legislative Black Caucus
Jackson, MS

Missouri Legislative Black Caucus
Foundation, Inc.
Jefferson City, MO

New Jersey Legislative Black Caucus
Trenton, NJ

North Carolina Legislative Black
Caucus
Raleigh, NC

Northwest Black Public Elected and
Appointed Officials
Seattle, WA

Oklahoma Legislative Black Caucus
Oklahoma City, OK

Pennsylvania Legislative Black
Caucus
Harrisburg, PA

Rhode Island Caucus of Black State
Legislators
Providence, RI

South Carolina Legislative Black
Caucus
Columbia, SC

Tennessee Black Caucus of State
Legislators
Nashville, TN

Texas Legislative Black Caucus
Austin, TX

Virginia Legislative Black Caucus
Norfolk, VA

Selected Black Organizations

A Better Chance
Boston, MA

Action Alliance of Black Managers
Columbus, OH

A. Philip Randolph Institute and A.
Philip Randolph Educational Fund
Washington, DC

African American Museums
Association
Washington, DC

African American Coalition
Washington, DC

African Heritage Studies Association
New York, NY

African Influence
Atadena, CA

African Methodist Episcopal Church
Washington, DC

African Methodist Episcopal Zion
Church
Charlotte, NC

Africare, Inc.
Washington, DC

Afro-American Historical and
Geneological Society
Washington, DC

Alliance of Black Entertainment
Technicians
Los Angeles, CA

Alpha Kappa Alpha Sorority,
Inc.
Chicago, IL

Alpha Phi Alpha Fraternity, Inc.
Baltimore, MD

Alpha Pi Chi Sorority, Inc.
Hyattsville, MD

American Association For Affirmative
Action
Atlanta, GA

American Association of Black Women
Entrepreneurs Corp.
Silver Spring, MD

American Association of Blacks In
  Energy
Washington, DC

American Bridge Association
Atlanta, GA

American Council on Education, Office
  of Minorities in Higher Education
Washington, DC

American Health and Beauty Aids
  Institute
Chicago, IL

American League of Financial
  Institutions
Washington, DC

Amisted Research Center
New Orleans, LA

Ancient Egyptian Arabic Order
  Nobles Mystic Shrine, Inc.
Detroit, MI

Associated Black Charities
New York, NY

Association For Multi-Cultural
  Counseling and Development
Alexandria, VA

Association For The Study of
  Afro-American Life and History
Washington, DC

Association of Black Admissions and
  Financial Aid Officers of the Ivy
  League and Sister Schools, Inc.
Cambridge, MA

Association of Black American
  Ambassadors
Washington, DC

Association of Black Foundation
  Executives
Washington, DC

Association of Black Psychologists
Washington, DC

Association of Black Sociologists
Washington, DC

Association of Black Women In
  Higher Education, Inc.
New York, NY

Association of Minority Enterprises of
  New York
Hempstead, NY

Audience Development Committee,
  Inc.
New York, NY

Bethume-DuBois Fund
Washington, DC

Black Agency Executives
New York, NY

Black American Response to The
  African Community
Pasadena, CA

Black Awareness In Television
Detroit, MI

Black Caucus of The American
  Library Association
Richmond, VA

Black Creative Professionals
  Association
Los Angeles, CA

Black Filmmakers Foundation
New York, NY

Black Psychiatrist of America
Oakland, CA

Black Retail Action Group, Inc.
New York, NY

Black United Front
Chicao, IL

Black Women's Forum
Los Angeles, CA

Black Women In Church and Society
Atlanta, GA

Black Women In Publishing, Inc.
New York, NY

Black Women's Network (Los
  Angeles)
Los Angeles, CA

Blacks In Government
Washington, DC

Booker T. Washington Foundation
Washington, DC

Business Policy Review Council
Washington, DC

Carato, Inc.
Columbus, OH

Career Expo Planning Committee,
Inc.
Boston, MA

Caribbean Action Lobby
Compton, CA

Caribbean-American Chamber of
Commerce
Brooklyn, NY

Carronsels, Inc.
Dallas, TX

Chi Eta Phi Sorority, Inc.
Washington, DC

Chums, Inc.
Washington, DC

Coalition of Black Trade Unionists
Washington, DC

Concerned Educators of Black
Students
Dayton, OH

Conference of Minority Public
Administrators
Washington, DC

Conference of Prince Hall Grand
Masters
South Minneapolis, MN

Congress of National Black Churches
Washington, DC

Congress of Racial Equality (CORE)
New York, NY

Congressional Black Associates, Inc.
Washington, DC

Congressional Black Caucus
Washington, DC

Congressional Black Caucus
Foundation, Inc.
Washington, DC

Consortium for Graduate Studies in
Management
Clayton, MO

Constituency For Africa
Washington, DC

Continental Societies, Inc.
Blackwood, NJ

Council of National Alumni
Associations
Delaware State College
Dover, Delaware

Delta Sigma Theta Sorority, Inc.
Washington, DC

Doll League, Inc.
Paterson, NJ

Drifters, Inc.
Neptune, NJ

EDGES GROUP, INC.
Woodbridge, NJ

Eta Phi Beta Sorority, Inc.
Detroit, MI

Executive Leadership Council
Washington, DC

Federation of Masons of the World of
Eastern Stars
Austin, TX

Federation of Southern Cooperatives
Land Assistance Fund
Atlanta, GA

Florida Endowment Fund
Tampa, FL

Frontiers International, Inc.
Philadelphia, PA

Girl Friends, Inc.
Portsmouth, VA

Gospel Music Workshop of America
Detroit, MI

Groove Phi Groove Social Fellowship,
Inc.
Silver Spring, MD

Holidays, Inc.
Laurel, MD

Ida Van Smith Flight Club, Inc.
Rochdale Village, NY

Improved Benevolent Protective
Order of Elks of the World
Winton, NC

Institute For American Business
Washington, DC

Institute For Independent
Education
Washington, DC

International Association of Black
Professional Fire Fighters
Washington, DC

International Benevolent Society, Inc.
Columbus, GA

International Black Writers
Chicago, IL

Interracial Council for Business
Opportunity
New York, NY

Iota Phi Lambda Sorority, Inc.
Montgomery, AL

Iota Phi Theta Fraternity, Inc.
Baltimore, MD

Jack and Jill of America, Inc.
Chattanooga, TN

Jackie Robinson Foundation
New York, NY

Joint Center For Political and
Economic Studies
Washington, DC

J.U.G.S., Inc.
Detroit, MI

KAPPA ALPHA PSI
FRATERNITY, INC.
Philadelphia, PA

Lambda Kappa Mu Sorority, Inc.
Randallstown, MD

Lawyers' Committee for Civil Rights
Under Law
Washington, DC

Leadership Conference on Civil
Rights
Washington, DC

Links, Inc.
Washington, DC

Low Income Housing Information
Service
Washington, DC

Marla Gibbs Crossroads National
Education Arts Center and Theatre
Los Angeles, CA

Martin Luther King, Jr. Celebration
Day & Scholarship Foundation
Washington, DC

Minority Agricultural Resources
Center
Sacramento, CA

Minority Business Enterprise Legal
Defense and Education Fund
Washington, DC

Modern Free and Accepted Masons of
the World, Inc.
Columbus, OH

Moles
Washington, DC

Moreland-Spingarn Research
Center
Washington, DC

Most Worshipful
National Grand Lodge Free and
Accepted Ancient York Masons
Prince Hall Origin, National
Compact, U.S.A., Inc.
Orangeburg, SC

National Action Council For
Minorities In Engineering
New York, NY

The National Alliance of Slack
Salesmen and Saleswomen
New York, NY

National Alliance of Black School
Educators
Washington, DC

National Alliance of Postal and
Federal Employees
Washington, DC

National Alliance of Third World
Journalists
Washington, DC

National Association for Equal
Opportunity in Higher Education
Washington, DC

National Association for Sickle Cell
Disease, Inc.
Los Angeles, CA

National Association for the
Advancement of Colored People
Baltimore, MD

NAACP Legal Defense and
Educational Fund, Inc.
New York, NY

National Association of Bench and Bar
Piedmont, CA

National Association of Black
Accountants, Inc.
Washington, DC

National Association of Black Catholic
Administrators
Rockville Centre, NY

National Association of Black
Consulting Engineers
Washington, DC

National Association of Black County
Officials
Washington, DC

National Association of Black
Hospitality Professionals, Inc.
Plainfield, NJ

National Association of Black
Journalists
Washington, DC

National Association of Black Reading
and Language Educators
Palo Alto, CA

National Association of Black Social
Workers, Inc.
Detroit, MI

National Association of Black Women
Attorneys, Inc.
Washington, DC

National Association of Black-Owned
Broadcasters
Washington, DC

National Association of Blacks in
Criminal Justice
Washington, DC

National Association of Colored
Women's Clubs
Washington, DC

National Association of Health Service
Executives
Washington, DC

National Association of Investment
Companies
Washington, DC

National Association of Market
Developers, Inc.
Atlanta, GA

National Association of Media
Women
Laurelton, NY

National Association of Milliners,
Dressmakers and Tailors, Inc.
New York, NY

National Association of Minority
Contractors
Washington, DC

National Association of Minority
Media Executives
Reston, VA

National Association of Minority
Political Women, USA, Inc.
Washington, DC

National Association of Negro
Business and Professional Women's
Clubs
Washington, DC

National Association of
Neighborhoods
Washington, DC

National Black Public Relations
Society of America
Los Angeles, CA

National Black Republican Council
Washington, DC

National Black United Fund, Inc.
Newark, NJ

National Black Women's
Consciousness-Raising Association
Baltimore, MD

National Bowling Association, Inc.
New York, NY

National Brotherhood of Skiers
South San Francisco, CA

National Business League
Washington, DC

National Catholic Conference for
Interracial Justice
Washington, DC

National Caucus and Center on Black
Aged, Inc.
Washington, DC

National Coalition of Black Meeting
Planners
Washington, DC

National Coalition of 100 Black
Women
New York, NY

National Conference of Black Mayors,
Inc.
Atlanta, GA

National Conference of Black Political
Scientists
Albany, GA

National Council of Negro Women,
Inc.
Washington, DC

National Dental Association
Washington, DC

National Association of University
Women
Washington, DC

National Association of Urban
Bankers, Inc.
Washington, DC

National Bankers Association
Washington, DC

National Baptist Convention of
America, Inc.
Shreveport, LA

National Baptist Convention, USA,
Inc.
Nashville, TN

National Bar Association
Washington, DC

National Beauty Culturists League,
Inc.
Washington, DC

National Black Catholic Congress
Baltimore, MD

National Black Caucus of Local
Elected Officials
Washington, DC

National Black Caucus of State
Legislators
Washington, DC

National Black Chambers of
Commerce
Oakland, CA

National Black Child Development
Institute
Washington, DC

National Black College Alumni Hall of
Fame Foundation
Atlanta, GA

National Black MBA Association, Inc.
Chicago, IL

National Black Media Coalition
Washington, DC

National Black Nurses Association,
Inc.
Washington, DC

National Black Police Association, Inc.
Washington, DC

National Black Programming
Consortium
Columbus, OH

National Economic Association
Michigan Business School
University of Michigan
Ann Arbor, MI

National Forum for Black Public
Administrators
Washington, DC

National Funeral Directors and
Morticians Association, Inc.
Mount Vernon, NY

National Insurance Association
Chicago, IL

National Medical Association
Washington, DC

National Minority Business Council,
Inc.
New York, NY

National Minority Suppliers
Development Council, Inc.
New York, NY

National Naval Officers Association
Washington, DC

National Newspaper Publishers
Association
Washington, DC

National Optometric Association
Chicago, IL

National Organization for the
Professional Advancement of Black
Chemists and Chemical Engineers
Howard University
Washington, DC

National Organization of Black County
Officials
Washington, DC

National Organization of Black Law
Enforcement Executives
Washington, DC

National Organization of Minority
Architects
Atlanta, GA

National Pan-Hellenic Council
Bloomington, IN

National Pharmaceutical Association
Washington, DC

National Political Congress of Black
Women, Inc.
Rancocas, NJ

National Student Business League
Kentland, MD

National Technical Association, Inc.
Washington, DC

National United Church Ushers
Association of America, Inc.
Washington, DC

National Urban Affairs Council
New York, NY

National Urban Coalition
Silver Spring, MD

National Urban League, Inc.
New York, NY

New Concept Self-Development
Center, Inc.
Milwaukee, WI

New Professional Theatre
New York, NY

New York African American Research
Institute
State University of New York
Albany, NY

Nigerian American Alliance
New York, NY

Office for the Advancement of Public
Black Colleges
Washington, DC

Omega Psi Phi Fraternity
Washington, DC

One Hundred Black Men
New York, NY

Opera North
Philadelphia, PA

Operation PUSH (People United to
Serve Humanity)
Chicago, IL

Opportunities Industrialization
Centers of America, Inc.
Philadelphia, PA

Organization of Black Airline Pilots,
Inc.
Flushing, NY

Phelph Stokes Fund
New York, NY

Phi Beta Sigma Fraternity, Inc.
Washington, NY

Phi Delta Kapps, Inc.
Chicago, IL

Pinochle Bugs Social & Civic Club
Charlotte, NC

Progressive National Baptist
Convention, Inc.
Washington, DC

Schomburg Center for Research in
Black Culture
New York, NY

Sickle Cell Anemia Foundation of
Greater New York
New York, NY

Sigma Gamma Rho Sorority, Inc.
Chicago, IL

Sigma Pi Phi Fraternity
("The Boule")
New York, NY

Southern Christian Leadership
Conference
Atlanta, GA

Southern Poverty Law Center
Montgomery, AL

Southern Regional Council
Atlanta, GA

Student National Medical Association,
Inc.
Washington, DC

369th Veterans Association, Inc.
New York, NY

Thurgood Marshall Scholarship Fund
Washington, DC

Trans Africa, Inc.
Washington, DC

Tuskegee Airmen, Inc.
Detroit, MI

Twenty-First Century Foundation
Teaneck, NH

United American Progress
Association
Chicago, IL

United Black Church Appeal
Bronx, NY

United Church of Christ, Commission
for Racial Justice
Cleveland, OH

United Negro College Fund, Inc.
New York, NY

UNCF's National Alumni Council
New York, NY

Voter Education Project, Inc.
Atlanta, GA

World Institute of Black
Communications, Inc.
New York, NY

Zeta Delta Phi Sorority, Inc.
Bronx, NY

Zeta Phi Beta Sorority, Inc.
Washington, DC

Black Colleges and Universities

Alabama A & M University
Huntsville, AL

Alabama State University
Montgomery, AL

Bishop State Community College
Mobile, AL

Concordia College
Selma, AL

Lawson State Community College
Birmingham, AL

Miles College
Birmingham, AL

Oakwood College
Huntsville, AL

Selma University
Selma, AL

Stillman College
Tuscaloosa, AL

Talladega College
Talladega, AL

Trenholm State Technical College
Montgomery, AL

Tuskegee University
Tuskegee, AL

Arkansas Baptist College
Little Rock, AR

Philander Smith College
Little Rock, AR

Shorter College
North Little Rock, AR

University of Arkansas, Pine Bluff
Pine Bluff, AR

Charles R. Drew University of
   Medicine and Science
Los Angeles, CA

Compton Community College
Compton, CA

Delaware State University
Dover, DE

Howard University
Washington, DC

University of the District of Columbia
Washington, DC

Bethune-Cookman College
Daytona Beach, FL

Edward Waters College
Jacksonville, FL

Florida A & M University
Tallahassee, FL

Florida Memorial College
Miami, FL

Albany State College
Albany, GA

Atlanta Metropolitan Junior College
Atlanta, GA

Clark Atlanta University
Atlanta, GA

Fort Valley State College
Fort Valley, GA

Morehouse College
Atlanta, GA

Morehouse School of Medicine
Atlanta, GA

Morris Brown College
Atlanta, GA

Paine College
Augusta, GA

Savannah State College
Savannah, GA

Spellman College
Atlanta, GA

Chicago State University
Chicago, IL

Kennedy-King College
Chicago, IL

Kentucky State University
Frankfurt, KY

Simmons Bible College
Louisville, KY

Dillard University
New Orleans, LA

Grambling State University
Grambling, LA

Southern University and A&M
   System College
Baton Rouge, LA

Southern University and A&M
   College at Baton Rouge
Baton Rouge, LA

Southern University at New Orleans
New Orleans, LA

Southern University at Shreveport
Shreveport, LA

Xavier University
New Orleans, LA

Bowie State College
Bowie, MD

Coppin State College
Baltimore, MD

Morgan State University
Baltimore, MD

Sojourner-Douglass College
Baltimore, MD

University of Maryland Eastern Shore
Princess Anne, MD

Roxbury Community College
Boston, MA

Lewis College of Business
Detroit, MI

Alcorn State University
Lorman, MS

Coahoma Community College
Clarksdale, MS

Jackson State University
Jackson, MS

Mary Holmes College
West Point, MS

Mississippi Valley State University
Itta Bena, MS

Natchez Junior College
Natchez, MS

Rust College
Holly Springs, MS

Tougaloo College
Tougaloo, MS

Utica Campus/Hinds Junior College
Utica, MS

Harris-Stowe State College
St. Louis, MO

Lincoln University
Jefferson City, MO

Medger Evers College
Brooklyn, NY

Baber-Scotia College
Concord, NC

Bennett College
Greensboro, NC

Elizabeth City State University
Elizabeth City, NC

Fayetteville State University
Fayetteville, NC

Johnson C. Smith University
Charlotte, NC

Livingstone College
Salsbury, NC

North Carolina A & T State
University
Greensboro, NC

North Carolina Central University
Durham, NC

Saint Augustine's College
Raleigh, NC

Shaw University
Raleigh, NC

Winston-Salem State University
Winston-Salem, NC

Central State University
Wilberforce, OH

Cuyahaga Community College
Cleveland, OH

Wilberforce University
Wilberforce, OH

Langston University
Langston, OK

Cheyney University
Cheyney, PA

Lincoln University
Lincoln, PA

Allen University
Columbia, SC

Benedict College
Columbia, SC

Claflin College
Orangeburg, SC

Clinton Junior College
Rock Hill, SC

Denmark Technical College
Denmark, SC

Morris College
Sumter, SC

South Carolina State College
N.E. Orangeburg, SC

Voorhees College
Denmark, SC

Fisk University
Nashville, TN

Knoxville College
Knoxville, TN

Lane College
Jackson, TN

LeMoyne-Owen
Memphis, TN

Meharry Medical College
Nashville, TN

Tennessee State University
Nashville, TN

Huston-Tillotson College
Austin, TX

Jarvis Christian College
Hawkins, TX

Paul Quinn College
Dallas, TX

Prairie View A & M University
Prairie View, TX

Southwestern Christian
  College
Terrell, TX

Texas College
Tyler, TX

Texas Southern University
Houston, TX

Wiley College
Marshall, TX

University of the Virgin Islands
Saint Thomas, VI

Hampton University
Hampton, VA

Norfolk State University
Norfolk, VA

Virginia Seminary & College
Lynchburg, VA

Virginia State College
Petersburg, VA

Virginia Union University
Richmond, VA

West Virginia State College
Institute West, VA

APPENDIX I
Title VII: Prohibition of Employment Discrimination

Title VII of the Civil Rights Act of 1964, as amended, is the federal law that prohibits employment discrimination based on race, color, sex, religion, or national origin. Title VII was extended to cover federal, state, and local public employers and educational institutions by the Equal Employment Opportunity Act of 1972. This amendment to Title VII also gave the Equal Employment Opportunity Commission the authority to file suit in federal district court against employers in the private sector on behalf of individuals whose charges were not successfully conciliated.

In 1978, Title VII was amended to include the Pregnancy Discrimination Act, which requires employers to treat pregnancy and pregnancy-related medical conditions the same as any other medical disability with respect to all terms and conditions of employment, including employee health benefits.

Under Title VII employment discrimination by any of these groups having fifteen or more employees is prohibited:

- Private employers
- State and local governments
- Educational institutions
- Labor organizations

Employment discrimination by any of these groups also is prohibited:

- The federal government
- Private and public employment agencies
- Joint labor-management committees for apprenticeship and training

It is unlawful for an employer to discriminate with regard to:

- Job advertisements
- Recruitment
- Testing
- Hiring and firing
- Compensation, assignment, or classification of employees
- Transfer, promotion, layoff, or recall
- Use of company facilities
- Training and apprenticeship programs
- Fringe benefits such as life and health insurance
- Pay, retirement plans, and disability leave
- Causing or attempting to cause a union to discriminate
- Other terms and conditions of employment

It is unlawful for employment agencies to discriminate with regard to:
- Its own employees on the basis of race, color, religion, sex, or national origin
- Receiving, classifying, or referring applications for employment
- Job advertisements

It is unlawful for labor unions to discriminate with regard to:

- Applications for membership
- Segregation or classification of members
- Referrals for employment
- Training and apprenticeship programs
- Other discriminatory conduct, including causing or attempting to cause an employer to discriminate
- Job advertisements

It is unlawful for employers, employment agencies, and labor unions to retaliate against individuals who oppose unlawful employment practices or attempt to exercise their rights under the statute.

Filing a Charge

You must file an employment discrimination charge within 180 days of the alleged discriminatory act. Where there is a state or local Fair Employment Practices Agency in your area, you have up to 240 days, and in some cases you may have up to 300 days, to file your charge with the commission. A charge may be filed either by or on behalf of an aggrieved individual or "class." A charge may be filed in person or by mail with any of EEOC's field offices.

If you are a federal employee, you must file a complaint of discrimination with your own agency. Your EEO counselor generally must be contacted within 30 days of the alleged discriminatory act.

Remedies Available Under Title VII

Remedies under Title VII are tailored to specific findings of discrimination by EEOC or by the federal district courts. These remedies may include requiring an employer to end discriminatory practices and systems, institute equal employment practices and systems, and in some cases, provide specific make-whole compensation for victims of discrimination.

Remedies may involve reinstatement, hiring, reassignment, promotion, training, seniority rights, back pay and other compensation and benefits. (Back pay awards under Title VII cannot accrue from a date more than two years prior to the filing of a charge.)

In pursuing its mission of eradicating discrimination in the workplace, the commission intends that its enforcement be predictable, provide effective relief for those affected by discrimination, allow remedies designed to correct the sources of discrimination, and prevent its recurrence.

EEO has offices in the following cities:

Albuquerque, N.M.*	Memphis, Tenn.
Atlanta, Ga.	Miami, Fla.
Baltimore, Md.	Milwaukee, Wis.
Birmingham, Ala.	Minneapolis, Minn.**
Boston, Mass.	Nashville, Tenn.*
Buffalo, N.Y.**	Newark, N.J.*
Charlotte, N.C.	New Orleans, La.
Chicago, Ill.	New York, N.Y.
Cincinnati, Ohio*	Norfolk, Va.*
Cleveland, Ohio	Oakland, Calif.**
Dallas, Tex.	Oklahoma City, Okla.*
Denver, Colo.	Philadelphia, Pa.
Detroit, Mich.	Phoenix, Ariz.
El Paso, Tex.**	Pittsburgh, Pa.*
Fresno, Calif.**	Raleigh, N.C.*
Greensboro, N.C.**	Richmond, Va.*
Greenville, S.C.**	San Antonio, Tex.
Houston, Tex.	San Diego, Calif.**
Indianapolis, Ind.	San Francisco, Calif.
Jackson, Miss.*	San Jose, Calif.**
Kansas City, Mo.*	Seattle, Wash.
Little Rock, Ark.*	St. Louis, Mo.
Los Angeles, Calif.	Tampa, Fla.*
Louisville, Ken.*	Washington, D.C.*

*Area offices
**Local offices

APPENDIX II

Average Income by State
as Reported by the
Commerce Department in 1992

A study of median income* of households by state as reported by the Commerce Department in 1993. Median income of households—in 1992 adjusted dollars—by state: 1990, 1991, and 1992.

State	Average Median 1991–1992	Average Median 1990–1991
Alabama	$25,119	$24,343
Alaska	$41,291	$40,782
Arizona	$30,165	$30,595
Arkansas	$23,664	$23,590
California	$34,419	$34,177
Colorado	$32,108	$31,763
Connecticut	$41,607	$41,330

*Statistics herein contained do not include figures for standard error.

State	Average Median 1991–1992	Average Median 1990–1991
Delaware	$34,162	$32,343
District of Col.	$30,121	$29,215
Florida	$27,354	$27,530
Georgia	$28,051	$27,966
Hawaii	$39,709	$38,902
Idaho	$26,950	$26,243
Illinois	$31,796	$32,898
Indiana	$27,876	$27,575
Iowa	$28,717	$28,495
Kansas	$29,871	$30,235
Kentucky	$23,666	$24,793
Louisiana	$25,389	$24,323
Maine	$28,787	$28,244
Maryland	$37,120	$38,722
Massachusetts	$36,136	$36,743
Michigan	$32,232	$31,657
Minnesota	$30,278	$31,134
Mississippi	$20,030	$20,251
Missouri	$27,708	$28,204
Montana	$25,715	$24,593
Nebraska	$29,863	$29,094
Nevada	$32,482	$33,154
New Hampshire	$37,838	$39,277
New Jersey	$39,638	$40,206
New Mexico	$26,349	$26,316
New York	$31,524	$32,357
North Carolina	$27,344	$27,145
North Dakota	$26,499	$26,110
Ohio	$30,635	$30,533
Oklahoma	$25,413	$25,436
Oregon	$31,152	$30,352
Pennsylvania	$30,193	$30,296
Rhode Island	$30,736	$32,075
South Carolina	$27,565	$28,704
South Dakota	$25,495	$25,122
Tennessee	$24,396	$23,998

State	Average Median 1991–1992	Average Median 1990–1991
Texas	$28,008	$28,574
Utah	$31,225	$29,713
Vermont	$30,992	$30,781
Virginia	$37,180	$36,343
Washington	$34,017	$33,717
West Virginia	$21,724	$23,108
Wisconsin	$32,274	$31,568
Wyoming	$29,715	$29,875
Los Angeles (CMSA)	$35,005	$34,694
New York (CMSA)	$34,832	$35,704

RECOMMENDED READING

Managing for the Future: The 1990s and Beyond
Peter F. Drucker. Truman Talley Books/Plume Printing, November, 1993

Live Your Dreams. Les Brown. William Morrow and Company, Inc., 1992

Black Life in Corporate America: Swimming in the Mainstream. George Davis and Glegg Watson. Doubleday and Co., 1985

Understand Those Financial Reports: Question-and-Answer Guide for Investors and Nonfinancial Managers. Raymond J. Lipay. John Wiley & Sons, 1984

The Black Manager: Making It in the Corporate World. Floyd Dickens, Jr., and Jacqueline B. Dickens. AMACOM, 1991

The Peter Pyramid. Dr. Laurence J. Peter. Bantam Books, 1986

Corporate Cultures: The Rites and Rituals of Corporate Life. By Terrence E. Deal and Allen A. Kennedy. Addison-Wesley Publishing Co., 1982

Managing Paperwork: A Key to Productivity. Frank M. Know. Thomond Press: An Elsevier Professional Publication, 1980

Getting Unstuck: An Essential Planning Guide for Anyone Who Wants a New Beginning. Iris W. Randall. NB Publications, 1986. 6219 Lafayette Rd., PO Box 1332 Medina, OH 44256

Business Week's Guide to Careers. P.O. Box 7819, West Trenton, NJ 08628.

Harvard Business Review. A bimonthly journal for professional managers. Sodiers Field, Boston, MA 02163.

The Prentice Hall Directory of Executive Search Firms. Over 1,800 Executive Search Firms Arranged by Field and Location Plus, How to Find and Use a "Headhunter." By William Lewis & Carol Milano, Prentice Hall, 1986

The Nonprofit Management Handbook: Operating Policies and Procedures. Edited by Tracy Daniel Connors. John Wiley & Sons, Inc., 1992.

Financial and Strategic Management for Nonprofit Organizations (Second Edition). Herrington J. Bryce. Prentice Hall, Inc., 1991.

Ageless Body, Timeless Mind: The Quantum Alternative to Growing Old. Deepak Chopra, M.D. Harmony/Crown Books, 1993.

Leadership. James MacGregor Burns. Torchbooks/Harper Collins, 1982

The McGraw-Hill Guide to Starting Your Own Business: A Step-by-step Blueprint for the First-Time Entrepreneur. Stephen C. Harper. McGraw-Hill, Inc., 1991.

Getting To Yes: Negotiating Agreement Without Giving In (Second Edition). Roger Fisher and William L. Ury. Penguin, 1991.

Reengineering the Corporation: A Manifesto for Business Revolution. Michael Hammer and James Champy. Harper Business, 1993.

The Team Building Tool Kit. Deborah Harrington-Mackin. AMACOM, 1994.

INDEX

A

Accomplishments, listing major, 175
Achievement needs, 37, 185
Action plan for job hunting, 146
Affiliation needs, 37, 185
Affirmative action, xi, xii
Agee, William, 156
Agricultural jobs, xvi
Alcohol consumption, 54, 149–50
Alertness as a networking characteristic, 110
Ambitious employees, 93
American Manufacturers Directory, 224
America's Top-Rated Cities, 224
Approaching people to network, 112
Asians, 215, 240–42, 248–49
Attitude
  cultivating opportunities with a positive, 60
  right, 14–16
  societal attitudes reflected in corporations,' 7–8
Automation, 203

B

Bachelor's degree, 221
Bank officers/managers, 206
Bendix Corporation, 156
Biological scientists, 206–7

Black Americans Information Directory, 224
Blacks, 1–2
  colleges/universities for, 261–64
  corporate culture or racism towards, 40–45
  disappearance of executives who are, xi-xiii
  dress code and, 17–18
  family support for, 168–69
  image assassination of, 82–85
  individual spirit of, 16
  interviewing for a position/promotion, 130
  labor force entrants and, 215
  mentoring relationship and, 6
  newspapers oriented towards, 234–38
  organizations representing, 254–61
  relocation and, 199
  stress and, 164
Body language, 131
Boyce, William M., 49–50
Bureau of Labor Statistics, xvii, 201, 207
Business cards, 112

C

Career Opportunities in the Music Industry (Field), 224
Career planning, 177–78. *See also Job headings*

Career planning (Cont'd.)
  changing jobs, 66–69
  choice and, 197–98
  colleges/universities and information on,
    230–31
  lateral career move, 191–95
  problem solving and, 65
Careers in Medicine (Rucker & Keller),
  224–25
CEOs
  consultants used by, 50
  job hunting and checking out, 51
  management make-up and, xvii
  values/perceptions of, 49
Challenges, anticipating, 172–73, 190–91
Choice in career paths, 197–98
Civil Rights Act of 1964, 85, 265
Clothing. See Dress code
Cocaine, 156–57
Colleges and universities
  Black, 261–64
  business-related studies in, 36
  career planning/networking
    opportunities and, 230–31
  coping skills for corporate culture shock
    and, 4–5
  trade association industry and, 179
Community as a job resource, 232
Competition, 161
Computer systems analysts, 204
Conformity within corporations, 16
Consultants, xviii, 8
  corporate culture, monitoring, 49–50
  increasing demand for, 203
  job attack and, 94
Consumer Guide: Best-Rated Retirement
  Cities and Towns, 225
Contacts for networking, 108, 113–14
Contingency plans, 12, 189, 197
Cooperative approach to managing people,
  52
Coping skills for corporate culture shock,
  4–5
"Corporate Noble Truths," 12
  attitude, right, 14–16
  dress code, 16–18
  politics, company, 25–26
  presentation skills, 22–25
  speaking skills, 18–20
  writing skills, 21–22
Corporations, 10, 11
  conformity within, 16
  cultivating opportunities within, 60–64
  culture within. See Culture, corporate
  disappearance of blacks from, xi–xiii
  image within. See "Corporate Noble
    Truths"
  influential players in, 33

informational grapevines in, 35–36
  pitfalls in, 77–82
  power and privileges in, 37–39, 41–42
  profit-centered departments in, 202
  renewal process for, 64–65, 104–5, 187–88
  rules/regulations within, 33–34
  severance/settlement packages provided
    by, 69–76
  social responsibility practiced by, 6–8,
    119–20
  success in, checklist for, 55–59
Cost-of-living comparisons in lateral career
  move, 193, 194
Co-workers
  avoiding destructive, 27
  isolated from, 86–92
  job hunting using, 50–51
  job responsibilities confirmed by,
    45–46
  orientation period and, 52
  right attitude from, opinion on, 14
  sexual harassment discussed with, 79
  speaking skills borrowed from, 20
  stress relief from, 166
Culture, corporate, xiv, 39–40
  checklist for dealing with, 50–52
  consultants monitoring, 49–50
  inadequate preparation for, 2–4, 8
  job hunting and, 68
  racism or, 40–48
Cunningham, Mary, 156

D
Data collection, 94, 171–72, 174, 185
Dating on the job, 151–52
Debating skills, 19
Deep-breathing exercises, 166
Defensive strategies against job attack,
  96–99
Desire as a networking characteristic, 109
Desperation and job hunting, 59, 136,
  142–43
Diet, balanced, 102, 165
Diplomacy in networking, 110
Directories, 224–30
Directory of Public Interest Legal
  Internships, 225
Disagreeing with others, 19
Discharging your feelings, 101
Discretion, 36, 110, 111–12
Discrimination, employment, 265–68
Documentation, 80, 81, 111, 184
Double standard for male and female
  behavior, 152
Downsizing, xvi, 59, 187–88, 199
Dress code, 16
  Hispanics/Blacks and, 17–18
  while interviewing for a job, 138–39

networking and, 109
presentations and, 23
Drug usage, 54, 156–59

E
Economic trends. *See* Employment/
economic trends through 2005
Education
bachelor's degree needed for
employment, 221
job growth and, 217
salaries and, 213
Ego-gratifying experience of power, 42
Employment agency, private, 231
Employment/economic trends through
2005
gross national product, 211
industries, 207–9
labor force entrants, 214–16
occupational groups, 217
occupations, specific, 203–7, 218–21
salaries, 213
Encyclopedia of Associations, 225–26
Enthusiasm, 60
Equal Employment Opportunity Act of
1972, 265
Equal Employment Opportunity
Commission (EEOC), 80–82, 184, 265,
267–68
Evaluating data on a job attack, 95
Evaluation process for job hunting, 146–47
Examinations, medical, 165
Exchanging favors, 110–11
Executive privileges and power, 37–39, 42
Exercising, 101–2, 166
Expectations, realistic, 57

F
Facial hair, 17–18
Failure, learning from, 53, 57, 135–36,
196–97
Fairness, 52
Family-owned/operated companies, 155
Family support for minority employees,
168–69
Fashion magazines, 17
Favors, exchanging, 110–11
Feelings, discharging your, 101
Financial independence, 160
Financial services industry, 202
Five-year written plan, 11, 169–76
Flexibility and good management, 53
(Florida) Job Bank, 1992 (Adams), 226
Forecasting five years in the future, 11,
169–76
Freelance talent, xviii
Friendliness, 130–32
Fry, Art, 65–66

Future employment/economic trends
through 2005, 210
gross national product, 211
industries, 207–9
labor force entrants, 214–16
occupational groups, 217
occupations, specific, 203–7, 218–21
salaries, 213

G
Gamesmanship, corporate, 57
Gherman, E. M., 164, 165
Goals, identifying, 12, 175–76
Godfather Game, 57
Goods-producing to service sector,
employment shift from, 212
Government
reshaping of business prompted by, xvii,
4
social responsibility of corporations
prompted by, 6–7
training and education programs,
subsidizing, 180
Great Society, xii, xiii
Grooming habits, 17
Gross national product (GNP), 201, 211
Group pressure, 97
Growth opportunities, 68

H
Hand gestures, 19
Health care industry, 202, 205, 207
*Hispanic Americans Information
Directory* (Smith), 227
Hispanics
corporate culture or racism towards,
45–48
dress code and, 17–18
family support for, 168
individual spirit of, 16
interpersonal skills and, 82–85
interviewing for a position/promotion,
130
labor force entrants and, 214–15
magazines/directories/periodicals
oriented towards, 239
newspapers oriented towards, 238–39
organizations representing, 249–53
relocation and, 199
Home health care, 202
Hotel managers and assistants, 205
*How to Get A Job in the New York Metro
Area* (Camden & Fleming–Holland),
227
Human Resources Department, 61
Human Rights Commission, 80
Humor, 102
Hypertension, 167

I

Image, professional. *See also* "Corporate Noble Truths"
  assassination of, 82–85
  job attack hurting, 96, 98–99, 100
  networking and, 117–19
  success and, 56
Impatience and success, 197
Indians, American, 240, 247–48
Individualism, 16
Informal meetings with senior executives, 114–16
Information grapevines/pipelines, 35–36
Information society, 5–6
Intelligence as a networking characteristic, 109
International Internships and Volunteer Programs (Cantrell & Modderno), 227
Internships, 1994, 227
Internships (Fry)
  Accounting, Banking, Brokerage, Finance, and Insurance (Volume 3), 228
  Advertising, Marketing, Public Relations, and Sales (Volume 1), 227
  Newspapers, Magazines, and Book Publishing (Volume 2), 228
  Radio and Television, Broadcasting and Production (Volume 5), 228
  Travel and Hospitality Industries, The (Volume 4), 228
Interpersonal skills, 82–85
Interviewing
  friendliness and, 130–32
  interviewers, what they're looking for, 179–80
  rejection and, 135–36
  self-critique process and, 136–37
  tips on, important personnel, 138–40, 179–80
Investing outside your company, 54, 162
Isolated from co-workers, 86–92

J

Job attack, 92–93, 185–86
  case history on a, 103–6
  defensive strategies against, 96–99
  evaluation/recommendation stage and, 95–96
  offensive strategies against, 99–100
  protecting your welfare during, 100–103
  researching information on a, 94, 185–86
  risks involved in a, 94
Job description, 182–83
Job hunting, 8, 132, 180
  corporate culture and, 50–51
  having a job while, 59, 136, 142–43
  interview process while, tips on, 138–40, 179–80

planning for successful, 144–47
  rejection during, 135–36
  research for, 68–69
  salary negotiations and, 141–44
  self-confidence and, 133–34
  self-critique while, 136–37
Job(s). *See also* Career planning
  changing, 47–48, 66–69, 186–87
  dating on the, 151–52
  difficulty in finding, 178–79
  discrimination, 265–68
  future trends in. *See* Future
  employment/economic trends through 2005
  losing your, xii–xiii, xvi, 187–90
  relocating to another, 193–95, 199
  satisfaction, 53, 67–68
  scanning for future of a, 11–12
  searching for a. *See* Job hunting
  security, 181, 202
  unemployment, xii–xiii, xv–xviii, 201
Job Seeker's Guide to Private and Public Companies (Dorgan & Mast), 228
Jobs in Paradise (Maltzman), 228–29

K

"King." *See* CEOs

L

Labor. *See Job* headings
Laser technology, 202
Last in, first out method of reorganization, 4
Lateral career move, 191–95
Laughter, 102
Lawyers, 205–6
Layoffs, xii–xiii, xvi, 187–90
Lesly's Public Relations Handbook (Lesly), 119
Lifecycle of the company, 68
Life In America's Small Cities (Thomas), 229
Limitations, knowing your, 56
Listening skills, 56, 96
Location of your workplace, 68

M

Magazines/periodicals, 17, 239–42
Makeup, 17
Management
  adversarial, 46–48
  good managers, 52–54
  informal meetings with, 114–16
  job attack and intervention of, 97
  job security for, 202
  lean and aggressive, xvii
  marketing your skills using, 63
  planning by executives respected by, 12

prospects in the 1990s, 206
severance/settlement packages and
attitude of, 69–76
survival instincts respected by, 28
Manufacturing trends, 201–2, 220
Marketing your skills/personality, 27–31,
58, 62–64
Marriage partners at work, 155–56
Mathematicians, 204–5
McClelland, David C., 37
McLuhan, Marshall, 5–6
Mechanical engineers, 203–4
Meditation, 102, 166
Medium-size/small corporations, 7
Mentoring relationships
corporate culture and, 40
job attack and, 186
networking and, 125–29
racism and, 29
subjective criteria negotiated using, 6
Middle-management, 140, 199, 202
Mistakes, learning from, 196–97
Motivation, 37, 53, 199–200

N
National Directory of Arts Internships
(Christensen), 229
National Directory of Minority-Owned
Business Firms, 229
National Job Bank, 1992: A
Comprehensive Guide to Major
Employers In the United States
(Smith), 229–30
Native Americans, 240, 247–48
Need for achievement/power/affiliation, 37,
185
Networking, 3, 8
corporate culture information and, 51
defining, 107–8
friendliness and, 130–32
image creation and, 117–19
job hunting and, 51, 132–47
learning phases in, 111–16
mentoring relationships and, 125–29
organizations and, minority, 247–64
overexposure through, 122–23
planning for success and, 10–11, 12
press release and, 123–25
professional associations and, 121–22
trade organizations and, 120–21
twelve top characteristics in, 109–10
volunteering and, 119–20
New Careers: A Directory of Jobs and
Internships In Technology and
Society (Helfand), 230
Newspapers, 232–34
black-oriented, 234–38
Hispanic-oriented, 238–39

New York Times, 51
1990s, socioeconomic issues and
expectations in the, 201–3. See also
Future employment/economic trends
through 2005
Non-Profit Employer Directory, 1991, 230
Nuclear engineers, 204
Nursing professionals, 203

O
Objectives and planning process, 11–12, 13,
175–76
Offensive strategies against job attack,
99–100
100 Best Small Towns In America, The
(Crampton), 230
Only Retirement Guide You'll Ever Need,
The, 230
On-time habits, 21, 139
Open door policy, 114
Opportunity, cultivating, 60–64
Organizations, minority, 247–64
Orientation period, 52, 85–92
Overexposure through networking, 122–23

P
Packaging your corporate image, 12–26
Patience and success, 197
Pay scales. See Salary and benefits
Peer pressure, 97
Performance appraisals/reviews, 183
Personal/career data, 172, 174
Personality
A & B types, 165
marketing your, 27–31, 58, 62–64
as a networking characteristic, 109
Personal life
alcohol consumption, 54, 149–50
dating on the job, 151–52
drug usage, 54, 156–59
family support, 168–69
five-year written plan, 169–76
married and working together, 155–56
sex used for promotions, 153–54
stress, 164–68
weekly paycheck syndrome, 160–64
Personnel department and sexual
harassment, 79–80
Personnel files, 34
Petroleum engineers, 204
Photo opportunities, 64
Physical exercise, 101–2, 166
Pitfalls, corporate, 77–82
Planning for success, 9–12, 184–85
checklist on, 55–59
by good management, 53
information gathering. See Reference
sources

Planning for success (Cont'd.)
  job hunting and, 144-47
  marketing skills/personality, 27-31
  motivation and, 199-200
  rules/regulations within corporations
    and, 33-34
  seven corporate noble truths and, 12-26
  thoughts for career wisdom and, 196-97
Political caucuses, state, 253-54
Political skill as a networking
  characteristic, 109
Politics, company, 25-26
Power, need for, 37, 185
Power brokers, 8, 109
Power/privileges, executive, 37-39, 41-42
Practice of Public Relations, The (Seitel),
  119
Pregnancy Discrimination Act of 1978, 265
Preparation time for job hunting, 145
Presentation skills, 22-25
Press release, 123-25
Private employment agencies, 231
Privileges/power, executive, 37-39, 41-42
Problem solving, 65
Professional organizations/associations, 30,
  121-22
Profit-centered departments, 202
Profits, declining, xvii
Promotions, 54, 59
  departments within corporations leading
    to, 181-82
  lateral career move and, 192
  mentors and, 126
  roadblocks to black, xii
  sex used for, 153-54
Prosperity, corporations as key to
  America's, 36
Psychologists, 207
Public relations, 64, 117-19, 123-25
Public resources, 231

Q
Question-and-answer sessions, 24

R
Race
  employment discrimination and, 265-68
  labor force entrants and, 214-15
Racism, xiii-xiv, 1-2
  corporate culture or, 40-48
  personality strengths needed to deal
    with, 29
Radio/television stations,
  minority-oriented, 242-47
Randall, Iris, 190
Reading, industry-related, 62
Reagan, Ronald, xi
Reciprocation in networking, 110-11

Recognition, personal, 53
Recommendation stage and job attack,
  95-96
Record-keeping, 80, 81, 111, 184
Reference sources, 223
  directories, 224-30
  magazines/directories/periodicals,
    239-42
  newspapers, 232-39
  organizations, minority, 247-64
  television/radio stations, minority
    oriented, 242-47
  where to look for information, 230-32
Rehearsing for presentations, 24
Rejection during job hunt, 135-36
Relocation, 193-95, 199
Renewal process for corporations,
  xvii-xviii, 4, 64-65, 104-5, 187-88
Research. See also Reference sources
  corporate culture information and, 51
  job attack and, 94, 185-86
  job hunting and, 50-51, 68-69, 144-47
  lateral career move and, 191
  objectives within planning process and,
    11-12
  personnel practices and, 34
  relocation lateral move and, 194
  risk taking and, 199
  salary negotiations and, 143-44
Reshaping business, xvii-xviii, 4, 64-65,
  104-5, 187-88
Resumes, 171, 180
Risk taking, 66
  job attack and, 94
  mentoring relationships and, 128
  relocation and, 199
  studying art of, 56
Robotic industry, 202-3
Rules/regulations within corporations,
  33-34

S
Salary and benefits
  of corporations compared to other fields,
    36
  future trends in, 213
  injustices in, 140
  job hunting and, 68
  lateral career move and, 193
  negotiating, 141-44
  pay raises, decline in, xviii
  severance/settlement packages, 69-76
  state by state report on, 269-71
  weekly paycheck syndrome, 160-64
Savings, 58, 163
Secretiveness in networking, 110, 111-12
Self-confidence, xviii-xix, 19, 30, 133-34
Self-control, 19, 27-28

Self-critique during job hunt, 136–37
Self-determination, 196
Self-employment, xii, 161–62, 195
Self-motivation, 53, 199–200
Self-worth/esteem, 67–68
Services sector, 212
Setting the stage for presentations, 24–25
Severance/settlement packages, 69–76
Sexual harassment, 78–82, 183–84
Sex used for promotions, 153–54
Short-term quick fix approach to business, xvii
Skills, marketing your, 27–31, 58, 62–64
Socializing for networking purposes, 111
Social/professional data, 172, 174
Social responsibility of corporations, 6–8, 119–20
Socioeconomic issues and expectations, 201–3
Sociologists, 207
Speaking skills, 18–20, 109, 139
Special assignments, taking on, 30
Spradley, J. P., 164
Standard Directory of Advertisers, 230
State political caucuses, 253–54
Strengths, identifying your, 175
Stress, 57
    coping with, 164–68
    job attack and, 100–103
    lateral career move and, 193
Success. See Planning for success
Survival instincts, 28

T
Taylor, R. William, 179
Team player, 53
Television/radio stations,
    minority–oriented, 242–47
Temporary employees, xviii, 203

Third party endorsement concept, 63
Three-motive theory of psychological
    motivation, 37
Time, getting to work on, 21, 139
Timing when combating job attack, 98
Trade organizations/publications, 30, 62,
    64, 120–21, 179
Trainees and interpersonal skills,
    management, 82–85
Training/retraining, professional, 61–62,
    180–81
Travel expenses, 62

U
Unemployment, xii-xiii, xv-xviii, 201
Unwritten policy, 34
Upward mobility. See Promotions

V
Vacations, 166–68
Venings, R. L., 164
Visual backup support for presentations,
    24
Vocabulary skills, 20
Volunteering, 60–61, 119–20

W
Wall Street Journal, 51
Weekly paycheck syndrome, 160–64
Women
    challenges for, 190–91
    double standard pertaining to, 152
    dress code and, 17
    labor force entrants, 214, 216
    Pregnancy Discrimination Act of 1972,
        265
    sex for promotions issue, aware of, 154
    sexual harassment of, 78–82, 183–84
Writing skills, 21–22, 30

ABOUT THE AUTHOR

Randolph W. Cameron is founder and president of Cameron Enterprises, a New York-based management consulting firm with client experience that includes Avon Products, Grey Advertising, The Children's Aid Society, United Way of New York City, New York City Mission Society, The Council of Churches of the City of New York, The Concord Baptist Church of Christ, Institute of Church Administration and Management, General Board of Global Ministries, The United Methodist Church, Yale University, and The New York State Division for Youth. He was also the director of marketing and communications for Avon Products, Inc., for thirteen years. Before joining Avon, he was vice president of marketing and public affairs at D. Parke Gibson Associates, an international management consulting firm. In that position, Mr. Cameron served such clients as Columbia Pictures, Mobil Oil, Canadian World's Fair, and the Government of Bermuda.